2015 SUPPLEMENT TO CASES AND MATERIALS ON

CONSTITUTIONAL LAW

THEMES FOR THE CONSTITUTION'S THIRD CENTURY

Fifth Edition

■ ■ ■

Daniel A. Farber

Sho Sato Professor of Law
University of California, Berkeley

William N. Eskridge, Jr.

John A. Garver Professor of Jurisprudence
Yale University

Jane S. Schacter

William Nelson Cromwell Professor of Law
Stanford Law School

D1611030

AMERICAN CASEBOOK SERIES®

WEST
ACADEMIC
PUBLISHING

American Casebook Series is a trademark registered in the U.S. Patent and Trademark Office.

© 2013 LEG, Inc. d/b/a West Academic Publishing
© 2014 LEG, Inc. d/b/a West Academic
© 2015 LEG, Inc. d/b/a West Academic
      444 Cedar Street, Suite 700
      St. Paul, MN 55101
      1-877-888-1330

West, West Academic Publishing, and West Academic are trademarks of West Publishing Corporation, used under license.

Printed in the United States of America

ISBN: 978-1-63459-694-7

TABLE OF CONTENTS

TABLE OF CASES

The principal cases are in bold type.

2015 SUPPLEMENT TO
CASES AND MATERIALS ON

CONSTITUTIONAL LAW

THEMES FOR THE CONSTITUTION'S THIRD CENTURY

Fifth Edition

CHAPTER 3

THE CONSTITUTION AND RACIAL DISCRIMINATION

■ ■ ■

SECTION 3. THE AFFIRMATIVE ACTION CONTROVERSY: BENIGN RACIAL CLASSIFICATIONS OR REVERSE DISCRIMINATION?

B. THE EVOLUTION OF THE MODERN CASE LAW, 1980–1995

Page 314. Add before Section C:

In a high profile case involving the meaning of a major federal statute, the Court in *Texas Department of Housing Community Affairs v. Inclusive Communities Project, Inc.*, ___ U.S. ___, 135 S.Ct. 2507 (2015) ruled that plaintiffs have a claim for disparate impact under the Fair Housing Act. Writing for a 5-member majority, Justice Kennedy reached the result as a matter of statutory interpretation. At several points in the opinion, however, he alluded to the need to narrow disparate impact liability under the Act because of lurking constitutional concerns of the kind flagged in *Ricci*. He noted, for example, that "disparate-impact liability has always been properly limited in key respects that avoid the serious constitutional questions that might arise under the FHA, for instance, if such liability were imposed based solely on a showing of a statistical disparity."

C. REVISITING THE DIVERSITY RATIONALE AND ADMISSION TO STATE UNIVERSITY PROFESSIONAL SCHOOLS

Page 332. Delete Note 4 and insert the following material at the end of Section 3 C:

In the following case, the Court issued its first major decision on affirmative action in higher education since *Grutter* and *Gratz*.

FISHER V. UNIVERSITY OF TEXAS AT AUSTIN
570 U.S. ___, 133 S.Ct. 2411 (2013)

JUSTICE KENNEDY delivered the opinion of the Court.

Located in Austin, Texas, on the most renowned campus of the Texas state university system, the University is one of the leading institutions of higher education in the Nation. Admission is prized and competitive. In 2008, when petitioner sought admission to the University's entering class, she was 1 of 29,501 applicants. From this group 12,843 were admitted, and 6,715 accepted and enrolled. Petitioner was denied admission.

In recent years the University has used three different programs to evaluate candidates for admission. The first is the program it used for some years before 1997, when the University considered two factors: a numerical score reflecting an applicant's test scores and academic performance in high school (Academic Index or AI), and the applicant's race. In 1996, this system was held unconstitutional by the United States Court of Appeals for the Fifth Circuit. It ruled the University's consideration of race violated the Equal Protection Clause because it did not further any compelling government interest. *Hopwood v. Texas.*

The second program was adopted to comply with the *Hopwood* decision. The University stopped considering race in admissions and substituted instead a new holistic metric of a candidate's potential contribution to the University, to be used in conjunction with the Academic Index. This "Personal Achievement Index" (PAI) measures a student's leadership and work experience, awards, extracurricular activities, community service, and other special circumstances that give insight into a student's background. These included growing up in a single-parent home, speaking a language other than English at home, significant family responsibilities assumed by the applicant, and the general socioeconomic condition of the student's family. Seeking to address the decline in minority enrollment after *Hopwood,* the University also expanded its outreach programs.

The Texas State Legislature also responded to the *Hopwood* decision. It enacted a measure known as the Top Ten Percent Law [that] grants automatic admission to any public state college, including the University, to all students in the top 10% of their class at high schools in Texas that comply with certain standards.

The University's revised admissions process, coupled with the operation of the Top Ten Percent Law, resulted in a more racially diverse environment at the University. Before the admissions program at issue in this case, in the last year under the post-*Hopwood* AI/PAI system that did not consider race, the entering class was 4.5% African-American and 16.9% Hispanic. This is in contrast with the 1996 pre-*Hopwood* and Top Ten

Percent regime, when race was explicitly considered, and the University's entering freshman class was 4.1% African-American and 14.5% Hispanic.

Following this Court's decisions in *Grutter v. Bollinger* and *Gratz v. Bollinger,* the University adopted a third admissions program, the 2004 program in which the University reverted to explicit consideration of race. This is the program here at issue. In *Grutter,* the Court upheld the use of race as one of many "plus factors" in an admissions program that considered the overall individual contribution of each candidate. In *Gratz,* by contrast, the Court held unconstitutional Michigan's undergraduate admissions program, which automatically awarded points to applicants from certain racial minorities.

The University's plan to resume race-conscious admissions was given formal expression in June 2004 in an internal document entitled Proposal to Consider Race and Ethnicity in Admissions (Proposal). The Proposal relied in substantial part on a study of a subset of undergraduate classes containing between 5 and 24 students. It showed that few of these classes had significant enrollment by members of racial minorities. In addition the Proposal relied on what it called "anecdotal" reports from students regarding their "interaction in the classroom." The Proposal concluded that the University lacked a "critical mass" of minority students and that to remedy the deficiency it was necessary to give explicit consideration to race in the undergraduate admissions program.

To implement the Proposal the University included a student's race as a component of the PAI score, beginning with applicants in the fall of 2004. The University asks students to classify themselves from among five predefined racial categories on the application. Race is not assigned an explicit numerical value, but it is undisputed that race is a meaningful factor.

Once applications have been scored, they are plotted on a grid with the Academic Index on the x-axis and the Personal Achievement Index on the y-axis. On that grid students are assigned to so-called cells based on their individual scores. All students in the cells falling above a certain line are admitted. All students below the line are not. Each college—such as Liberal Arts or Engineering—admits students separately. So a student is considered initially for her first-choice college, then for her second choice, and finally for general admission as an undeclared major.

Petitioner applied for admission to the University's 2008 entering class and was rejected. She sued the University and various University officials. * * *

Among the Court's cases involving racial classifications in education, there are three decisions that directly address the question of considering racial minority status as a positive or favorable factor in a university's admissions process, with the goal of achieving the educational benefits of a more diverse student body: *Bakke, Gratz*; and *Grutter*. We take those cases as given for purposes of deciding this case. * * *

[In *Bakke*, Justice Powell's central point] was that this interest in securing diversity's benefits, although a permissible objective, is complex. "It is not an interest in simple ethnic diversity, in which a specified percentage of the student body is in effect guaranteed to be members of selected ethnic groups, with the remaining percentage an undifferentiated aggregation of students. The diversity that furthers a compelling state interest encompasses a far broader array of qualifications and characteristics of which racial or ethnic origin is but a single though important element." * * *

In *Grutter,* the Court reaffirmed [the] conclusion that obtaining the educational benefits of "student body diversity is a compelling state interest that can justify the use of race in university admissions."

As *Gratz* and *Grutter* observed, however, this follows only if a clear precondition is met: The particular admissions process used for this objective is subject to judicial review. Race may not be considered unless the admissions process can withstand strict scrutiny. * * * Strict scrutiny requires the university to demonstrate with clarity that its "purpose or interest is both constitutionally permissible and substantial, and that its use of the classification is necessary. . . to the accomplishment of its purpose."

While these are the cases that most specifically address the central issue in this case, additional guidance may be found in the Court's broader equal protection jurisprudence which applies in this context. "Distinctions between citizens solely because of their ancestry are by their very nature odious to a free people," *Rice v. Cayetano*, and therefore "are contrary to our traditions and hence constitutionally suspect," *Bolling v. Sharpe* " '[B]ecause racial characteristics so seldom provide a relevant basis for disparate treatment,' " "the Equal Protection Clause demands that racial classifications . . . be subjected to the 'most rigid scrutiny.' " *Loving v. Virginia.*

According to *Grutter,* a university's "educational judgment that such diversity is essential to its educational mission is one to which we defer." * * * A court, of course, should ensure that there is a reasoned, principled explanation for the academic decision. On this point, the District Court and Court of Appeals were correct in finding that *Grutter* calls for deference to the University's conclusion, " 'based on its experience and expertise,' " that a diverse student body would serve its educational goals. There is disagreement about whether *Grutter* was consistent with the principles of equal protection in approving this compelling interest in diversity. [Justice Kennedy cited to the separate opinions of Justices Scalia, Thomas, and

Ginsburg.] But the parties here do not ask the Court to revisit that aspect of *Grutter*'s holding.

A university is not permitted to define diversity as "some specified percentage of a particular group merely because of its race or ethnic origin." "That would amount to outright racial balancing, which is patently unconstitutional." Racial balancing is not transformed from 'patently unconstitutional' to a compelling state interest simply by relabeling it 'racial diversity.'" *Parents Involved in Community Schools v. Seattle School Dist. No. 1.*

Once the University has established that its goal of diversity is consistent with strict scrutiny, however, there must still be a further judicial determination that the admissions process meets strict scrutiny in its implementation. The University must prove that the means chosen by the University to attain diversity are narrowly tailored to that goal. On this point, the University receives no deference. *Grutter* made clear that it is for the courts, not for university administrators, to ensure that "[t]he means chosen to accomplish the [government's] asserted purpose must be specifically and narrowly framed to accomplish that purpose." True, a court can take account of a university's experience and expertise in adopting or rejecting certain admissions processes. But, as the Court said in *Grutter,* it remains at all times the University's obligation to demonstrate, and the Judiciary's obligation to determine, that admissions processes "ensure that each applicant is evaluated as an individual and not in a way that makes an applicant's race or ethnicity the defining feature of his or her application."

Narrow tailoring also requires that the reviewing court verify that it is "necessary" for a university to use race to achieve the educational benefits of diversity. This involves a careful judicial inquiry into whether a university could achieve sufficient diversity without using racial classifications. Although "[n]arrow tailoring does not require exhaustion of every *conceivable* race-neutral alternative," strict scrutiny does require a court to examine with care, and not defer to, a university's "serious, good faith consideration of workable race-neutral alternatives." Consideration by the university is of course necessary, but it is not sufficient to satisfy strict scrutiny: The reviewing court must ultimately be satisfied that no workable race-neutral alternatives would produce the educational benefits of diversity. If " 'a nonracial approach . . . could promote the substantial interest about as well and at tolerable administrative expense,'" then the university may not consider race. A plaintiff, of course, bears the burden of placing the validity of a university's adoption of an affirmative action plan in issue. But strict scrutiny imposes on the university the ultimate burden of demonstrating, before turning to racial classifications, that available, workable race-neutral alternatives do not suffice.

Rather than perform this searching examination, however, the Court of Appeals held petitioner could challenge only "whether [the University's] decision to reintroduce race as a factor in admissions was made in good faith." * * *

Grutter did not hold that good faith would forgive an impermissible consideration of race. It must be remembered that "the mere recitation of a 'benign' or legitimate purpose for a racial classification is entitled to little or no weight." Strict scrutiny does not permit a court to accept a school's assertion that its admissions process uses race in a permissible way without a court giving close analysis to the evidence of how the process works in practice.

The higher education dynamic does not change the narrow tailoring analysis of strict scrutiny applicable in other contexts. * * *

The District Court and Court of Appeals confined the strict scrutiny inquiry in too narrow a way by deferring to the University's good faith in its use of racial classifications and affirming the grant of summary judgment on that basis. The Court vacates that judgment, but fairness to the litigants and the courts that heard the case requires that it be remanded so that the admissions process can be considered and judged under a correct analysis. Unlike *Grutter,* which was decided after trial, this case arises from cross-motions for summary judgment. * * * Whether this record—and not "simple . . . assurances of good intention,"—is sufficient is a question for the Court of Appeals in the first instance.

Strict scrutiny must not be " 'strict in theory, but fatal in fact.' " But the opposite is also true. Strict scrutiny must not be strict in theory but feeble in fact. * * *

JUSTICE KAGAN took no part in the consideration or decision of this case.

JUSTICE SCALIA, concurring.

[Justice Scalia first reiterated views he had expressed in dissent in *Grutter*.] The petitioner in this case did not ask us to overrule *Grutter*'s holding that a "compelling interest" in the educational benefits of diversity can justify racial preferences in university admissions. I therefore join the Court's opinion in full.

JUSTICE THOMAS, concurring.

I join the Court's opinion because I agree that the Court of Appeals did not apply strict scrutiny to [the University's] use of racial discrimination in admissions decisions. I write separately to explain that I would overrule *Grutter v. Bollinger,* and hold that a State's use of race in higher education admissions decisions is categorically prohibited by the Equal Protection Clause. * * *

The Court first articulated the strict-scrutiny standard in *Korematsu v. United States.* There, we held that "[p]ressing public necessity may sometimes justify the existence of [racial discrimination]; racial antagonism never can." Aside from *Grutter,* the Court has recognized only two instances in which a "[p]ressing public necessity" may justify racial discrimination by the government. First, in *Korematsu,* the Court recognized that protecting national security may satisfy this exacting standard. In that case, the Court upheld an evacuation order directed at "all persons of Japanese ancestry" on the grounds that the Nation was at war with Japan and that the order had "a definite and close relationship to the prevention of espionage and sabotage." Second, the Court has recognized that the government has a compelling interest in remedying past discrimination for which it is responsible, but we have stressed that a government wishing to use race must provide "a 'strong basis in evidence for its conclusion that remedial action [is] necessary.' "

Grutter was a radical departure from our strict-scrutiny precedents. * * * Contrary to the very meaning of strict scrutiny, the Court *deferred* to the Law School's determination that this interest was sufficiently compelling to justify racial discrimination. * * *

The University claims that the District Court found that it has a compelling interest in attaining "a diverse student body and the educational benefits flowing from such diversity." The use of the conjunction, "and," implies that the University believes its discrimination furthers two distinct interests. The first is an interest in attaining diversity for its own sake. The second is an interest in attaining educational benefits that allegedly flow from diversity.

Attaining diversity for its own sake is a nonstarter. As even *Grutter* recognized, the pursuit of diversity as an end is nothing more than impermissible "racial balancing." * * * Rather, diversity can only be the *means* by which the University obtains educational benefits; it cannot be an end pursued for its own sake. Therefore, the *educational benefits* allegedly produced by diversity must rise to the level of a compelling state interest in order for the program to survive strict scrutiny.

Unfortunately for the University, the educational benefits flowing from student body diversity—assuming they exist—hardly qualify as a compelling state interest. Indeed, the argument that educational benefits justify racial discrimination was advanced in support of racial segregation in the 1950's, but emphatically rejected by this Court. And just as the alleged educational benefits of segregation were insufficient to justify racial discrimination then, see *Brown v. Board of Education*, the alleged educational benefits of diversity cannot justify racial discrimination today.

Our desegregation cases establish that the Constitution prohibits public schools from discriminating based on race, even if discrimination is necessary to the schools' survival. In *Davis v. School Bd. of Prince Edward Cty.,* decided with *Brown,* the school board argued that if the Court found segregation unconstitutional, white students would migrate to private schools, funding for public schools would decrease, and public schools would either decline in quality or cease to exist altogether. * * *The true victims of desegregation, the school board asserted, would be black students, who would be unable to afford private school. See [Brief of School Board] at 31 ("[W]ith the demise of segregation, education in Virginia would receive a serious setback. Those who would suffer most would be the Negroes who, by and large, would be economically less able to afford the private school"). * * *.

Unmoved by this sky-is-falling argument, we held that segregation violates the principle of equality enshrined in the Fourteenth Amendment. See *Brown.* * * * Within a matter of years, the warning became reality: After being ordered to desegregate, Prince Edward County closed its public schools from the summer of 1959 until the fall of 1964. Despite this fact, the Court never backed down from its rigid enforcement of the Equal Protection Clause's antidiscrimination principle.

In this case, of course, Texas has not alleged that the University will close if it is prohibited from discriminating based on race. But even if it had, the foregoing cases make clear that even that consequence would not justify its use of racial discrimination. It follows, *a fortiori,* that the putative educational benefits of student body diversity cannot justify racial discrimination * * * If the Court were actually applying strict scrutiny, it would require Texas either to close the University or to stop discriminating against applicants based on their race. The Court has put other schools to that choice, and there is no reason to treat the University differently.

It is also noteworthy that, in our desegregation cases, we rejected arguments that are virtually identical to those advanced by the University today. The University asserts, for instance, that the diversity obtained through its discriminatory admissions program prepares its students to become leaders in a diverse society. The segregationists likewise defended segregation on the ground that it provided more leadership opportunities for blacks. See, *e.g.,* Brief for Respondents in *Sweatt* 96 ("[A] very large group of Northern Negroes [comes] South to attend separate colleges, suggesting that the Negro does not secure as well-rounded a college life at a mixed college, and that the separate college offers him positive advantages; that there is a more normal social life for the Negro in a separate college; that there is a greater opportunity for full participation and for the development of leadership; that the Negro is inwardly more 'secure' at a college of his own people"). * * * This argument was unavailing. It is irrelevant under the Fourteenth Amendment whether segregated or mixed schools produce better leaders. Indeed, no court today would accept the suggestion that segregation is permissible because historically black colleges produced Booker T. Washington, Thurgood Marshall, Martin Luther King, Jr., and other prominent leaders. Likewise, the University's racial discrimination cannot be justified on the ground that it will produce better leaders. * * *

The Constitution does not pander to faddish theories about whether race mixing is in the public interest. The Equal Protection Clause strips States of all authority to use race as a factor in providing education. All applicants must be treated equally under the law, and no benefit in the eye of the beholder can justify racial discrimination. * * *

I would overrule *Grutter* and hold that the University's admissions program violates the Equal Protection Clause because the University has not put forward a compelling interest that could possibly justify racial discrimination.

While I find the theory advanced by the University to justify racial discrimination facially inadequate, I also believe that its use of race has little to do with the alleged educational benefits of diversity. I suspect that the University's program is instead based on the benighted notion that it is possible to tell when discrimination helps, rather than hurts, racial minorities. [See Justice Ginsburg's dissent] ("[G]overnment actors, including state universities, need not be blind to the lingering effects of 'an overtly discriminatory past,' the legacy of 'centuries of law-sanctioned inequality' "). But "[h]istory should teach greater humility." The worst forms of racial discrimination in this Nation have always been accompanied by straight-faced representations that discrimination helped minorities.

Slaveholders argued that slavery was a "positive good" that civilized blacks and elevated them in every dimension of life. See, *e.g.,* Calhoun, Speech in the U.S. Senate, 1837, in P. Finkelman, Defending Slavery 54, 58–59 (2003) ("Never before has the black race of Central Africa, from the dawn of history to the present day, attained a condition so civilized and so improved, not only physically, but morally and intellectually. . . . [T]he relation now existing in the slaveholding States between the two [races], is, instead of an evil, a good—a positive good"); Harper, Memoir on Slavery, in The Ideology of Slavery 78, 115–116 (D. Faust ed. 1981) ("Slavery, as it is said in an eloquent article published in a Southern periodical work . . . 'has done more to elevate a degraded race in the scale of humanity; to tame the savage; to civilize the barbarous; to soften the ferocious; to enlighten the ignorant, and to spread the blessings of [C]hristianity among the heathen, than all the missionaries that philanthropy and religion have ever sent forth' "); Hammond, The Mudsill Speech, 1858, in Defending Slavery, *supra,* at 80, 87 ("They are elevated from the condition in which God first created them, by being made our slaves").

A century later, segregationists similarly asserted that segregation was not only benign, but good for black students. They argued, for example, that separate schools protected black children from racist white students and teachers. * * *

Following in these inauspicious footsteps, the University would have us believe that its discrimination is likewise benign. I think the lesson of history is clear enough: Racial discrimination is never benign. * * *

While it does not, for constitutional purposes, matter whether the University's racial discrimination is benign, I note that racial engineering does in fact have insidious consequences. There can be no doubt that the University's discrimination injures white and Asian applicants who are denied admission because of their race. But I believe the injury to those admitted under the University's discriminatory admissions program is even more harmful.

Blacks and Hispanics admitted to the University as a result of racial discrimination are, on average, far less prepared than their white and Asian classmates. In the University's entering class of 2009, for example, among the students admitted outside the Top Ten Percent plan, blacks scored at the 52d percentile of 2009 SAT takers nationwide, while Asians scored at the 93d percentile. Brief for Richard Sander et al. as *Amici Curiae* 3–4, and n. 4. Blacks had a mean GPA of 2.57 and a mean SAT score of 1524; Hispanics had a mean GPA of 2.83 and a mean SAT score of 1794; whites had a mean GPA of 3.04 and a mean SAT score of 1914; and Asians had a mean GPA of 3.07 and a mean SAT score of 1991. *Ibid.*

Tellingly, neither the University nor any of the 73 *amici* briefs in support of racial discrimination has presented a shred of evidence that black and Hispanic students are able to close this substantial gap during their time at the University. . . .There is no reason to believe this is not the case at the University. The University and its dozens of *amici* are deafeningly silent on this point.

Furthermore, the University's discrimination does nothing to increase the number of blacks and Hispanics who have access to a college education generally. Instead, the University's discrimination has a pervasive shifting effect. See T. Sowell, Affirmative Action Around the World 145–146 (2004). The University admits minorities who otherwise would have attended less selective colleges where they would have been more evenly matched. * * *

The Court of Appeals believed that the University needed to enroll more blacks and Hispanics because they remained "clustered in certain programs." * * * These students may well drift towards less competitive majors because the mismatch caused by racial discrimination in admissions makes it difficult for them to compete in more rigorous majors.

Moreover, the University's discrimination "stamp[s] [blacks and Hispanics] with a badge of inferiority." It taints the accomplishments of all those who are admitted as a result of racial discrimination. * * * Although cloaked in good intentions, the University's racial tinkering harms the very people it claims to be helping.

JUSTICE GINSBURG, dissenting.

[The University] is candid about what it is endeavoring to do: It seeks to achieve student-body diversity through an admissions policy patterned after the Harvard plan referenced as exemplary in Justice Powell's opinion in *Bakke.* The University has steered clear of a quota system like the one struck down in *Bakke,* which excluded all nonminority candidates from competition for a fixed number of seats. And, like so many educational institutions across the Nation, the University has taken care to follow the model approved by the Court in *Grutter.* * * *

Petitioner urges that Texas' Top Ten Percent Law and race-blind holistic review of each application achieve significant diversity, so the University must be content with those alternatives. I have said before and reiterate here that only an ostrich could regard the supposedly neutral alternatives as race unconscious. As Justice Souter observed, the vaunted alternatives suffer from "the disadvantage of deliberate obfuscation."

Texas' percentage plan was adopted with racially segregated neighborhoods and schools front and center stage. See House Research Organization, Bill Analysis, HB 588, pp. 4–5 (Apr. 15, 1997) ("Many regions of the state, school districts, and high schools in Texas are still predominantly composed of people from a single racial or ethnic group. Because of the persistence of this segregation, admitting the top 10 percent of all high schools would provide a diverse population and ensure that a large, well-qualified pool of minority students was admitted to Texas universities."). It is race consciousness, not blindness to race, that drives such plans. As for holistic review, if universities cannot explicitly include race as a factor, many may "resort to camouflage" to "maintain their minority enrollment."

I have several times explained why government actors, including state universities, need not be blind to the lingering effects of "an overtly discriminatory past," the legacy of "centuries of law-sanctioned inequality." Among constitutionally permissible options, I remain convinced, "those that candidly disclose their consideration of race [are] preferable to those that conceal it."

Accordingly, I would not return this case for a second look. As the thorough opinions below show, the University's admissions policy flexibly considers race only as a "factor of a factor of a factor of a factor" in the calculus, followed a yearlong review through which the University reached the reasonable, good-faith judgment that supposedly race-neutral initiatives were insufficient to achieve, in appropriate measure, the educational benefits of student-body diversity, and is subject to periodic review to ensure that the consideration of race remains necessary and proper to achieve the University's educational objectives. Justice Powell's opinion in *Bakke* and the Court's decision in *Grutter* require no further determinations. * * *

NOTES

1. *A Surprise 7–1 Opinion on Affirmative Action.* In light of Justice Kagan's recusal, *Fisher* was decided by an eight-member court. Given how contentious debates over affirmative action have been, many observers expected a closely divided decision. Indeed, *Shelby County v. Holder*, the other major decision of the October 2012 Term addressing race (see Chapter 7 of this Supplement), fell along familiar 5–4 lines. What do you make of the fact that seven members of the Court coalesced behind the majority opinion? Is it significant that several Justices note that Abigail Fisher's attorneys did not expressly ask for *Grutter* to be overruled?

2. *Victory for Affirmative Action or* Fisher *as* Casey? What do you read *Fisher* to mean for the future of affirmative action? The Court reaffirmed the vitality of diversity as a compelling state interest and repeatedly cited *Grutter* and Justice Powell's opinion in *Bakke* as settled law on the framework for analyzing affirmative action in education. Yet, the Court also pointedly restricted the extent to which deference may be given to the educational judgment of schools in constructing their admissions policies. More significantly, perhaps, the opinion emphasized the need for "a careful judicial inquiry into whether a university could achieve sufficient diversity without using racial classifications," noting at one point that "[t]he reviewing court must ultimately be satisfied that no workable race-neutral alternatives would produce the educational benefits of diversity." *Fisher* might thus usher in a more exacting version of strict scrutiny that makes it more difficult for universities to defend the use of race-conscious mechanisms. If *Fisher* has this effect, it might one day be broadly analogized to *Planned Parenthood of Southeastern Pennsylvania v. Casey* (Casebook, p. 646), a decision on abortion rights in which the Court famously declined to overrule *Roe v. Wade*, but revised the framework for reviewing abortion laws in ways that have made it easier for states to restrict access to abortion through regulation. Note that *Casey* relaxed the standard of review, while *Fisher* may tighten it, but the ideological effect on two hotly-contested areas of policy may prove to be similar.

3. *Justice Thomas' Concurrence.* Justice Thomas deploys several highly controversial analogies in his concurring opinion. Some of his argument is reminiscent of the debate among the justices in *Parents Involved in Community Schools v. Seattle School District No. 1* (Casebook, p. 333) about the "true" meaning of *Brown*. But he goes well beyond that when he provocatively alludes to the institution of slavery, noting in the course of doing so that "the worst forms of racial discrimination in this Nation have always

been accompanied by straight-faced representations that discrimination helped minorities." How do you assess his dissent?

4. *Justice Thomas' Embrace of the "Mismatch" Thesis.* Note that Justice Thomas asserts as fact the "mismatch" thesis associated with the work of Professor Richard Sander and, more recently, his co-author, Stuart Taylor. The concurrence says, for example, that "as a result of the mismatching, many blacks and Hispanics who likely would have excelled at less elite schools are placed in a position where underperformance is all but inevitable because they are less academically prepared than the white and Asian students with whom they must compete." This idea of mismatch, however, has been widely criticized by various social scientists who question many aspects of the work. For a succinct overview of the authors' argument, as well as social science-based critiques of it, see Kali Borkoski, *Ask the author: Richard Sander and Stuart Taylor, Jr. on Mismatch*, SCOTUSblog (Oct. 16, 2012, 9:39 AM), http://www.scotusblog.com/2012/10/ask-the-author-richard-sander-and-stuart-taylor-jr-on-mismatch/ and Richard Lempert, William Kidder, and Felice Levine, *All hat, no cattle? Mismatch and Fisher v. University of Texas at Austin*, SCOTUSblog (Nov. 5, 2012, 12:06 PM), http://www.scotusblog.com/2012/11/all-hat-no-cattle-mismatch-and-fisher-v-university-of-texas-at-austin/.

5. *Justice Ginsburg's Dissent and the Aesthetics of Affirmative Action.* Justice Ginsburg pointedly contests the idea that the Texas Top Ten Percent Plan is "race unconscious," suggesting that "only an ostrich" could reach that conclusion. Is she correct? Is it significant, as she notes, that the plan was designed in the context of well-established residential racial segregation in Texas? Consider Problems 3–11 and 3–12 (Casebook, p. 365) in light of *Fisher*. What do the *Fisher* opinions suggest about how Justices Kennedy, Thomas and Ginsburg would each approach and answer Problem 3–11, which probes possible constitutional challenges to the Top Ten Percent Plan?

6. *Return Date for Fisher.* On remand, the Fifth Circuit upheld the University's plan and found it to be narrowly tailored. *Fisher v. Univ. of Texas at Austin*, 758 F. 2d 633 (5th Cir. 2014). Shortly before this Supplement went to press, the Court granted *certiorari* to review the Texas policy, and the Fifth Circuit's decision upholding it, once again.

Just a year after the remand of *Fisher*, the Court returned to the issue of affirmative action, but this time its focus was on the permissibility of a state ballot measure designed to ban affirmative action in a state.

SCHUETTE V. COALITION TO DEFEND AFFIRMATIVE ACTION
572 U.S. ___, 134 S.Ct. 1623 (2014)

JUSTICE KENNEDY announced the judgment of the Court and delivered an opinion in which **THE CHIEF JUSTICE** and **JUSTICE ALITO** join.

[After the Supreme Court's decisions in the Michigan affirmative action cases (Casebook p. 314), the voters of Michigan enacted Proposal 2, a measure that amended the state constitution to ban affirmative action. Proposal 2, codified as § 26, provided that the state and its universities "shall not discriminate against, or grant preferential treatment to, any individual or group on the basis of race, sex, color, ethnicity or national origin in the operation of public employment, public education, or public contracting." Sitting *en banc*, the Sixth Circuit struck down the ballot measure as a violation of the Equal Protection Clause. That court relied heavily on cases about unconstitutional restrictions on the political process, especially *Washington v. Seattle School District No. 1* (Casebook, p. 347 and 485) (striking down a ballot measure limiting the use of mandatory busing for school integration) and *Hunter v. Erickson* (Casebook p. 485) (striking down a ballot measure banning city council passage of non-discrimination ordinances). The Sixth Circuit held that Michigan had created a scheme that subjected only racial minorities to the onerous burden of amending the state constitution to secure favorable policy on university admissions, while other groups could use the ordinary political process to pursue their desired policy].

Before the Court addresses the question presented, it is important to note what this case is not about. It is not about the constitutionality, or the merits, of race-conscious admissions policies in higher education. The consideration of race in admissions presents complex questions, in part addressed last Term in *Fisher*. In *Fisher,* the Court did not disturb the principle that the consideration of race in admissions is permissible, provided that certain conditions are met. In this case, as in *Fisher,* that principle is not challenged. The question here concerns not the permissibility of race-conscious admissions policies under the Constitution but whether, and in what manner, voters in the States may choose to prohibit the consideration of racial preferences in governmental decisions, in particular with respect to school admissions.

This Court has noted that some States have decided to prohibit race-conscious admissions policies. In *Grutter,* the Court noted: "Universities in California, Florida, and Washington State, where racial preferences in admissions are prohibited by state law, are currently engaged in experimenting with a wide variety of alternative approaches. Universities in other States can and should draw on the most promising aspects of these race-neutral alternatives as they develop." In this way, *Grutter* acknowledged the significance of a dialogue regarding this contested and complex policy question among and within States. There was recognition that our federal structure "permits 'innovation and experimentation'" and "enables greater citizen 'involvement in democratic processes.'" While this case arises in Michigan, the decision by the State's voters reflects in part the national dialogue regarding the wisdom and practicality of race-conscious admissions policies in higher education.

In Michigan, the State Constitution invests independent boards of trustees with plenary authority over public universities, including admissions policies. Although the members of the boards are elected, some evidence in the record suggests they delegated authority over admissions policy to the faculty. But whether the boards or the faculty set the specific policy, Michigan's public universities did consider race as a factor in admissions decisions before 2006.

In holding § 26 invalid in the context of student admissions at state universities, the Court of Appeals relied in primary part on *Seattle,* which it deemed to control the case. But that determination extends *Seattle's* holding in a case presenting quite different issues to reach a conclusion that is mistaken here. * * *

Seattle stated that where a government policy "inures primarily to the benefit of the minority" and "minorities . . . consider" the policy to be " 'in their interest,' " then any state action that "place[s] effective decisionmaking authority over" that policy "at a different level of government" must be reviewed under strict scrutiny. In essence, according to the broad reading of *Seattle*, any state action with a "racial focus" that makes it "more difficult for certain racial minorities than for other groups" to "achieve legislation that is in their interest" is subject to strict scrutiny. It is this reading of *Seattle* that the Court of Appeals found to be controlling here. And that reading must be rejected.

* * * The expansive reading of *Seattle* has no principled limitation and raises serious questions of compatibility with the Court's settled equal protection jurisprudence. * * *

In cautioning against "impermissible racial stereotypes," this Court has rejected the assumption that "members of the same racial group— regardless of their age, education, economic status, or the community in which they live—think alike, share the same political interests, and will prefer the same candidates at the polls." It cannot be entertained as a serious proposition that all individuals of the same race think alike. Yet that proposition would be a necessary beginning point were the *Seattle* formulation to control, as the Court of Appeals held it did in this case. And if it were deemed necessary to probe how some races define their own interest in political matters, still another beginning point would be to define individuals according to race. But in a society in which those lines are becoming more blurred, the attempt to define race-based categories also raises serious questions of its own. Government action that classifies individuals on the basis of race is inherently suspect and carries the danger of perpetuating the very racial divisions the polity seeks to transcend. Were courts to embark upon this venture not only would it be undertaken with no clear legal standards or accepted sources to guide judicial decision but also it would result in, or at least impose a high risk of, inquiries and categories dependent upon demeaning stereotypes, classifications of questionable constitutionality on their own terms. * * *

There would be no apparent limiting standards defining what public policies should be included in what *Seattle* called policies that "inur[e] primarily to the benefit of the minority" and that "minorities . . . consider" to be " 'in their interest.' * * * Tax policy, housing subsidies, wage regulations, and even the naming of public schools, highways, and monuments are just a few examples of what could become a list of subjects that some organizations could insist should be beyond the power of voters to decide, or beyond the power of a legislature to decide when enacting limits on the power of local authorities or other governmental entities to address certain subjects. Racial division would be validated, not discouraged, were the *Seattle* formulation, and the reasoning of the Court of Appeals in this case, to remain in force. * * *

Michigan voters exercised their privilege to enact laws as a basic exercise of their democratic power. In the federal system States "respond, through the enactment of positive law, to the initiative of those who seek a voice in shaping the destiny of their own times." Michigan voters used the initiative system to bypass public officials who were deemed not responsive to the concerns of a majority of the voters with respect to a policy of granting race-based preferences that raises difficult and delicate issues.

* * * [F]reedom does not stop with individual rights. Our constitutional system embraces, too, the right of citizens to debate so they can learn and decide and then, through the political process, act in concert to try to shape the course of their own times and the course of a nation that must strive always to make freedom ever greater and more secure. Here Michigan voters acted in concert and statewide to seek consensus and adopt a policy on a difficult subject against a historical background of race in America that has been a source of tragedy and persisting injustice. That history demands that we continue to learn, to listen, and to remain open to new approaches if we are to aspire always to a constitutional order in which all persons are treated with fairness and equal dignity. Were the Court to rule that the question addressed by Michigan voters is too sensitive or complex to be within the grasp of the electorate; or that the policies at issue remain too delicate to be resolved save by university officials or faculties, acting at some remove from immediate public scrutiny and control; or that these matters are so arcane that the electorate's power must be limited because the people cannot prudently exercise that power even after a full debate, that holding would be an unprecedented restriction on the exercise of a fundamental right held not just by one person but by all in common. It is the right to speak and debate and learn and then, as a matter of political will, to act through a lawful electoral process.

The respondents in this case insist that a difficult question of public policy must be taken from the reach of the voters, and thus removed from the realm of public discussion, dialogue, and debate in an election campaign. Quite in addition to the serious First Amendment implications of that position with respect to any particular election, it is inconsistent with the underlying premises of a responsible, functioning democracy. One of those premises is that a democracy has the capacity—and the duty—to learn from its past mistakes; to discover and confront persisting biases; and by respectful, rationale (sic) deliberation to rise above those flaws and injustices. That process is impeded, not advanced, by court decrees based on the proposition that the public cannot have the requisite repose to discuss certain issues. It is demeaning to the democratic process to presume that the voters are not capable of deciding an issue of this sensitivity on decent and rational grounds. * * *

These precepts are not inconsistent with the well-established principle that when hurt or injury is inflicted on racial minorities by the encouragement or command of laws or other state action, the Constitution requires redress by the courts. * * *

For reasons already discussed, [the political process cases] are not precedents that stand for the conclusion that Michigan's voters must be disempowered from acting. Those cases were ones in which the political restriction in question was designed to be used, or was likely to be used, to encourage infliction of injury by reason of race. What is at stake here is not whether injury will be inflicted but whether government can be instructed not to follow a course that entails, first, the definition of racial categories and, second, the grant of favored status to persons in some racial categories and not others. The electorate's instruction to governmental entities not to embark upon the course of race-defined and race-based preferences was adopted, we must assume, because the voters deemed a preference system to be unwise, on account of what voters may deem its latent potential to become itself a source of the very resentments and hostilities based on race that this Nation seeks to put behind it. Whether those adverse results would follow is, and should be, the subject of debate. Voters might likewise consider, after debate and reflection, that programs designed to increase diversity—consistent with the Constitution—are a necessary part of progress to transcend the stigma of past racism.

CHIEF JUSTICE ROBERTS, concurring.

The dissent devotes 11 pages to expounding its own policy preferences in favor of taking race into account in college admissions, while nonetheless concluding that it "do[es] not mean to suggest that the virtues of adopting race-sensitive admissions policies should inform the legal question before the Court." (opinion of SOTOMAYOR, J.). The dissent concedes that the governing boards of the State's various universities could have implemented a policy making it illegal to "discriminate against, or grant preferential treatment to," any individual on the basis of race. On the dissent's view, if the governing boards conclude that drawing racial distinctions in university admissions is undesirable or counterproductive, they are permissibly exercising their policymaking authority. But others who might reach the same conclusion are failing to take race seriously.

The dissent states that "[t]he way to stop discrimination on the basis of race is to speak openly and candidly on the subject of race." And it urges that "[r]ace matters because of the slights, the snickers, the silent judgments that reinforce that most crippling of thoughts: 'I do not belong here.' " But it is not "out of touch with reality" to conclude that racial preferences may themselves have the debilitating effect of reinforcing precisely that doubt, and—if so—that the preferences do more harm than good. To disagree with the dissent's views on the costs and benefits of racial preferences is not to "wish away, rather than confront" racial inequality. People can disagree in good faith on this issue, but it similarly does more harm than good to question the openness and candor of those on either side of the debate.

JUSTICE SCALIA, with whom **JUSTICE THOMAS** joins, concurring in the judgment.

It has come to this. Called upon to explore the jurisprudential twilight zone between two errant lines of precedent, we confront a frighteningly bizarre question: Does the Equal Protection Clause of the Fourteenth Amendment *forbid* what its text plainly *requires*? Needless to say (except that this case obliges us to say it), the question answers itself. * * *

Even taking this Court's sorry line of race-based-admissions cases as a given, I find the question presented only slightly less strange: Does the Equal Protection Clause forbid a State from banning a practice that the Clause barely—and only provisionally—permits? Reacting to those race-based-admissions decisions, some States—whether deterred by the prospect of costly litigation; aware that *Grutter*'s bell may soon toll; or simply opposed in principle to the notion of "benign" racial discrimination—have gotten out of the racial-preferences business altogether. * * *

But the battleground for this case is not the constitutionality of race-based admissions—at least, not quite. Rather, it is the so-called political-process doctrine, derived from this Court's opinions in *Washington v. Seattle School Dist. No. 1* and *Hunter v. Erickson*. I agree with those parts of the plurality opinion that repudiate this doctrine. But I do not agree with its reinterpretation of *Seattle* and *Hunter*, which makes them stand in part for the cloudy and doctrinally anomalous proposition that whenever state action poses "the serious risk . . . of causing specific injuries on account of race," it denies equal protection. I would instead reaffirm that the "ordinary principles of our law [and] of our democratic heritage" require "plaintiffs alleging equal protection violations" stemming from facially neutral acts to "prove intent and causation and not merely the existence of racial disparity." I would further hold that a law directing state actors to provide equal protection is (to say the least) facially neutral, and cannot violate the Constitution. Section 26 of the Michigan Constitution (formerly Proposal 2) rightly stands. * * *

The dissent trots out the old saw, derived from dictum in a footnote, that legislation motivated by " 'prejudice against discrete and insular minorities' " merits " 'more exacting judicial scrutiny.' " (quoting *United States v. Carolene Products,* 304 U.S. 144, 152–153, n. 4). I say derived from that dictum (expressed by the four-Justice majority of a seven-Justice Court) because the dictum itself merely said *"[n]or need we enquire . . . whether prejudice against discrete and insular minorities may be a special condition."* (emphasis added). The dissent does not argue, of course, that such "prejudice" produced § 26. Nor does it explain why certain racial minorities in Michigan qualify as " 'insular,' " meaning that "other groups will not form coalitions with them—and, critically, not because of lack of common interests but because of 'prejudice.' " Strauss, Is *Carolene Products* Obsolete? 2010 U. Ill. L.Rev. 1251, 1257. Nor does it even make the case that a group's "discreteness" and "insularity" are political *liabilities* rather than political *strengths*—a serious question that alone demonstrates the prudence of the *Carolene Products* dictumizers in leaving the "enquir[y]" for another day. As for the question whether "legislation which restricts those political processes which can ordinarily be expected to bring about repeal of undesirable legislation . . . is to be subjected to more exacting judicial scrutiny," the *Carolene Products* Court found it "unnecessary to consider [that] now." If the dissent thinks that worth considering today, it should explain why the election of a university's governing board is a "political process which can ordinarily be expected to bring about repeal of undesirable legislation," but Michigan voters' ability to amend their Constitution is not. It seems to me quite the opposite. Amending the Constitution requires the approval of only "a majority of the electors voting on the question." Mich. Const., Art. XII, § 2. By contrast, voting in a favorable board (each of which has eight members) at the three major public universities requires electing by majority vote at least 15 different candidates, several of whom would be running during different election cycles. So if Michigan voters, instead of amending their Constitution, had pursued the dissent's preferred path of electing board members promising to "abolish race-sensitive admissions policies," it would have been *harder,* not easier, for racial minorities favoring affirmative action to overturn that decision. But the more important point is that we should not design our jurisprudence to conform to dictum in a footnote in a four-Justice opinion. * * *

I part ways with *Hunter, Seattle,* and (I think) the plurality for an additional reason: Each endorses a version of the proposition that a facially neutral law may deny equal protection solely because it has a disparate racial impact. Few equal-protection theories have been so squarely and soundly rejected. * * *

Notwithstanding our dozens of cases confirming the exceptionless nature of the *Washington v. Davis* rule, the plurality opinion leaves ajar an effects-test escape hatch modeled after *Hunter* and *Seattle,* suggesting that state action denies equal protection when it "ha[s] the *serious risk,* if not purpose, of causing specific injuries on account of race," or is either "designed to be used, or . . . *likely to be used,* to encourage infliction of injury by reason of race." (emphasis added). Since these formulations enable a determination of an equal-protection violation where there is no discriminatory intent, they are inconsistent with the long *Washington v. Davis* line of cases.

JUSTICE BREYER, concurring in the judgment.

I continue to believe that the Constitution permits, though it does not require, the use of the kind of race-conscious programs that are now barred by the Michigan Constitution. The serious educational problems that faced Americans at the time this Court decided *Grutter* endure. And low educational achievement continues to be correlated with income and race. [Justice Breyer then provided citations for these propositions]. * * *

The Constitution allows local, state, and national communities to adopt narrowly tailored race-conscious programs designed to bring about greater inclusion and diversity. But the Constitution foresees the ballot box, not the courts, as the normal instrument for resolving differences and debates about the merits of these programs. * * *

[C]ases such as [*Hunter* and *Seattle*] reflect an important principle, namely, that an individual's ability to participate meaningfully in the political process should be independent of his race. Although racial minorities, like other political minorities, will not always succeed at the polls, they must have the same opportunity as others to secure through the ballot box policies that reflect their preferences. In my view, however, neither *Hunter* nor *Seattle* applies here. * * *

Hunter and *Seattle* involved efforts to manipulate the political process in a way not here at issue. Both cases involved a restructuring of the political process that changed the political level at which policies were enacted. In *Hunter,* decisionmaking was moved from the elected city council to the local electorate at large. And in *Seattle,* decisionmaking by an elected school board was replaced with decisionmaking by the state legislature and electorate at large.

This case, in contrast, does not involve a reordering of the *political* process; it does not in fact involve the movement of decisionmaking from one political level to another. Rather, here, Michigan law delegated broad policymaking authority to elected university boards, but those boards delegated admissions-related decisionmaking authority to unelected university faculty members and administrators. Although the boards unquestionably retained the *power* to set policy regarding race-conscious admissions, see *post,* at 1664–1667 (SOTOMAYOR J., dissenting), in *fact* faculty members and administrators set the race-conscious admissions policies in question. (It is often true that elected bodies—including, for example, school boards, city councils, and state legislatures—have the power to enact policies, but in fact delegate that power to administrators.) Although at limited times the university boards were advised of the content of their race-conscious admissions policies, to my knowledge no board voted to accept or reject any of those policies. Thus, unelected faculty members and administrators, not voters or their elected representatives, adopted the race-conscious admissions programs affected by Michigan's constitutional amendment. The amendment took decisionmaking authority away from these unelected actors and placed it in the hands of the voters.

Why does this matter? For one thing, considered conceptually, the doctrine set forth in *Hunter* and *Seattle* does not easily fit this case. In those cases minorities had participated in the political process and they had won. The majority's subsequent reordering of the political process repealed the minority's successes and made it more difficult for the minority to succeed in the future. The majority thereby diminished the minority's ability to participate meaningfully in the electoral process. But one cannot as easily characterize the movement of the decisionmaking mechanism at issue here—from an administrative process to an electoral process—as diminishing the minority's ability to participate meaningfully in the *political* process. There is no prior electoral process in which the minority participated.

For another thing, to extend the holding of *Hunter* and *Seattle* to reach situations in which decisionmaking authority is moved from an administrative body to a political one would pose significant difficulties. The administrative process encompasses vast numbers of decisionmakers answering numerous policy questions in hosts of different fields. * * *

[M]y discussion here is limited to circumstances in which decisionmaking is moved from an unelected administrative body to a politically responsive one, and in which the targeted race-conscious admissions programs consider race solely in order to obtain the educational benefits of a diverse student body. We need now decide no more than whether the Federal Constitution permits Michigan to apply its constitutional amendment in those circumstances. I would hold that it does.

JUSTICE SOTOMAYOR, with whom JUSTICE GINSBURG joins, dissenting.

We are fortunate to live in a democratic society. But without checks, democratically approved legislation can oppress minority groups. For that reason, our Constitution places limits on what a majority of the people may do. This case implicates one such limit: the guarantee of equal protection of the laws. Although that guarantee is traditionally understood to prohibit intentional discrimination under existing laws, equal protection does not end there. Another fundamental strand of our equal protection jurisprudence focuses on process, securing to all citizens the right to participate meaningfully and equally in self-government. That right is the bedrock of our democracy, for it preserves all other rights.

Yet to know the history of our Nation is to understand its long and lamentable record of stymieing the right of racial minorities to participate in the political process. * * *

This case involves [discriminatory political restructuring]: A majority of the Michigan electorate changed the basic rules of the political process in that State in a manner that uniquely disadvantaged racial minorities. Prior to the enactment of the constitutional initiative at issue here, all of the admissions policies of Michigan's public colleges and universities— including race-sensitive admissions policies—were in the hands of each institution's governing board. The members of those boards are nominated by political parties and elected by the citizenry in statewide elections. After over a century of being shut out of Michigan's institutions of higher education, racial minorities in Michigan had succeeded in persuading the elected board representatives to adopt admissions policies that took into account the benefits of racial diversity. And this Court twice blessed such efforts—first in *Regents of Univ. of Cal. v. Bakke* (1978), and again in *Grutter v. Bollinger* (2003), a case that itself concerned a Michigan admissions policy.

In the wake of *Grutter,* some voters in Michigan set out to eliminate the use of race-sensitive admissions policies. Those voters were of course free to pursue this end in any number of ways. For example, they could have persuaded existing board members to change their minds through individual or grassroots lobbying efforts, or through general public awareness campaigns. Or they could have mobilized efforts to vote uncooperative board members out of office, replacing them with members who would share their desire to abolish race-sensitive admissions policies. When this Court holds that the Constitution permits a particular policy, nothing prevents a majority of a State's voters from choosing not to adopt that policy. Our system of government encourages—and indeed, depends on—that type of democratic action.

But instead, the majority of Michigan voters changed the rules in the middle of the game, reconfiguring the existing political process in Michigan in a manner that burdened racial minorities. * * *

As a result of § 26, there are now two very different processes through which a Michigan citizen is permitted to influence the admissions policies of the State's universities: one for persons interested in race-sensitive admissions policies and one for everyone else. A citizen who is a University of Michigan alumnus, for instance, can advocate for an admissions policy that considers an applicant's legacy status by meeting individually with members of the Board of Regents to convince them of her views, by joining with other legacy parents to lobby the Board, or by voting for and supporting Board candidates who share her position. The same options are available to a citizen who wants the Board to adopt admissions policies that consider athleticism, geography, area of study, and so on. The one and only policy a Michigan citizen may not seek through this long-established process is a race-sensitive admissions policy that considers race in an individualized manner when it is clear that race-neutral alternatives are not adequate to achieve diversity. For that policy alone, the citizens of Michigan must undertake the daunting task of amending the State Constitution.

Our precedents do not permit political restructurings that create one process for racial minorities and a separate, less burdensome process for everyone else. * * *

Like the plurality, I have faith that our citizenry will continue to learn from this Nation's regrettable history; that it will strive to move beyond those injustices towards a future of equality. And I, too, believe in the importance of public discourse on matters of public policy. But I part ways with the plurality when it suggests that judicial intervention in this case "impede[s]" rather than "advance[s]" the democratic process and the ultimate hope of equality. I firmly believe that our role as judges includes policing the process of self-government and stepping in when necessary to secure the constitutional guarantee of equal protection. * * *

[The right to participate meaningfully and equally in the process of government] is the bedrock of our democracy, recognized from its very inception. See J. Ely, Democracy and Distrust 87 (1980) (the Constitution "is overwhelmingly concerned, on the one hand, with procedural fairness in the resolution of individual disputes," and on the other, "with ensuring broad participation in the processes and distributions of government"). * * *

[Justice Sotomayor then reviewed *Carolene Products*, footnote 4]. The values identified in *Carolene Products* lie at the heart of the political-process doctrine. Indeed, *Seattle* explicitly relied on *Carolene Products*. These values are central tenets of our equal protection jurisprudence. * * *

My colleagues are of the view that we should leave race out of the picture entirely and let the voters sort it out. We have seen this reasoning before. See *Parents Involved,* 551 U.S., at 748, 127 S.Ct. 2738 ("The way to stop discrimination on the basis of race is to stop discriminating on the basis of race"). It is a sentiment out of touch with reality. * * *

Race matters. Race matters in part because of the long history of racial minorities' being denied access to the political process. * * * And although we have made great strides, "voting discrimination still exists; no one doubts that." *Shelby County.*

Race also matters because of persistent racial inequality in society—inequality that cannot be ignored and that has produced stark socioeconomic disparities. * * *

And race matters for reasons that really are only skin deep, that cannot be discussed any other way, and that cannot be wished away. Race matters to a young man's view of society when he spends his teenage years watching others tense up as he passes, no matter the neighborhood where he grew up. Race matters to a young woman's sense of self when she states her hometown, and then is pressed, "No, where are you *really* from?", regardless of how many generations her family has been in the country. Race matters to a young person addressed by a stranger in a foreign language, which he does not understand because only English was spoken at home. Race matters because of the slights, the snickers, the silent judgments that reinforce that most crippling of thoughts: "I do not belong here."

In my colleagues' view, examining the racial impact of legislation only perpetuates racial discrimination. This refusal to accept the stark reality that race matters is regrettable. The way to stop discrimination on the basis of race is to speak openly and candidly on the subject of race, and to apply the Constitution with eyes open to the unfortunate effects of centuries of racial discrimination. As members of the judiciary tasked with intervening to carry out the guarantee of equal protection, we ought not sit back and wish away, rather than confront, the racial inequality that exists in our society. It is this view that works harm, by perpetuating the facile notion that what makes race matter is acknowledging the simple truth that race *does* matter. * * *

[While acknowledging that the constitutionality of affirmative action was not at issue in this case, Justice Sotomayor noted that, because other justices had suggested that "race-sensitive admissions policies have the 'potential to become . . . the source of the very resentments and hostilities based on race that this Nation seeks to put behind it,' " she would "speak in response." Her dissent went on to offer a lengthy examination of affirmative action in university admissions, including statistics showing reduced minority enrollments in states with measures like Proposal 2, as well as an extended functional defense of diversity]. Colleges and universities must be free to prioritize the goal of diversity. They must be free to immerse their students in a multiracial environment that fosters frequent and meaningful interactions with students of other races, and thereby pushes such students to transcend any assumptions they may hold on the basis of skin color. Without race-sensitive admissions policies, this might well be impossible. The statistics I have described make that fact glaringly obvious. We should not turn a blind eye to something we cannot help but see. * * *

NOTES ON SCHUETTE

1.   *The Political Process Theory.* The *Hunter-Seattle* "political process" theory on which *Schuette* turned has been rarely used by the Supreme Court, and some had questioned the continued vitality of the doctrine. Both the plurality opinion and Justice Breyer's concurrence chose to limit, rather than overrule, that doctrine. How do the formulations in these two opinions differ? Does one leave a more defensible role for the political process doctrine than the other?

2.   *Voter Initiatives and Equal Protection.* While not overruling the political process doctrine, the plurality opinion's praise of voter initiatives left little doubt that it was unwilling to allow the doctrine to become a significant impediment to the use of ballot measures. Was the plurality too sanguine about the deliberative virtues of direct democracy? About the effect of ballot measures on minorities? (As you consider these questions, you might wish to consult the Note on Judicial Review of Popular Initiatives and Referenda, Casebook p. 485.)

3.   *The Intellectual Roots of the Political Process Theory.* While the *Hunter-Seattle* doctrine itself has been of limited significance, it is derived from the broad ideas of representation-reinforcement embedded in *Carolene Products* footnote 4 and the work of Professor Ely. Those ideas have pervaded and critically shaped the jurisprudence of equal protection. Justices Scalia and Sotomayor engage in a rare and extended face-off on footnote 4, which Justice Scalia casts as "an old saw" and a mere "dictum." Who has the better of this debate?

4.   *Justice Sotomayor's Dissent.* Justice Sotomayor's dissent ran to 58 pages, and is the longest of her tenure as a justice. Among its most salient elements is the pointed response to Chief Justice Roberts' much-quoted comment in *Parents Involved* that the "way to stop discrimination on the basis of race is to stop discriminating on the basis of race." (Casebook p. 342). Justice Sotomayor bluntly calls this sentiment "out of touch with reality" and offers an impassioned argument about how and why "race matters." The Chief Justice characterizes the dissent as "expounding its own policy preferences" and asserts that it "does more harm than good to question the openness and candor of those on either side of the debate." This might be seen as a proxy battle between the forces of realism (championed by Sotomayor) and formalism

(championed by Roberts) in approaching questions of race and constitutional equality. Does their debate shed any light on the virtues or vices of the colorblindness ideal?

5.   *Implications for the Court's Jurisprudence of Race.* The *Schuette* ruling itself is unlikely to change the Court's doctrine in any significant way. As the justices agreed, the case did not squarely concern the constitutionality of affirmative action in admissions. But the opinions offer a frank and revealing window on the fissures among the justices on questions of race. Given that *Fisher* will now be back before the Court after the Fifth Circuit upheld the Texas affirmative action policy on remand, what do the different *Schuette* opinions suggest about how that renewed challenge will come out?

CHAPTER 4

SEX AND GENDER DISCRIMINATION AND OTHER EQUAL PROTECTION CONCERNS

■ ■ ■

SECTION 3. WHAT LEVEL OF SCRUTINY FOR OTHER "SUSPICIOUS" CLASSIFICATIONS?

D. SEXUAL ORIENTATION

Page 506. Insert the following after Problem 4–5:

In 2013, the constitutionality of both California's Proposition 8 (at issue in *Perry v. Brown*, Casebook, p. 494) and Section 3 of the Defense of Marriage Act (addressed in the Holder Letter, Casebook, p. 503) came before the Supreme Court. Both decisions were highly anticipated. In *Hollingsworth v. Perry*, ___ U.S. ___, 133 S.Ct. 2652 (2013), the Court declined to reach the constitutionality of Prop 8. Recall that the ballot measure had been struck down by both District Judge Vaughn Walker in 2010 and by a panel of the Ninth Circuit in 2012. Because none of the California officials named as defendants in the case elected to appeal the district court's judgment, it was the measure's ballot sponsors who had appealed to the Ninth Circuit and then petitioned for certiorari in the case. By a 5–4 vote, the Court found that these ballot sponsors lacked Article III standing to appeal on behalf of the state (see Chapter 9 of this Supplement). The effect of that ruling was to vacate the Ninth Circuit's decision and reinstate Judge Vaughn Walker's opinion invalidating that measure, including the permanent injunction against enforcement of Prop 8. Although there was some debate about the scope of Judge Walker's order, and who precisely was bound by that permanent injunction, same-sex marriages resumed around the state only days after the ruling. Based on their reading of the district court's order, the Governor and Attorney General instructed county clerks to resume issuing marriage licenses to same-sex couples as soon as the Ninth Circuit lifted the stay it had imposed pending Supreme Court resolution, and that stay was lifted quickly. In late June 2013, California became the 13th state to allow same-sex couples to wed.

In the next case, the justices rejected Article III challenges to an appeal from a ruling that sec. 3 of DOMA was unconstitutional (see Chapter 9 of this Supplement), and reached the constitutional question posed in that case.

UNITED STATES V. WINDSOR

570 U.S. ___, 133 S.Ct. 2675 (2013)

JUSTICE KENNEDY delivered the opinion of the Court.

In 1996, as some States were beginning to consider the concept of same-sex marriage, and before any State had acted to permit it, Congress enacted the Defense of Marriage Act (DOMA). DOMA contains two operative sections: Section 2, which has not been challenged here, allows States to refuse to recognize same-sex marriages performed under the laws of other States.

Section 3 is at issue here. It amends the Dictionary Act in Title 1, § 7, of the United States Code to provide a federal definition of "marriage" and "spouse." Section 3 of DOMA provides as follows:

> In determining the meaning of any Act of Congress, or of any ruling, regulation, or interpretation of the various administrative bureaus and agencies of the United States, the word 'marriage' means only a legal union between one man and one woman as husband and wife, and the word 'spouse' refers only to a person of the opposite sex who is a husband or a wife.

The definitional provision does not by its terms forbid States from enacting laws permitting same-sex marriages or civil unions or providing state benefits to residents in that status. The enactment's comprehensive definition of marriage for purposes of all federal statutes and other regulations or directives covered by its terms, however, does control over 1,000 federal laws in which marital or spousal status is addressed as a matter of federal law.

Edith Windsor and Thea Spyer met in New York City in 1963 and began a long-term relationship. Windsor and Spyer registered as domestic partners when New York City gave that right to same-sex couples in 1993. Concerned about Spyer's health, the couple made the 2007 trip to Canada for their marriage, but they continued to reside in New York City. The State of New York deems their Ontario marriage to be a valid one.

Spyer died in February 2009, and left her entire estate to Windsor. Because DOMA denies federal recognition to same-sex spouses, Windsor did not qualify for the marital exemption from the federal estate tax, which excludes from taxation "any interest in property which passes or has passed from the decedent to his surviving spouse." Windsor paid $363,053 in estate taxes and sought a refund. The Internal Revenue Service denied the refund, concluding that, under DOMA, Windsor was not a "surviving spouse." Windsor commenced this refund suit, [contending] that DOMA violates the guarantee of equal protection, as applied to the Federal Government through the Fifth Amendment.

While the tax refund suit was pending, the Attorney General of the United States notified the Speaker of the House of Representatives that the Department of Justice would no longer defend the constitutionality of DOMA's § 3. [See Holder Letter, Casebook p. 503] * * *

[The opinion first addressed the jurisdictional question under Article III that the Court had asked the parties to brief. In portions of the opinion excerpted in Chapter 9 of this Supplement, the majority found the case properly before the Court].

It seems fair to conclude that, until recent years, many citizens had not even considered the possibility that two persons of the same sex might aspire to occupy the same status and dignity as that of a man and woman in lawful marriage. For marriage between a man and a woman no doubt had been thought of by most people as essential to the very definition of that term and to its role and function throughout the history of civilization. That belief, for many who long have held it, became even more urgent, more cherished when challenged. For others, however, came the beginnings of a new perspective, a new insight. Accordingly some States concluded that same-sex marriage ought to be given recognition and validity in the law for those same-sex couples who wish to define themselves by their commitment to each other. The limitation of lawful marriage to heterosexual couples, which for centuries had been deemed both necessary and fundamental, came to be seen in New York and certain other States as an unjust exclusion.

Slowly at first and then in rapid course, the laws of New York came to acknowledge the urgency of this issue for same-sex couples who wanted to affirm their commitment to one another before their children, their family, their friends, and their community. And so New York recognized same-sex marriages performed elsewhere; and then it later amended its own marriage laws to permit same-sex marriage. * * *

Against this background of lawful same-sex marriage in some States, the design, purpose, and effect of DOMA should be considered as the beginning point in deciding whether it is valid under the Constitution. * * * [DOMA's] operation is directed to a class of persons that the laws of New York, and of [Massachusetts, Iowa, Vermont, Connecticut, New Hampshire, Washington, Maine, Maryland, Delaware, Rhode Island, and the District of Columbia] have sought to protect. [As reflected in the portions of Justice Kennedy's opinions reproduced in chapter 7 of this Supplement, the Court emphasized the extent to which states, not the federal government, have traditionally defined and regulated marriage].

The States' interest in defining and regulating the marital relation, subject to constitutional guarantees, stems from the understanding that marriage is more than a routine classification for purposes of certain statutory benefits. Private, consensual sexual intimacy between two adult persons of the same sex may not be punished by the State, and it can form "but one element in a personal bond that is more enduring." *Lawrence v. Texas* [Casebook, p. 677]. By its recognition of the validity of same-sex marriages performed in other jurisdictions and then by authorizing same-sex unions and same-sex marriages, New York sought to give further protection and dignity to that bond. For same-sex couples who wished to be married, the State acted to give their lawful conduct a lawful status. This status is a far-reaching legal acknowledgment of the intimate relationship between two people, a relationship deemed by the State worthy of dignity in the community equal with all other marriages. It reflects both the community's considered perspective on the historical roots of the institution of marriage and its evolving understanding of the meaning of equality.

DOMA seeks to injure the very class New York seeks to protect. By doing so it violates basic due process and equal protection principles applicable to the Federal Government [citing the Fifth Amendment]. The Constitution's guarantee of equality "must at the very least mean that a bare congressional desire to harm a politically unpopular group cannot" justify disparate treatment of that group. In determining whether a law is motivated by an improper animus or purpose, " '[d]iscriminations of an unusual character' " especially require careful consideration (quoting *Romer*). DOMA cannot survive under these principles. The responsibility of the States for the regulation of domestic relations is an important indicator of the substantial societal impact the State's classifications have in the daily lives and customs of its people. DOMA's unusual deviation from the usual tradition of recognizing and accepting state definitions of marriage here operates to deprive same-sex couples of the benefits and responsibilities that come with the federal recognition of their marriages. This is strong evidence of a law having the purpose and effect of disapproval of that class. * * *

The history of DOMA's enactment and its own text demonstrate that interference with the equal dignity of same-sex marriages, a dignity conferred by the States in the exercise of their sovereign power, was more than an incidental effect of the federal statute. It was its essence. The House Report announced its conclusion that "it is both appropriate and necessary for Congress to do what it can to defend the institution of traditional heterosexual marriage. . . . H.R. 3396 is appropriately entitled the 'Defense of Marriage Act.' The effort to redefine 'marriage' to extend to homosexual couples is a truly radical proposal that would fundamentally alter the institution of marriage." H.R.Rep. No. 104–664, pp. 12–13 (1996). The House concluded that DOMA expresses "both moral disapproval of homosexuality, and a moral conviction that heterosexuality better comports with traditional (especially Judeo-Christian) morality." * * *

DOMA's operation in practice confirms this purpose. When New York adopted a law to permit same-sex marriage, it sought to eliminate inequality; but DOMA frustrates that objective through a system-wide enactment with no identified connection to any particular area of federal law. DOMA writes inequality into the entire United States Code. The particular case at hand concerns the estate tax, but DOMA is more than a simple determination of what should or should not be allowed as an estate tax refund. Among the over 1,000 statutes and numerous federal regulations that DOMA controls are laws pertaining to Social Security, housing, taxes, criminal sanctions, copyright, and veterans' benefits.

DOMA's principal effect is to identify a subset of state-sanctioned marriages and make them unequal. * * * The differentiation demeans the couple, whose moral and sexual choices the Constitution protects, see *Lawrence*, and whose relationship the State has sought to dignify. And it humiliates tens of thousands of children now being raised by same-sex couples. The law in question makes it even more difficult for the children to understand the integrity and closeness of their own family and its concord with other families in their community and in their daily lives. * * *

DOMA also brings financial harm to children of same-sex couples. It raises the cost of health care for families by taxing health benefits provided by employers to their workers' same-sex spouses. And it denies or reduces benefits allowed to families upon the loss of a spouse and parent, benefits that are an integral part of family security. * * *

The liberty protected by the Fifth Amendment's Due Process Clause contains within it the prohibition against denying to any person the equal protection of the laws. While the Fifth Amendment itself withdraws from Government the power to degrade or demean in the way this law does, the equal protection guarantee of the Fourteenth Amendment makes that Fifth Amendment right all the more specific and all the better understood and preserved. * * *

By seeking to displace [the protection granted by states allowing same-sex marriage] and treating those persons as living in marriages less respected than others, the federal statute is in violation of the Fifth Amendment. This opinion and its holding are confined to those lawful marriages.

CHIEF JUSTICE ROBERTS, dissenting.

The majority [points] out that the Federal Government has generally (though not uniformly) deferred to state definitions of marriage in the past. That is true, of course, but none of those prior state-by-state variations had involved differences over something—as the majority puts it—"thought of by most people as essential to the very definition of [marriage] and to its role and function throughout the history of civilization." That the Federal Government treated this fundamental question differently than it treated variations over consanguinity or minimum age is hardly surprising—and hardly enough to support a conclusion that the "principal purpose," of the 342 Representatives and 85 Senators who voted for it, and the President who signed it, was a bare desire to harm. Nor do the snippets of legislative history and the banal title of the Act to which the majority points suffice to make such a showing. At least without some more convincing evidence that the Act's principal purpose was to codify malice, and that it furthered *no* legitimate government interests, I would not tar the political branches with the brush of bigotry.

But while I disagree with the result to which the majority's analysis leads it in this case, I think it more important to point out that its analysis leads no further. The Court does not have before it, and the logic of its opinion does not decide, the distinct question whether the States, in the exercise of their "historic and essential authority to define the marital relation," may continue to utilize the traditional definition of marriage. * * *

The dominant theme of the majority opinion is that the Federal Government's intrusion into an area "central to state domestic relations law applicable to its residents and citizens" is sufficiently "unusual" to set off alarm bells. I think the majority goes off course, as I have said, but it is undeniable that its judgment is based on federalism. * * *

JUSTICE SCALIA, with whom **JUSTICE THOMAS** joins, and with whom **THE CHIEF JUSTICE** joins as to part I, dissenting. * * *

[II.][I]f this is meant to be an equal-protection opinion, it is a confusing one. The opinion does not resolve and indeed does not even mention what had been the central question in this litigation: whether, under the Equal Protection Clause, laws restricting marriage to a man and a woman are reviewed for more than mere rationality. That is the issue that divided the parties and the court below. In accord with my previously expressed skepticism about the Court's "tiers of scrutiny" approach, I would review this classification only for its rationality. As nearly as I can tell, the Court agrees with that; its opinion does not apply strict scrutiny, and its central propositions are taken from rational-basis cases like *Moreno*. But the Court certainly does not *apply* anything that resembles that deferential framework.

The majority opinion need not get into the strict-vs.-rational-basis scrutiny question, and need not justify its holding under either, because it says that DOMA is unconstitutional as "a deprivation of the liberty of the person protected by the Fifth Amendment of the Constitution"; that it violates "basic due process" principles; and that it inflicts an "injury and indignity" of a kind that denies "an essential part of the liberty protected by the Fifth Amendment". The majority never utters the dread words "substantive due process," perhaps sensing the disrepute into which that doctrine has fallen, but that is what those statements mean. Yet the opinion does not argue that same-sex marriage is "deeply rooted in this Nation's history and tradition," a claim that would of course be quite absurd. * * *

The penultimate sentence of the majority's opinion is a naked declaration that "[t]his opinion and its holding are confined" to those couples "joined in same-sex marriages made lawful by the State." I have heard such "bald, unreasoned disclaimer[s]" before. When the Court declared a constitutional right to homosexual sodomy, we were assured that the case had nothing, nothing at all to do with "whether the government must give formal recognition to any relationship that homosexual persons seek to enter." (citing *Lawrence*). Now we are told that DOMA is invalid because it "demeans the couple, whose moral and sexual choices the Constitution protects,"—with an accompanying citation of *Lawrence*. It takes real cheek for today's majority to assure us, as it is going out the door, that a constitutional requirement to give formal recognition to same-sex marriage is not at issue here—when what has preceded that assurance is a lecture on how superior the majority's moral judgment in favor of same-sex marriage is to the Congress's hateful moral judgment against it. I promise you this: The only thing that will "confine" the Court's holding is its sense of what it can get away with.

I do not mean to suggest disagreement with THE CHIEF JUSTICE'S view that lower federal courts and state courts can distinguish today's case when the issue before them is state denial of marital status to same-sex couples— or even that this Court could *theoretically* do so. Lord, an opinion with such scatter-shot rationales as this one (federalism noises among them) can be distinguished in many ways. And deserves to be. State and lower federal courts should take the Court at its word and distinguish away.

In my opinion, however, the view that *this* Court will take of state prohibition of same-sex marriage is indicated beyond mistaking by today's opinion. As I have said, the real rationale of today's opinion, whatever disappearing trail of its legalistic argle-bargle one chooses to follow, is that DOMA is motivated by " 'bare . . . desire to harm' " couples in same-sex marriages. How easy it is, indeed how inevitable, to reach the same conclusion with regard to state laws denying same-sex couples marital status. Consider how easy (inevitable) it is to make the following substitutions in a passage from today's opinion: * * *

> "[DOMA] *This state law* tells those couples, and all the world, that their otherwise valid ~~marriages~~ *relationships* are unworthy of ~~federal~~ *state* recognition. This places same-sex couples in an unstable position of being in a second-tier ~~marriage~~ *relationship*. The differentiation demeans the couple, whose moral and sexual choices the Constitution protects, see *Lawrence*, . . . "

Or this, which does not even require alteration, except as to the invented number:

> "And it humiliates ~~tens of~~ thousands of children now being raised by same-sex couples. The law in question makes it even more difficult for the children to understand the integrity and closeness of their own family and its concord with other families in their community and in their daily lives." * * *

Some will rejoice in today's decision, and some will despair at it; that is the nature of a controversy that matters so much to so many. But the Court has cheated both sides, robbing the winners of an honest victory, and the losers of the peace that comes from a fair defeat. We owed both of them better. I dissent.

JUSTICE ALITO, with whom **JUSTICE THOMAS** joins as to Parts II and III, dissenting.

[III.] Windsor and the United States are really seeking to have the Court resolve a debate between two competing views of marriage.

The first and older view, which I will call the "traditional" or "conjugal" view, sees marriage as an intrinsically opposite-sex institution. * * * [V]irtually every culture, including many not influenced by the Abrahamic religions, has limited marriage to people of the opposite sex. * * * While modern cultural changes have weakened the link between marriage and procreation in the popular mind, there is no doubt that, throughout human history and across many cultures, marriage has been viewed as an exclusively opposite-sex institution and as one inextricably linked to procreation and biological kinship.

The other, newer view is what I will call the "consent-based" vision of marriage, a vision that primarily defines marriage as the solemnization of mutual commitment—marked by strong emotional attachment and sexual attraction—between two persons. At least as it applies to heterosexual couples, this view of marriage now plays a very prominent role in the popular understanding of the institution. Indeed, our popular culture is infused with this understanding of marriage. Proponents of same-sex marriage argue that because gender differentiation is not relevant to this vision, the exclusion of same-sex couples from the institution of marriage is rank discrimination.

The Constitution does not codify either of these views of marriage (although I suspect it would have been hard at the time of the adoption of the Constitution or the Fifth Amendment to find Americans who did not take the traditional view for granted). The silence of the Constitution on this question should be enough to end the matter as far as the judiciary is concerned. * * *

NOTES

1. *The Dissenters' Critiques*. Notice that the dissents level several criticisms against the majority opinion in *Windsor*:

(a) That the opinion is missing key doctrinal elements, such as the standard of review it is applying, as well as a clear statement of whether the opinion relies on "liberty" as a means of imposing equal protection on the federal government (as suggested by the citations to *Bolling v. Sharpe*, Casebook p. 98) or means to invoke liberty as an independent constitutional norm;

(b) That the Court ought to leave the question of marriage equality to the political branches and public debate, which have been heavily engaged with the question in recent years;

(c) That the majority wrongly imputes bias and animus to those who enacted DOMA, rather than a good faith difference of opinion; and

(d) That, contrary to the disclaimer at the end of the majority opinion, the majority's rationale is unlikely to be limited to DOMA, as opposed to state laws that bar same-sex marriage.

Do you find merit in any of these critiques? Did Justice Kennedy answer them satisfactorily? Could a stronger opinion have been written in support of the result the Court reached? If so, how?

2. *Dignity*. The majority emphasizes its view that DOMA undermines the dignity of same-sex couples who are married under state law. Indeed, some form of the word "dignity" is used no fewer than ten times in Justice Kennedy's full opinion. What does he mean by dignity? How ought a claim of dignitary harm be demonstrated? Does the idea of dignity merit a special place in 14th Amendment jurisprudence? How might it apply in other contexts, such as disputes over abortion and affirmative action? Note that human dignity is a key concept in some other constitutions, such as Germany's Basic Law. The term is not used in the U.S. Constitution, but is the concept implicit?

3. *Connections to Romer and Lawrence*. Compare Justice Kennedy's opinion to the opinions he wrote previously in *Romer* (Casebook, p. 474) and *Lawrence* (Casebook, p. 677). Do you notice similarities? Among other things, consider the *Windsor* majority opinion's repeated emphasis on the idea of respect for gay persons (a theme stressed in *Lawrence*) and on the unfair singling out of gay persons alone for a broadly-drawn legal disability (a theme stressed in *Romer*).

* * *

Two years to the day after *Windsor*, in an opinion once again authored by Justice Kennedy, the Court returned to the issue of same-sex marriage in the landmark case of *Obergefell v. Hodges*, ___ U.S. ___, 135 S.Ct. 2584 (2015). *Obergefell* declared a broad right of marriage equality applicable in every state. The Court placed principal emphasis not on equal protection, but on the fundamental right to marry. For that reason, the case appears in Chapter 5 of this Supplement. While the opinion focuses on due process, you will note that the majority invokes the equal protection clause as part of its analysis. After you read *Obergefell* in the next chapter, consider the following Problem.

PROBLEM 4–6:
A BAN ON LESBIAN OR GAY GRADE SCHOOL TEACHERS

Suppose a state enacts a law banning gay or lesbian persons from becoming public school teachers in kindergarten through fifth grade classes. The state cites as its justification its desire to shield young children for as long as possible from the complex issues of sexual orientation. Gay and lesbian teachers challenge the law as a violation of equal protection. Consider the following questions.

(a) What tier of scrutiny will be applied to this policy? Review the argument made for heightened scrutiny in the context of sexual orientation-based discrimination in the Holder Letter on the federal Defense of Marriage Act (Casebook, pp. 503–505). What, if anything, does the *Obergefell* majority add on the issue of heightened scrutiny? Is it significant that Justice Kennedy's opinion in that case twice characterizes sexual orientation as immutable? That he begins his opinion by reviewing in detail the history of how American law has regarded homosexuality? Do you find anything else in the opinion that might bear on the tier of scrutiny a court would use?

(b) How might the language about equal protection in the *Obergefell* opinion bear on whether the ban on gay or lesbian teachers would pass muster under equal protection? How would this ban fare if strict or intermediate scrutiny is used? If neither form of heightened scrutiny is used, do you think the law would survive equal protection challenge? You will note that there is no mention in *Obergefell* of the idea of "animus" that was employed in *Romer* and *Windsor*. Will the absence of that term in *Obergefell* affect subsequent equal protection challenges to laws discriminating on the basis of sexual orientation? Or is *Obergefell* best seen as limited to state marriage laws?

CHAPTER 5

PROTECTING FUNDAMENTAL RIGHTS

■ ■ ■

SECTION 2. PROTECTING ECONOMIC LIBERTY AND PROPERTY

C. THE TAKINGS CLAUSE

Page 569. Insert before Section 3:

In *Horne v. Department of Agriculture*, ___ U.S. ___, 135 S.Ct. 2419 (2015), the Court held that the Takings Clause applies to personal property, just as it applies to real property. The case involved a challenge by raisin growers to a federal agricultural subsidy program that required them to set aside a percentage of their annual crop. The purpose of the program is to limit supply as a way to stabilize prices. Pursuant to the program, the government physically takes possession of the raisins mandated to be set aside. Chief Justice Roberts wrote that "the Government has a categorical duty to pay just compensation when it takes your car, just as when it takes your home." Language in *Lucas* suggesting a different approach to *regulatory takings* of personal versus real property is irrelevant, the Court said, to takings involving the physical appropriation of property.

SECTION 3. EQUAL PROTECTION AND "FUNDAMENTAL INTERESTS"

A. VOTING

Page 580. Insert after Problem 5–1: Political Gerrymandering:

One mechanism some states have used to control political gerrymandering is the creation of independent commissions to handle redistricting. The voters in Arizona pursued this course in 2000 by passing a state constitutional amendment that reallocated authority from the state legislature to the Arizona Independent Redistricting Commission. The state legislature challenged this measure as a violation of the Elections Clause, Art. I, § 4, cl. 1, which provides in relevant part that the "Times, Places and Manner of holding Elections for Senators and Representatives, shall be prescribed in each State by the *Legislature* thereof." (emphasis added). In *Arizona State Legislature v. Arizona Independent Redistricting Comm'n*, ___ U.S. ___, 135 S.Ct. 2652 (2015), the Court by a 5–4 majority rejected this challenge. The case turned on how to interpret the word "Legislature" in the Clause. Justice Ginsburg's opinion for the Court reasoned that when the legislative power of a state is given by state constitution to the people, acting through the initiative process, they constitute the "legislature" for purposes of the Elections Clause. The opinion emphasized the norm of self-government (noting that direct democracy is consistent with the idea of popular sovereignty that underlies the Constitution's creation of republican government) and the policy consequences that would flow from a contrary ruling (noting that many election-related laws passed directly by voters around the country would be jeopardized). In dissent, Chief Justice Roberts argued that Senators were chosen by state legislatures, not popular vote, under the original Constitution. If judges could legitimately read the word legislature in the Elections Clause to include the people acting in a legislative capacity, he suggested, there would have been no need for the Seventeenth Amendment because even a change as consequential as popular election of Senators could have been accomplished by an act of simple judicial interpretation.

SECTION 4. FUNDAMENTAL PRIVACY RIGHTS

D. THE RIGHT TO MARRY

Page 691. Delete Note on the Constitutional Right to Marry and insert the following material at the end of Section 4:

In a highly anticipated ruling near the end of the Term, the Supreme Court decided what seems destined to become one of the most significant cases in a generation or more. It inspired a heated debate among the justices about the appropriate role of courts.

OBERGEFELL V. HODGES
___ U.S.___, 135 S.Ct. 2584 (2015)

[Voters in Michigan, Kentucky, Ohio and Tennessee enacted state constitutional amendments defining marriage as a union between one man and one woman. Same-sex couples challenged the denial of their right to marry and to have out-of-state marriages that were valid where performed recognized in any of these states. The Sixth Circuit upheld the bans in 2014. That decision conflicted with decisions of several federal appellate courts in favor of marriage equality. Two Terms after it had struck down the federal Defense of Marriage Act as unconstitutional in *United States v. Windsor* (Chapter Four of this Supplement), the Supreme Court granted review to decide whether the Fourteenth Amendment requires states to license a marriage between two people of the same-sex and/or to recognize a same-sex marriage licensed in another state.]

JUSTICE KENNEDY delivered the opinion of the Court.

[II.] From their beginning to their most recent page, the annals of human history reveal the transcendent importance of marriage. The lifelong union of a man and a woman always has promised nobility and dignity to all persons, without regard to their station in life. Marriage is sacred to those who live by their religions and offers unique fulfillment to those who find meaning in the secular realm. Its dynamic allows two people to find a life that could not be found alone, for a marriage becomes greater than just the two persons. Rising from the most basic human needs, marriage is essential to our most profound hopes and aspirations.

The centrality of marriage to the human condition makes it unsurprising that the institution has existed for millennia and across civilizations. Since the dawn of history, marriage has transformed strangers into relatives, binding families and societies together. * * *

The petitioners acknowledge this history but contend that these cases cannot end there. * * * Far from seeking to devalue marriage, the petitioners seek it for themselves because of their respect—and need—for its privileges and responsibilities. And their immutable nature dictates that same-sex marriage is their only real path to this profound commitment.

Recounting the circumstances of three of these cases illustrates the urgency of the petitioners' cause from their perspective. Petitioner James Obergefell, a plaintiff in the Ohio case, met John Arthur over two decades ago. They fell in love and started a life together, establishing a lasting, committed relation. In 2011, however, Arthur was diagnosed with amyotrophic lateral sclerosis, or ALS. This debilitating disease is progressive, with no known cure. Two years ago, Obergefell and Arthur decided to commit to one another, resolving to marry before Arthur died. To fulfill their mutual promise, they traveled from Ohio to Maryland, where same-sex marriage was legal. It was difficult for Arthur to move, and so the couple were wed inside a medical transport plane as it remained on the tarmac in Baltimore. Three months later, Arthur died. Ohio law does not permit Obergefell to be listed as the surviving spouse on Arthur's death certificate. By statute, they must remain strangers even in death, a state-imposed separation Obergefell deems "hurtful for the rest of time." He brought suit to be shown as the surviving spouse on Arthur's death certificate.

April DeBoer and Jayne Rowse are co-plaintiffs in the case from Michigan. They celebrated a commitment ceremony to honor their permanent relation in 2007. They both work as nurses, DeBoer in a neonatal unit and Rowse in an emergency unit. In 2009, DeBoer and Rowse fostered and then adopted a baby boy. Later that same year, they welcomed another son into their family. The new baby, born prematurely and abandoned by his biological mother, required around-the-clock care. The next year, a baby girl with special needs joined their family. Michigan, however, permits only opposite-sex married couples or single individuals to adopt, so each child can have only one woman as his or her legal parent. If an emergency were to arise, schools and hospitals may treat the three children as if they had only one parent. And, were tragedy to befall either DeBoer or Rowse, the other would have no legal rights over the children she had not been permitted to adopt. This couple seeks relief from the continuing uncertainty their unmarried status creates in their lives.

Army Reserve Sergeant First Class Ijpe DeKoe and his partner Thomas Kostura, co-plaintiffs in the Tennessee case, fell in love. In 2011, DeKoe received orders to deploy to Afghanistan. Before leaving, he and Kostura married in New York. A week later, DeKoe began his deployment, which lasted for almost a year. When he returned, the two settled in Tennessee, where DeKoe works full-time for the Army Reserve. Their lawful marriage is stripped from them whenever they reside in Tennessee, returning and disappearing as they travel across state lines. DeKoe, who served this Nation to preserve the freedom the Constitution protects, must endure a substantial burden. * * *

The ancient origins of marriage confirm its centrality, but it has not stood in isolation from developments in law and society. The history of marriage is one of both continuity and change. That institution—even as confined to opposite-sex relations—has evolved over time.

For example, marriage was once viewed as an arrangement by the couple's parents based on political, religious, and financial concerns; but by the time of the Nation's founding it was understood to be a voluntary contract between a man and a woman. As the role and status of women changed, the institution further evolved. Under the centuries-old doctrine of coverture, a married man and woman were treated by the State as a single, male-dominated legal entity. As women gained legal, political, and property rights, and as society began to understand that women have their own equal dignity, the law of coverture was abandoned. These and other developments in the institution of marriage over the past centuries were not mere superficial changes. Rather, they worked deep transformations in its structure, affecting aspects of marriage long viewed by many as essential. * * *

These new insights have strengthened, not weakened, the institution of marriage. Indeed, changed understandings of marriage are characteristic of a Nation where new dimensions of freedom become apparent to new generations, often through perspectives that begin in pleas or protests and then are considered in the political sphere and the judicial process.

This dynamic can be seen in the Nation's experiences with the rights of gays and lesbians. Until the mid-20th century, same-sex intimacy long had been condemned as immoral by the state itself in most Western nations, a belief often embodied in the criminal law. For this reason, among others, many persons did not deem homosexuals to have dignity in their own distinct identity. A truthful declaration by same-sex couples of what was in their hearts had to remain unspoken. Even when a greater awareness of the humanity and integrity of homosexual persons came in the period after World War II, the argument that gays and lesbians had a just claim to dignity was in conflict with both law and widespread social conventions. Same-sex intimacy remained a crime in many States. Gays and lesbians were prohibited from most government employment, barred from military service, excluded under immigration laws, targeted by police, and burdened in their rights to associate.

For much of the 20th century, moreover, homosexuality was treated as an illness. When the American Psychiatric Association published the first Diagnostic and Statistical Manual of Mental Disorders in 1952, homosexuality was classified as a mental disorder, a position adhered to until 1973. Only in more recent years have psychiatrists and others recognized that sexual orientation is both a normal expression of human sexuality and immutable.

In the late 20th century, following substantial cultural and political developments, same-sex couples began to lead more open and public lives and to establish families. This development was followed by a quite extensive discussion of the issue in both governmental and private sectors and by a shift in public attitudes toward greater tolerance. As a result, questions about the rights of gays and lesbians soon reached the courts, where the issue could be discussed in the formal discourse of the law.

[Justice Kennedy first recounted the history of the Court's cases addressing "the legal status of homosexuals" in *Bowers v. Hardwick*, [Casebook, p. 675], *Romer v. Evans* [Casebook, p. 474], and *Lawrence v. Texas* [Casebook, p. 677]. He then reviewed the history of the same-sex marriage debate, highlighting the Hawaii Supreme Court's decision in *Baehr v. Lewin* [Casebook p. 507], which began the contemporary debate; the Massachusetts Supreme Judicial Court's decision in *Goodridge v. Department of Public Health* [Casebook, p. 487] finding for the first time that a state constitution protected the right of same-sex couples to wed; the Court's own 2013 decision in *United States v. Windsor*, invalidating DOMA to the extent it barred the Federal Government from treating a same-sex marriage as valid even when it was lawful in the state where it was licensed; and the many cases addressing marriage equality in federal appellate and district courts, as well as state supreme courts.] After years of litigation, legislation, referenda, and the discussions that attended these public acts, the States are now divided on the issue of same-sex marriage.

[III.] Under the Due Process Clause of the Fourteenth Amendment, no State shall "deprive any person of life, liberty, or property, without due process of law." The fundamental liberties protected by this Clause include most of the rights enumerated in the Bill of Rights. In addition these liberties extend to certain personal choices central to individual dignity and autonomy, including intimate choices that define personal identity and beliefs.

The identification and protection of fundamental rights is an enduring part of the judicial duty to interpret the Constitution. That responsibility, however, "has not been reduced to any formula." *Poe v. Ullman* (Harlan, J., dissenting) [Casebook, p. 613]. Rather, it requires courts to exercise reasoned judgment in identifying interests of the person so fundamental that the State must accord them its respect. That process is guided by many of the same considerations relevant to analysis of other constitutional provisions that set forth broad principles rather than specific requirements. History and tradition guide and discipline this inquiry but do not set its outer boundaries. See *Lawrence*. That method respects our history and learns from it without allowing the past alone to rule the present.

The nature of injustice is that we may not always see it in our own times. The generations that wrote and ratified the Bill of Rights and the Fourteenth Amendment did not presume to know the extent of freedom in all of its dimensions, and so they entrusted to future generations a charter protecting the right of all persons to enjoy liberty as we learn its meaning. When new insight reveals discord between the Constitution's central protections and a received legal stricture, a claim to liberty must be addressed.

Applying these established tenets, the Court has long held the right to marry is protected by the Constitution. In *Loving v. Virginia* [Casebook, p. 216], which invalidated bans on interracial unions, a unanimous Court held marriage is "one of the vital personal rights essential to the orderly pursuit of happiness by free men." The Court reaffirmed that holding in *Zablocki v. Redhail* [Casebook, p. 687], which held the right to marry was burdened by a law prohibiting fathers who were behind on child support from marrying. The Court again applied this principle in *Turner v. Safley* [Casebook, p. 688], which held the right to marry was abridged by regulations limiting the privilege of prison inmates to marry. Over time and in other contexts, the Court has reiterated that the right to marry is fundamental under the Due Process Clause. * * *

The four principles and traditions to be discussed demonstrate that the reasons marriage is fundamental under the Constitution apply with equal force to same-sex couples.

A first premise of the Court's relevant precedents is that the right to personal choice regarding marriage is inherent in the concept of individual autonomy. This abiding connection between marriage and liberty is why *Loving* invalidated interracial marriage bans under the Due Process Clause. Like choices concerning contraception, family relationships, procreation, and childrearing, all of which are protected by the Constitution, decisions concerning marriage are among the most intimate that an individual can make. * * *

A second principle in this Court's jurisprudence is that the right to marry is fundamental because it supports a two-person union unlike any other in its importance to the committed individuals. This point was central to *Griswold v. Connecticut,* which held the Constitution protects the right of married couples to use contraception. * * *

The right to marry thus dignifies couples who "wish to define themselves by their commitment to each other." *Windsor.* Marriage responds to the universal fear that a lonely person might call out only to find no one there. It offers the hope of companionship and understanding and assurance that while both still live there will be someone to care for the other. * * *

Lawrence confirmed a dimension of freedom that allows individuals to engage in intimate association without criminal liability, [but] it does not follow that freedom stops there. Outlaw to outcast may be a step forward, but it does not achieve the full promise of liberty.

A third basis for protecting the right to marry is that it safeguards children and families and thus draws meaning from related rights of childrearing, procreation, and education. See *Pierce v. Society of Sisters*; *Meyer v. Nebraska* [Casebook, pp. 609–611]. * * *

As all parties agree, many same-sex couples provide loving and nurturing homes to their children, whether biological or adopted. And hundreds of thousands of children are presently being raised by such couples. Most States have allowed gays and lesbians to adopt, either as individuals or as couples, and many adopted and foster children have same-sex parents. This provides powerful confirmation from the law itself that gays and lesbians can create loving, supportive families.

Excluding same-sex couples from marriage thus conflicts with a central premise of the right to marry. Without the recognition, stability, and predictability marriage offers, their children suffer the stigma of knowing their families are somehow lesser. They also suffer the significant material costs of being raised by unmarried parents, relegated through no fault of their own to a more difficult and uncertain family life. The marriage laws at issue here thus harm and humiliate the children of same-sex couples.

That is not to say the right to marry is less meaningful for those who do not or cannot have children. An ability, desire, or promise to procreate is not and has not been a prerequisite for a valid marriage in any State. In light of precedent protecting the right of a married couple not to procreate, it cannot be said the Court or the States have conditioned the right to marry on the capacity or commitment to procreate. The constitutional marriage right has many aspects, of which childbearing is only one.

Fourth and finally, this Court's cases and the Nation's traditions make clear that marriage is a keystone of our social order. * * *

[J]ust as a couple vows to support each other, so does society pledge to support the couple, offering symbolic recognition and material benefits to protect and nourish the union. Indeed, while the States are in general free to vary the benefits they confer on all married couples, they have throughout our history made marriage the basis for an expanding list of governmental rights, benefits, and responsibilities. These aspects of marital status include: taxation; inheritance and property rights; rules of intestate succession; spousal privilege in the law of evidence; hospital access; medical decisionmaking authority; adoption rights; the rights and benefits of survivors; birth and death certificates; professional ethics rules; campaign finance restrictions; workers' compensation benefits; health insurance; and child custody, support, and visitation rules. Valid marriage under state law is also a significant status for over a thousand provisions of federal law. See *Windsor*. The States have contributed to the fundamental character of the marriage right by placing that institution at the center of so many facets of the legal and social order.

There is no difference between same- and opposite-sex couples with respect to this principle. Yet by virtue of their exclusion from that institution, same-sex couples are denied the constellation of benefits that the States have linked to marriage. This harm results in more than just material burdens. * * * It demeans gays and lesbians for the State to lock them out of a central institution of the Nation's society. Same-sex couples, too, may aspire to the transcendent purposes of marriage and seek fulfillment in its highest meaning.

Objecting that this does not reflect an appropriate framing of the issue, the respondents refer to *Washington v. Glucksberg,* [Casebook, p. 692], which called for a " 'careful description' " of fundamental rights. They assert the petitioners do not seek to exercise the right to marry but rather a new and nonexistent "right to same-sex marriage." *Glucksberg* did insist that liberty under the Due Process Clause must be defined in a most circumscribed manner, with central reference to specific historical practices. Yet while that approach may have been appropriate for the asserted right there involved (physician-assisted suicide), it is inconsistent with the approach this Court has used in discussing other fundamental rights, including marriage and intimacy. *Loving* did not ask about a "right to interracial marriage"; *Turner* did not ask about a "right of inmates to marry"; and *Zablocki* did not ask about a "right of fathers with unpaid child support duties to marry." Rather, each case inquired about the right to marry in its comprehensive sense, asking if there was a sufficient justification for excluding the relevant class from the right.

That principle applies here. If rights were defined by who exercised them in the past, then received practices could serve as their own continued justification and new groups could not invoke rights once denied. This Court has rejected that approach, both with respect to the right to marry and the rights of gays and lesbians. See *Loving*; *Lawrence*. * * *

The right of same-sex couples to marry that is part of the liberty promised by the Fourteenth Amendment is derived, too, from that Amendment's guarantee of the equal protection of the laws. The Due Process Clause and the Equal Protection Clause are connected in a profound way, though they set forth independent principles. Rights implicit in liberty and rights secured by equal protection may rest on different precepts and are not always co-extensive, yet in some instances each may be instructive as to the meaning and reach of the other. In any particular case one Clause may be thought to capture the essence of the right in a more accurate and comprehensive way, even as the two Clauses may converge in the identification and definition of the right. This interrelation of the two principles furthers our understanding of what freedom is and must become.

The Court's cases touching upon the right to marry reflect this dynamic. In *Loving* the Court invalidated a prohibition on interracial marriage under both the Equal Protection Clause and the Due Process Clause. The Court first declared the prohibition invalid because of its unequal treatment of interracial couples. It stated: "There can be no doubt that restricting the freedom to marry solely because of racial classifications violates the central meaning of the Equal Protection Clause." With this link to equal protection the Court proceeded to hold the prohibition offended central precepts of liberty: "To deny this fundamental freedom on so unsupportable a basis as the racial classifications embodied in these statutes, classifications so directly subversive of the principle of equality at the heart of the Fourteenth Amendment, is surely to deprive all the State's citizens of liberty without due process of law." The reasons why marriage is a fundamental right became more clear and compelling from a full awareness and understanding of the hurt that resulted from laws barring interracial unions.

The synergy between the two protections is illustrated further in *Zablocki*. There the Court invoked the Equal Protection Clause as its basis for invalidating the challenged law, which, as already noted, barred fathers who were behind on child-support payments from marrying without judicial approval. The equal protection analysis depended in central part on the Court's holding that the law burdened a right "of fundamental importance." It was the essential nature of the marriage right, discussed at length in *Zablocki* that made apparent the law's incompatibility with requirements of equality. Each concept—liberty and equal protection—leads to a stronger understanding of the other.

Indeed, in interpreting the Equal Protection Clause, the Court has recognized that new insights and societal understandings can reveal unjustified inequality within our most fundamental institutions that once passed unnoticed and unchallenged. To take but one period, this occurred with respect to marriage in the 1970's and 1980's. Notwithstanding the gradual erosion of the doctrine of coverture, invidious sex-based classifications in marriage remained common through the mid-20th century. These classifications denied the equal dignity of men and women. One State's law, for example, provided in 1971 that "the husband is the head of the family and the wife is subject to him; her legal civil existence is merged in the husband, except so far as the law recognizes her separately, either for her own protection, or for her benefit." Responding to a new awareness, the Court invoked equal protection principles to invalidate laws imposing sex-based inequality on marriage. [Justice Kennedy collected here a set of gender discrimination cases decided in the 1970s and 1980s]. * * *

[*Lawrence* also] drew upon principles of liberty and equality to define and protect the rights of gays and lesbians, holding the State "cannot demean their existence or control their destiny by making their private sexual conduct a crime." * * *

Here the marriage laws enforced by the respondents are in essence unequal: same-sex couples are denied all the benefits afforded to opposite-sex couples and are barred from exercising a fundamental right. Especially against a long history of disapproval of their relationships, this denial to same-sex couples of the right to marry works a grave and continuing harm. * * *

These considerations lead to the conclusion that the right to marry is a fundamental right inherent in the liberty of the person, and under the Due Process and Equal Protection Clauses of the Fourteenth Amendment couples of the same-sex may not be deprived of that right and that liberty. The Court now holds that same-sex couples may exercise the fundamental right to marry. No longer may this liberty be denied to them. * * *

[IV]. There may be an initial inclination in these cases to proceed with caution—to await further legislation, litigation, and debate. The respondents warn there has been insufficient democratic discourse before deciding an issue so basic as the definition of marriage. In its ruling on the cases now before this Court, the majority opinion for the Court of Appeals made a cogent argument that it would be appropriate for the respondents' States to await further public discussion and political measures before licensing same-sex marriages. Yet there has been far more deliberation than this argument acknowledges. [The majority noted here the many "referenda, legislative debates, and grassroots campaigns, studies, as well as countless studies, papers, books, and other popular and scholarly writings," and the scores of amicus briefs filed in *Obergefell* itself. Justice Kennedy also attached to the opinion two appendices that listed state and federal litigation addressing, and state legislation legalizing, same-sex marriage.]

Of course, the Constitution contemplates that democracy is the appropriate process for change, so long as that process does not abridge fundamental rights. Last Term, a plurality of this Court reaffirmed the importance of the democratic principle in *Schuette v. BAMN*, noting the "right of citizens to debate so they can learn and decide and then, through the political process, act in concert to try to shape the course of their own times." Indeed, it is most often through democracy that liberty is preserved and protected in our lives. But as *Schuette* also said, "[t]he freedom secured by the Constitution consists, in one of its essential dimensions, of the right of the individual not to be injured by the unlawful exercise of governmental power." * * *

The idea of the Constitution "was to withdraw certain subjects from the vicissitudes of political controversy, to place them beyond the reach of majorities and officials and to establish them as legal principles to be applied by the courts." This is why "fundamental rights may not be submitted to a vote; they depend on the outcome of no elections." It is of no moment whether advocates of same-sex marriage now enjoy or lack momentum in the democratic process. * * *

The petitioners' stories make clear the urgency of the issue they present to the Court. * * *

The respondents also argue allowing same-sex couples to wed will harm marriage as an institution by leading to fewer opposite-sex marriages. This may occur, the respondents contend, because licensing same-sex marriage severs the connection between natural procreation and marriage. That argument, however, rests on a counterintuitive view of opposite-sex couple's decisionmaking processes regarding marriage and parenthood. Decisions about whether to marry and raise children are based on many personal, romantic, and practical considerations; and it is unrealistic to conclude that an opposite-sex couple would choose not to marry simply because same-sex couples may do so. * * *Indeed, with respect to this asserted basis for excluding same-sex couples from the right to marry, it is appropriate to observe these cases involve only the rights of two consenting adults whose marriages would pose no risk of harm to themselves or third parties.

Finally, it must be emphasized that religions, and those who adhere to religious doctrines, may continue to advocate with utmost, sincere conviction that, by divine precepts, same-sex marriage should not be condoned. The First Amendment ensures that religious organizations and persons are given proper protection as they seek to teach the principles that are so fulfilling and so central to their lives and faiths, and to their own deep aspirations to continue the family structure they have long revered. The same is true of those who oppose same-sex marriage for other reasons. In turn, those who believe allowing same-sex marriage is proper or indeed essential, whether as a matter of religious conviction or secular belief, may engage those who disagree with their view in an open and searching debate. The Constitution, however, does not permit the State to bar same-sex couples from marriage on the same terms as accorded to couples of the opposite sex.

[V. The Court then held that the same reasons cited for affording same-sex couples the right to marry also affords them the right to have an out-of-state marriage recognized.] * * *

It would misunderstand [the plaintiffs] to say they disrespect the idea of marriage. Their plea is that they do respect it, respect it so deeply that they seek to find its fulfillment for themselves. Their hope is not to be condemned to live in loneliness, excluded from one of civilization's oldest institutions. They ask for equal dignity in the eyes of the law. The Constitution grants them that right.

CHIEF JUSTICE ROBERTS, with whom **JUSTICE SCALIA** and **JUSTICE THOMAS** join, dissenting.

Petitioners make strong arguments rooted in social policy and considerations of fairness. They contend that same-sex couples should be allowed to affirm their love and commitment through marriage, just like opposite-sex couples. That position has undeniable appeal; over the past six years, voters and legislators in eleven States and the District of Columbia have revised their laws to allow marriage between two people of the same sex.

But this Court is not a legislature. Whether same-sex marriage is a good idea should be of no concern to us. Under the Constitution, judges have power to say what the law is, not what it should be. The people who ratified the Constitution authorized courts to exercise "neither force nor will but merely judgment." The Federalist No. 78, p. 465

Although the policy arguments for extending marriage to same-sex couples may be compelling, the legal arguments for requiring such an extension are not. The fundamental right to marry does not include a right to make a State change its definition of marriage. * * *

Today, however, the Court takes the extraordinary step of ordering every State to license and recognize same-sex marriage. Many people will rejoice at this decision, and I begrudge none their celebration. But for those who believe in a government of laws, not of men, the majority's approach is deeply disheartening. Supporters of same-sex marriage have achieved considerable success persuading their fellow citizens—through the democratic process—to adopt their view. That ends today. Five lawyers have closed the debate and enacted their own vision of marriage as a matter of constitutional law. Stealing this issue from the people will for many cast a cloud over same-sex marriage, making a dramatic social change that much more difficult to accept.

The majority's decision is an act of will, not legal judgment. The right it announces has no basis in the Constitution or this Court's precedent. The majority expressly disclaims judicial "caution" and omits even a pretense of humility, openly relying on its desire to remake society according to its own "new insight" into the "nature of injustice." As a result, the Court invalidates the marriage laws of more than half the States and orders the transformation of a social institution that has formed the basis of human society for millennia, for the Kalahari Bushmen and the Han Chinese, the Carthaginians and the Aztecs. Just who do we think we are? * * *

[I.] [The] universal definition of marriage as the union of a man and a woman is no historical coincidence. Marriage did not come about as a result of a political movement, discovery, disease, war, religious doctrine, or any other moving force of world history—and certainly not as a result of a prehistoric decision to exclude gays and lesbians. It arose in the nature of things to meet a vital need: ensuring that children are conceived by a mother and father committed to raising them in the stable conditions of a lifelong relationship. * * *

The human race must procreate to survive. Procreation occurs through sexual relations between a man and a woman. When sexual relations result in the conception of a child, that child's prospects are generally better if the mother and father stay together rather than going their separate ways. Therefore, for the good of children and society, sexual relations that can lead to procreation should occur only between a man and a woman committed to a lasting bond.

Society has recognized that bond as marriage. And by bestowing a respected status and material benefits on married couples, society encourages men and women to conduct sexual relations within marriage rather than without. * * *

There is no dispute that every State at the founding—and every State throughout our history until a dozen years ago—defined marriage in the traditional, biologically rooted way. * * *

[II.] Petitioners' "fundamental right" claim falls into the most sensitive category of constitutional adjudication. Petitioners do not contend that their States' marriage laws violate an *enumerated* constitutional right, such as the freedom of speech protected by the First Amendment. There is, after all, no "Companionship and Understanding" or "Nobility and Dignity" Clause in the Constitution. They argue instead that the laws violate a right *implied* by the Fourteenth Amendment's requirement that "liberty" may not be deprived without "due process of law." * * *

Allowing unelected federal judges to select which unenumerated rights rank as "fundamental"—and to strike down state laws on the basis of that determination—raises obvious concerns about the judicial role. Our precedents have accordingly insisted that judges "exercise the utmost care" in identifying implied fundamental rights, "lest the liberty protected by the Due Process Clause be subtly transformed into the policy preferences of the Members of this Court." *Washington v. Glucksberg.*

The need for restraint in administering the strong medicine of substantive due process is a lesson this Court has learned the hard way. The Court first applied substantive due process to strike down a statute in *Dred Scott.* There the Court invalidated the Missouri Compromise on the ground that legislation restricting the institution of slavery violated the implied rights of slaveholders. The Court relied on its own conception of liberty and property in doing so. * * *

Dred Scott's holding was overruled on the battlefields of the Civil War and by constitutional amendment after Appomattox, but its approach to the Due Process Clause reappeared. In a series of early 20th-century cases, most prominently *Lochner v. New York,* this Court invalidated state statutes that presented "meddlesome interferences with the rights of the individual," and "undue interference with liberty of person and freedom of contract." In *Lochner* itself, the Court struck down a New York law setting maximum hours for bakery employees, because there was "in our judgment, no reasonable foundation for holding this to be necessary or appropriate as a health law."

The dissenting Justices in *Lochner* explained that the New York law could be viewed as a reasonable response to legislative concern about the health of bakery employees, an issue on which there was at least "room for debate and for an honest difference of opinion." (opinion of Harlan, J.). The majority's contrary conclusion required adopting as constitutional law "an economic theory which a large part of the country does not entertain." (opinion of Holmes, J.). As Justice Holmes memorably put it, "The Fourteenth Amendment does not enact Mr. Herbert Spencer's Social

Statics," a leading work on the philosophy of Social Darwinism. The Constitution "is not intended to embody a particular economic theory. . . . It is made for people of fundamentally differing views, and the accident of our finding certain opinions natural and familiar or novel and even shocking ought not to conclude our judgment upon the question whether statutes embodying them conflict with the Constitution."

In the decades after *Lochner,* the Court struck down nearly 200 laws as violations of individual liberty, often over strong dissents contending that "[t]he criterion of constitutionality is not whether we believe the law to be for the public good." * * *

Eventually, the Court recognized its error and vowed not to repeat it. * * *[I]t has become an accepted rule that the Court will not hold laws unconstitutional simply because we find them "unwise, improvident, or out of harmony with a particular school of thought." *Williamson v. Lee Optical of Okla., Inc.* [Casebook, p. 550]. * * *

None of the laws at issue in [the cases cited by the majority finding a fundamental right to marry] purported to change the core definition of marriage as the union of a man and a woman. * * * The laws challenged in *Zablocki* and *Turner* did not define marriage as "the union of a man and a woman, *where neither party owes child support or is in prison.*" Nor did the interracial marriage ban at issue in *Loving* define marriage as "the union of a man and a woman *of the same race.*" Removing racial barriers to marriage therefore did not change what a marriage was any more than integrating schools changed what a school was. As the majority admits, the institution of "marriage" discussed in every one of these cases "presumed a relationship involving opposite-sex partners." * * *

Neither *Lawrence* nor any other precedent in the privacy line of cases supports the right that petitioners assert here. Unlike criminal laws banning contraceptives and sodomy, the marriage laws at issue here involve no government intrusion. They create no crime and impose no punishment. * * *

Perhaps recognizing how little support it can derive from precedent, the majority goes out of its way to jettison the "careful" approach to implied fundamental rights taken by this Court in *Glucksberg*. It is revealing that the majority's position requires it to effectively overrule *Glucksberg*, the leading modern case setting the bounds of substantive due process. At least this part of the majority opinion has the virtue of candor. Nobody could rightly accuse the majority of taking a careful approach. * * *

One immediate question invited by the majority's position is whether States may retain the definition of marriage as a union of two people. Although the majority randomly inserts the adjective "two" in various places, it offers no reason at all why the two-person element of the core definition of marriage may be preserved while the man-woman element may not. Indeed, from the standpoint of history and tradition, a leap from opposite-sex marriage to same-sex marriage is much greater than one from a two-person union to plural unions, which have deep roots in some cultures around the world. If the majority is willing to take the big leap, it is hard to see how it can say no to the shorter one.

It is striking how much of the majority's reasoning would apply with equal force to the claim of a fundamental right to plural marriage. If "[t]here is dignity in the bond between two men or two women who seek to marry and in their autonomy to make such profound choices," why would there be any less dignity in the bond between three people who, in exercising their autonomy, seek to make the profound choice to marry? If a same-sex couple has the constitutional right to marry because their children would otherwise "suffer the stigma of knowing their families are somehow lesser," why wouldn't the same reasoning apply to a family of three or more persons raising children? If not having the opportunity to marry "serves to disrespect and subordinate" gay and lesbian couples, why wouldn't the same "imposition of this disability," serve to disrespect and subordinate people who find fulfillment in polyamorous relationships? * * *

Near the end of its opinion, the majority offers perhaps the clearest insight into its decision. Expanding marriage to include same-sex couples, the majority insists, would "pose no risk of harm to themselves or third parties." * * *

Then and now, this assertion of the "harm principle" sounds more in philosophy than law. The elevation of the fullest individual self-realization over the constraints that society has expressed in law may or may not be attractive moral philosophy. But a Justice's commission does not confer any special moral, philosophical, or social insight sufficient to justify imposing those perceptions on fellow citizens under the pretense of "due process." There is indeed a process due the people on issues of this sort—the democratic process. Respecting that understanding requires the Court to be guided by law, not any particular school of social thought. As Judge Henry Friendly once put it, echoing Justice Holmes's dissent in *Lochner,* the Fourteenth Amendment does not enact John Stuart Mill's On Liberty any more than it enacts Herbert Spencer's Social Statics. And it certainly does not enact any one concept of marriage. * * *

[III.] In addition to their due process argument, petitioners contend that the Equal Protection Clause requires their States to license and recognize same-sex marriages. The majority does not seriously engage with this claim. Its discussion is, quite frankly, difficult to follow. The central point seems to be that there is a "synergy between" the Equal Protection Clause and the Due Process Clause, and that some precedents relying on one Clause have also relied on the other. Absent from this portion of the opinion, however, is anything resembling our usual framework for deciding equal protection cases. It is casebook doctrine that the "modern Supreme Court's treatment of equal protection claims has used a means-ends methodology in which judges ask whether the classification the government is using is sufficiently related to the goals it is pursuing." * * *

Those who founded our country would not recognize the majority's conception of the judicial role. They after all risked their lives and fortunes for the precious right to govern themselves. They would never have imagined yielding that right on a question of social policy to unaccountable and unelected judges. * * * In our democracy, debate about the content of the law is not an exhaustion requirement to be checked off before courts can impose their will. * * *

By deciding this question under the Constitution, the Court removes it from the realm of democratic decision. There will be consequences to shutting down the political process on an issue of such profound public significance. Closing debate tends to close minds. People denied a voice are less likely to accept the ruling of a court on an issue that does not seem to be the sort of thing courts usually decide. As a thoughtful commentator observed about another issue, "The political process was moving . . . , not swiftly enough for advocates of quick, complete change, but majoritarian institutions were listening and acting. Heavy-handed judicial intervention was difficult to justify and appears to have provoked, not resolved, conflict." Ginsburg, Some Thoughts on Autonomy and Equality in Relation to *Roe* v. *Wade,* 63 N.C.L.Rev. 375, 385–386 (1985) (footnote omitted). Indeed, however heartened the proponents of same-sex marriage might be on this day, it is worth acknowledging what they have lost, and lost forever: the opportunity to win the true acceptance that comes from persuading their fellow citizens of the justice of their cause. And they lose this just when the winds of change were freshening at their backs. * * *

Respect for sincere religious conviction has led voters and legislators in every State that has adopted same-sex marriage democratically to include accommodations for religious practice. The majority's decision imposing same-sex marriage cannot, of course, create any such accommodations. The majority graciously suggests that religious believers may continue to "advocate" and "teach" their views of marriage. The First Amendment guarantees, however, the freedom to "*exercise*" religion. Ominously, that is not a word the majority uses. * * *

If you are among the many Americans—of whatever sexual orientation—who favor expanding same-sex marriage, by all means celebrate today's decision. Celebrate the achievement of a desired goal. Celebrate the opportunity for a new expression of commitment to a partner. Celebrate the availability of new benefits. But do not celebrate the Constitution. It had nothing to do with it.

JUSTICE SCALIA, with whom JUSTICE THOMAS joins, dissenting.

When the Fourteenth Amendment was ratified in 1868, every State limited marriage to one man and one woman, and no one doubted the constitutionality of doing so. That resolves these cases. When it comes to determining the meaning of a vague constitutional provision—such as "due process of law" or "equal protection of the laws"—it is unquestionable that the People who ratified that provision did not understand it to prohibit a practice that remained both universal and uncontroversial in the years after ratification. We have no basis for striking down a practice that is not expressly prohibited by the Fourteenth Amendment's text, and that bears the endorsement of a long tradition of open, widespread, and unchallenged use dating back to the Amendment's ratification. Since there is no doubt whatever that the People never decided to prohibit the limitation of marriage to opposite-sex couples, the public debate over same-sex marriage must be allowed to continue. * * *

Judges are selected precisely for their skill as lawyers; whether they reflect the policy views of a particular constituency is not (or should not be) relevant. Not surprisingly then, the Federal Judiciary is hardly a cross-section of America. Take, for example, this Court, which consists of only nine men and women, all of them successful lawyers who studied at Harvard or Yale Law School. Four of the nine are natives of New York City. Eight of them grew up in east- and west-coast States. Only one hails from the vast expanse in-between. Not a single Southwesterner or even, to tell the truth, a genuine Westerner (California does not count). Not a single evangelical Christian (a group that comprises about one quarter of Americans), or even a Protestant of any denomination. The strikingly unrepresentative character of the body voting on today's social upheaval would be irrelevant if they were functioning as *judges,* answering the legal question whether the American people had ever ratified a constitutional provision that was understood to proscribe the traditional definition of marriage. But of course the Justices in today's majority are not voting on that basis; *they say they are not.* And to allow the policy question of same-sex marriage to be considered and resolved by a select, patrician, highly unrepresentative panel of nine is to violate a principle even more fundamental than no taxation without representation: no social transformation without representation.

[II.] But what really astounds is the hubris reflected in today's judicial Putsch. The five Justices who compose today's majority are entirely comfortable concluding that every State violated the Constitution for all of the 135 years between the Fourteenth Amendment's ratification and Massachusetts' permitting of same-sex marriages in 2003. They have discovered in the Fourteenth Amendment a "fundamental right" overlooked by every person alive at the time of ratification, and almost everyone else in the time since. * * *

JUSTICE THOMAS, with whom JUSTICE SCALIA joins, dissenting.

As used in the Due Process Clauses, "liberty" most likely refers to "the power of locomotion, of changing situation, or removing one's person to whatsoever place one's own inclination may direct; without imprisonment or restraint, unless by due course of law." 1 W. Blackstone, Commentaries on the Laws of England 130 (1769) (Blackstone). That definition is drawn from the historical roots of the Clauses and is consistent with our Constitution's text and structure. * * *

Even assuming that the "liberty" in those Clauses encompasses something more than freedom from physical restraint, it would not include the types of rights claimed by the majority. In the American legal tradition, liberty has long been understood as individual freedom *from* governmental action, not as a right *to* a particular governmental entitlement.

The founding-era understanding of liberty was heavily influenced by John Locke, whose writings "on natural rights and on the social and governmental contract" were cited "[i]n pamphlet after pamphlet" by American writers. * * * Because [the] state of nature left men insecure in their persons and property, they entered civil society, trading a portion of their natural liberty for an increase in their security. Upon consenting to that order, men obtained civil liberty, or the freedom "to be under no other legislative power but that established by consent in the commonwealth; nor under the dominion of any will or restraint of any law, but what that legislative shall enact according to the trust put in it." * * *

Petitioners cannot claim, under the most plausible definition of "liberty," that they have been imprisoned or physically restrained by the States for participating in same-sex relationships. To the contrary, they have been able to cohabitate and raise their children in peace. They have been able to hold civil marriage ceremonies in States that recognize same-sex marriages and private religious ceremonies in all States. They have been able to travel freely around the country, making their homes where they please. Far from being incarcerated or physically restrained, petitioners have been left alone to order their lives as they see fit. * * *

Instead, the States have refused to grant them governmental entitlements. Petitioners claim that as a matter of "liberty," they are entitled to access privileges and benefits that exist solely *because of* the government. They want, for example, to receive the State's *imprimatur* on their marriages—on state issued marriage licenses, death certificates, or other official forms. And they want to receive various monetary benefits, including reduced inheritance taxes upon the death of a spouse, compensation if a spouse dies as a result of a work-related injury, or loss of consortium damages in tort suits. But receiving governmental recognition and benefits has nothing to do with any understanding of "liberty" that the Framers would have recognized. * * *

Petitioners' misconception of liberty carries over into their discussion of our precedents identifying a right to marry, not one of which has expanded the concept of "liberty" beyond the concept of negative liberty. Those precedents all involved absolute prohibitions on private actions associated with marriage. *Loving v. Virginia,* for example, involved a couple who was criminally prosecuted for marrying in the District of Columbia and cohabiting in Virginia. They were each sentenced to a year of imprisonment, suspended for a term of 25 years on the condition that they not reenter the Commonwealth together during that time. In a similar vein, *Zablocki v. Redhail* involved a man who was prohibited, on pain of criminal penalty, from "marry[ing] in Wisconsin or elsewhere" because of his outstanding child-support obligations. And *Turner v. Safley* involved state inmates who were prohibited from entering marriages without the permission of the superintendent of the prison, permission that could not be granted absent compelling reasons. In *none* of those cases were individuals denied solely governmental recognition and benefits associated with marriage. * * *

[IV.] Human dignity has long been understood in this country to be innate. When the Framers proclaimed in the Declaration of Independence that "all men are created equal" and "endowed by their Creator with certain unalienable Rights," they referred to a vision of mankind in which all humans are created in the image of God and therefore of inherent worth. That vision is the foundation upon which this Nation was built.

The corollary of that principle is that human dignity cannot be taken away by the government. Slaves did not lose their dignity (any more than they lost their humanity) because the government allowed them to be enslaved. Those held in internment camps did not lose their dignity because the government confined them. And those denied governmental benefits certainly do not lose their dignity because the government denies them those benefits. The government cannot bestow dignity, and it cannot take it away. * * *

JUSTICE ALITO, with whom **JUSTICE SCALIA** and **JUSTICE THOMAS** join, dissenting.

Today's decision usurps the constitutional right of the people to decide whether to keep or alter the traditional understanding of marriage. The decision will also have other important consequences.

It will be used to vilify Americans who are unwilling to assent to the new orthodoxy. In the course of its opinion, the majority compares traditional marriage laws to laws that denied equal treatment for African-Americans and women. The implications of this analogy will be exploited by those who are determined to stamp out every vestige of dissent.

Perhaps recognizing how its reasoning may be used, the majority attempts, toward the end of its opinion, to reassure those who oppose same-sex marriage that their rights of conscience will be protected. We will soon see whether this proves to be true. I assume that those who cling to old beliefs will be able to whisper their thoughts in the recesses of their homes, but if they repeat those views in public, they will risk being labeled as bigots and treated as such by governments, employers, and schools.

The system of federalism established by our Constitution provides a way for people with different beliefs to live together in a single nation. If the issue of same-sex marriage had been left to the people of the States, it is likely that some States would recognize same-sex marriage and others would not. It is also possible that some States would tie recognition to protection for conscience rights. The majority today makes that impossible. By imposing its own views on the entire country, the majority facilitates the marginalization of the many Americans who have traditional ideas. Recalling the harsh treatment of gays and lesbians in the past, some may think that turnabout is fair play. But if that sentiment prevails, the Nation will experience bitter and lasting wounds. * * *

NOTES

1. *Possible Rationales.* The parties and amici in *Obergefell* presented the Court with several ways to find bans on same-sex marriage unconstitutional under the Fourteenth Amendment. The principal theories argued that the bans:

- Violated the fundamental right to marry grounded in the due process clause;

- Violated the fundamental right to marry (or interest in marriage) grounded in the equal protection clause;

- Violated the equal protection clause by discriminating against same-sex couples based on their sexual orientation; and

- Violated the equal protection clause by discriminating against same-sex couples based on gender.

The first of these alternatives plainly forms a core part of the opinion, which says explicitly that same-sex couples have a fundamental right to marry as part of the liberty protected by the due process clause. Given Justice Kennedy's invocation of equal protection, as well, do you read the opinion to bring in any of the other rationales? Do you think Justice Kennedy chose the strongest framing for the right vindicated in the case?

2. *Strict Scrutiny?* As you consider the fundamental right to marry identified in the opinion, recall that under established doctrine, a finding that a right is fundamental triggers strict scrutiny. Strict scrutiny, in turn, requires the reviewing court to determine whether the state has a compelling interest and has used the least restrictive alternative in the challenged policy. Puzzlingly, there is no explicit application of strict scrutiny in the opinion. Note that the opinion, in section IV, does discuss what might be seen as three state

interests: the interest in allowing a state's democratic process to define marriage; the interest in linking marriage to procreation as a way to channel birth parents into marriage; and the interest in protecting the religious liberties of those opposing same-sex marriage. Is the first of these three—letting majorities decide—a cognizable state "interest" at all? As to all three, does the majority's rejection of them serve as a version of strict, or at least heightened, scrutiny? If so, does it matter that the relevant doctrinal language about compelling interests and narrow tailoring is never used? What should lower courts take away from this approach? Is this what heightened scrutiny in the realm of due process now looks like? Recall that *Lawrence* and *Windsor* were also doctrinally idiosyncratic, although *Obergefell* is clearer than they were in saying unambiguously that a fundamental right is involved.

3. *Synergy Between Liberty and Equality.* What does Justice Kennedy mean when he links due process and equal protection in the opinion and speaks of a "synergy" between them? This is not a new idea, as his discussion of *Loving* and *Lawrence*, among others, suggests. For scholarly elaborations of this idea, see Rebecca L. Brown, *Liberty, the New Equality*, 77 N.Y.U. L. REV. 1491 (2002); Cary Franklin, *Marrying Liberty and Equality: The New Jurisprudence of Gay Rights*, 100 VA. L. REV. 817 (2014); Reva B. Siegel, *Dignity and the Politics of Protection: Abortion Restrictions Under Casey/Carhart*, 117 YALE L.J. 1694 (2008); Laurence H. Tribe, *Lawrence v. Texas: The "Fundamental Right" that Dare Not Speak Its Name*, 117 HARV. L. REV. 1893 (2004); Kenji Yoshino, *The New Equal Protection*, 124 HARV. L. REV. 747 (2011). How, if at all, does Justice Kennedy's use of equal protection language change the due process holding in this case? Does it suggest that the Court has now embraced a new understanding of liberty itself? Does the liberty-equality synergy implicate any of the other legal theories listed in note 1 above?

4. *Role of Justice Kennedy.* It is both striking and unusual that Justice Kennedy has written all four of the major LGBT rights opinions decided by the Supreme Court since *Romer*, in 1996. *Obergefell* contains some of the hallmarks of the jurisprudence he has created through *Romer*, *Lawrence*, *Windsor*, especially his focus on rejecting laws that demean gays and lesbians and on protecting the dignity of this group. From the institutional perspective of the Court, would it be preferable for more than one justice to write major opinions in a highly salient and controversial area like this one?

5. *Praise of Marriage.* Justice Kennedy is lavish in his praise of marriage as an institution, calling it, for example, of "transcendent importance," "sacred," "offer[ing] unique fulfillment," "essential to our most profound hopes and aspirations," and a "keystone of our social order." Does he go too far? Is he overreaching when he twice casts marriage as the antidote to "loneliness?" Does the rhetoric in the opinion stigmatize those who are not married?

6. *Bitterness on the Court.* After *Obergefell* was decided, various observers, including former Solicitor Generals from both parties, noted that some of the dissents contained particularly bitter language. See Nina

Totenberg, Liberal Minority Won Over Conservatives in Historic Supreme
Court Term, July 6, 2015, http://www.npr.org/sections/itsallpolitics/2015/07/
06/420289254/liberal-minority-won-over-conservatives-in-historic-supreme-
court-term (quoting Charles Fried, who served in the Reagan Administration
and Walter Dellinger, who served in the Clinton Administration). In addition
to what is in the excerpts above, the dissents by Chief Justice Roberts and
Justice Scalia both called the majority opinion "pretentious," and Scalia said
he would "hide [his] head in a bag" before joining any opinion with such
language. Former Solicitor General Fried suggested that Justice Kennedy
might have helped to provoke that reaction by aiming more for poetry than
precedent laid out in a straightforward way. Does the heated rhetoric suggest
that not much is left to the norm of civility on the Court, at least on the part of
some Justices? Or is the problem merely a reflection of growing polarization in
society as a whole? Or, perhaps, an indication that Justices may be directing
parts of their opinions at a public (rather than professional) audience? And is
the problem merely an issue of etiquette or something that may affect the
Court's institutional functioning and legitimacy?

7. *Links to Roe.* Given the Chief Justice's emphasis on the perils of
"Lochnerizing," is it surprising that he did he not invoke *Roe v. Wade* as an
example of this danger? *Roe*, after all, has been the most controversial of the
modern Court's substantive due process cases. The closest he comes is citing
an article by Justice Ginsburg suggesting how the Court could have avoided
some of the controversy generated by *Roe*. How do you think Justice Ginsburg
might respond to the parallel Roberts draws here? Do you think *Obergefell* will
be controversial in the way *Roe* has been? Is it relevant to consider the rapid
recent shift of public opinion in favor of marriage equality, and, especially the
strong generational tilt in favor? See Chris Cillizza, *How Unbelievably Quickly
Public Opinion Changed on Gay Marriage, in 5 Charts*, Washington Post, June
26, 2015 (http://www.washingtonpost.com/blogs/the-fix/wp/2015/06/26/how-
unbelievably-quickly-public-opinion-changed-on-gay-marriage-in-6-charts/).

8. *Theories of Interpretation.* The opinions in the case offer a rich basis
for exploring theories of constitutional interpretation. The justices divide along
familiar jurisprudential lines; the majority espouses the virtues of living
constitutionalism, while the dissents counter with arguments grounded in
originalism and excoriate what they see as illegitimate judicial activism. Two
of us have examined how the marriage debate can be understood in terms of a
range of constitutional theories. For an argument that there is an
unappreciated originalist case *in favor of* marriage equality, see William N.
Eskridge, Jr., The Nineteenth Annual Frankel Lecture, *Original Meaning and
Marriage Equality*, 52 HOUSTON L. REV. 1067 (2015); see also Steven G.
Calabresi and Hannah Begley, *Originalism and Same-Sex Marriage*, http://
papers.ssrn.com/sol3/papers.cfm?abstract_id=2509443. For an argument
about the interlocking roles of popular and living constitutionalism in the
debate, see Jane S. Schacter, Commentary, *What Marriage Equality Can Tell
Us About Popular Constitutionalism (and Vice-Versa), 52* HOUSTON L. REV.
1147 (2015).

9. *Glucksberg.* Note the focus on *Washington v. Glucksberg* (Casebook p. 692), the next major case in this unit. *Glucksberg* emphasizes the normative weight of history and tradition in substantive due process analysis. The *Obergefell* majority says that "history and tradition guide and discipline this inquiry but do not set its outer boundaries." As you read *Glucksberg*, consider what this language means for the role of history in this area of doctrine and, indeed, how much remains of *Glucksberg* in the wake of *Obergefell*.

PROBLEM 5–4(a):
PLURAL MARRIAGE

In 1878, the Supreme Court rejected a challenge to a federal ban on bigamy. In *Reynolds v. United States*, 98 U.S. 145 (1879), the Court ruled that this ban did not violate the free exercise rights of Mormon men who, at the time, wished to have multiple wives. Chief Justice Roberts's *Obergefell* dissent argues that the logic of Justice Kennedy's majority opinion suggests constitutional protection under the Fourteenth Amendment for plural marriage. The dissent cited a newspaper story about three lesbians who consider themselves married, and who plan to raise together the baby carried by one of them. See *Married Lesbian "Throuple" Expecting First Child*, N.Y. Post, Apr. 23, 2014. Two of the women were legally married in Massachusetts, but the three cohabitate, divide household labor, are supported by the wages of one, and intend to co-parent. Suppose these three women seek to be recognized as married to one another, and challenge as unconstitutional Massachusetts law permitting only two persons to be recognized as legal spouses. What arguments will each side make under *Obergefell*, and how do you think a court would and should rule? After you set out your arguments, you may wish to consult recent scholarly analysis of this question. See *Symposium: Polygamous Unions? Charting the Contours of Marriage Law's Frontier*, 64 Emory L.J. 1669 *et seq.* (2015). The Roberts dissent cited one article from this collection: Otter, *Three May Not Be a Crowd: The Case for a Constitutional Right to Plural Marriage*, 64 Emory L.J.1977 (2015).

CHAPTER 6

THE FIRST AMENDMENT

∎ ∎ ∎

SECTION 1. FREE SPEECH AND COMPETING VALUES

Page 728. Insert before Section 1:

The Court further refined the test for content neutrality in the following case. Unlike the preceding cases, which dealt with controversial actions like flag burning, this one involved the far more mundane issue of location signs for public events.

REED v. TOWN OF GILBERT

___ U.S. ___, 135 S.Ct. 2218 (2015)

JUSTICE THOMAS delivered the opinion of the Court.

The town of Gilbert, Arizona (or Town), has adopted a comprehensive code governing the manner in which people may display outdoor signs. The Sign Code identifies various categories of signs based on the type of information they convey, then subjects each category to different restrictions. One of the categories is "Temporary Directional Signs Relating to a Qualifying Event," loosely defined as signs directing the public to a meeting of a nonprofit group. The Code imposes more stringent restrictions on these signs than it does on signs conveying other messages. We hold that these provisions are content-based regulations of speech that cannot survive strict scrutiny.

The Sign Code prohibits the display of outdoor signs anywhere within the Town without a permit, but it then exempts 23 categories of signs from that requirement. These exemptions include everything from bazaar signs to flying banners. Three categories of exempt signs are particularly relevant here.

The first is "Ideological Sign[s]." This category includes any "sign communicating a message or ideas for noncommercial purposes that is not a Construction Sign, Directional Sign, Temporary Directional Sign Relating to a Qualifying Event, Political Sign, Garage Sale Sign, or a sign owned or required by a governmental agency." Of the three categories discussed here, the Code treats ideological signs most favorably, allowing them to be up to 20 square feet in area and to be placed in all "zoning districts" without time limits.

The second category is "Political Sign[s]." This includes any "temporary sign designed to influence the outcome of an election called by a public body." The Code treats these signs less favorably than ideological signs. The Code allows the placement of political signs up to 16 square feet on residential property and up to 32 square feet on nonresidential property, undeveloped municipal property, and "rights-of-way." These signs may be displayed up to 60 days before a primary election and up to 15 days following a general election.

The third category is "Temporary Directional Signs Relating to a Qualifying Event." * * * The Code treats temporary directional signs even less favorably than political signs. Temporary directional signs may be no larger than six square feet. They may be placed on private property or on a public right-of-way, but no more than four signs may be placed on a single property at any time. And, they may be displayed no more than 12 hours before the "qualifying event" and no more than 1 hour afterward. * * *

Government regulation of speech is content based if a law applies to particular speech because of the topic discussed or the idea or message expressed. This commonsense meaning of the phrase "content based" requires a court to consider whether a regulation of speech "on its face" draws distinctions based on the message a speaker conveys. Some facial distinctions based on a message are obvious, defining regulated speech by particular subject matter, and others are more subtle, defining regulated speech by its function or purpose. Both are distinctions drawn based on the message a speaker conveys, and, therefore, are subject to strict scrutiny.

Our precedents have also recognized a separate and additional category of laws that, though facially content neutral, will be considered content-based regulations of speech: laws that cannot be " 'justified without reference to the content of the regulated speech,' " or that were adopted by the government "because of disagreement with the message [the speech] conveys." Those laws, like those that are content based on their face, must also satisfy strict scrutiny.

The Town's Sign Code is content based on its face. It defines "Temporary Directional Signs" on the basis of whether a sign conveys the message of directing the public to church or some other "qualifying event." It defines "Political Signs" on the basis of whether a sign's message is "designed to influence the outcome of an election." And it defines "Ideological Signs" on the basis of whether a sign "communicat[es] a message or ideas" that do not fit within the Code's other categories. It then subjects each of these categories to different restrictions.

The restrictions in the Sign Code that apply to any given sign thus depend entirely on the communicative content of the sign. * * * On its face, the Sign Code is a content-based regulation of speech. We thus have no need to consider the government's justifications or purposes for enacting the Code to determine whether it is subject to strict scrutiny.

Because the Town's Sign Code imposes content-based restrictions on speech, those provisions can stand only if they survive strict scrutiny * * *. Thus, it is the Town's burden to demonstrate that the Code's differentiation between temporary directional signs and other types of signs, such as political signs and ideological signs, furthers a compelling governmental interest and is narrowly tailored to that end.

The Town cannot do so. It has offered only two governmental interests in support of the distinctions the Sign Code draws: preserving the Town's aesthetic appeal and traffic safety. Assuming for the sake of argument that those are compelling governmental interests, the Code's distinctions fail as hopelessly underinclusive. * * *

We acknowledge that a city might reasonably view the general regulation of signs as necessary because signs "take up space and may obstruct views, distract motorists, displace alternative uses for land, and pose other problems that legitimately call for regulation." At the same time, the presence of certain signs may be essential, both for vehicles and pedestrians, to guide traffic or to identify hazards and ensure safety. A sign ordinance narrowly tailored to the challenges of protecting the safety of pedestrians, drivers, and passengers—such as warning signs marking hazards on private property, signs directing traffic, or street numbers associated with private houses—well might survive strict scrutiny. The signs at issue in this case, including political and ideological signs and signs for events, are far removed from those purposes. As discussed above, they are facially content based and are neither justified by traditional safety concerns nor narrowly tailored.

JUSTICE BREYER, concurring in the judgment.

The better approach is to generally treat content discrimination as a strong reason weighing against the constitutionality of a rule where a traditional public forum, or where viewpoint discrimination, is threatened, but elsewhere treat it as a rule of thumb, finding it a helpful, but not determinative legal tool, in an appropriate case, to determine the strength of a justification. I would use content discrimination as a supplement to a more basic analysis, which, tracking most of our First Amendment cases, asks whether the regulation at issue works harm to First Amendment interests that is disproportionate in light of the relevant regulatory objectives. Answering this question requires examining the seriousness of the harm to speech, the importance of the countervailing objectives, the extent to which the law will achieve those objectives, and whether there are other, less restrictive ways of doing so. But it does permit the government to regulate speech in numerous instances where the voters have authorized the government to regulate and where courts should hesitate to substitute judicial judgment for that of administrators.

Here, regulation of signage along the roadside, for purposes of safety and beautification is at issue. There is no traditional public forum nor do I find any general effort to censor a particular viewpoint. Consequently, the specific regulation at issue does not warrant "strict scrutiny."

JUSTICE KAGAN, joined by **JUSTICE GINSBURG** and **JUSTICE BREYER**, concurring in the judgment.

Countless cities and towns across America have adopted ordinances regulating the posting of signs, while exempting certain categories of signs based on their subject matter. For example, some municipalities generally prohibit illuminated signs in residential neighborhoods, but lift that ban for signs that identify the address of a home or the name of its owner or occupant. In other municipalities, safety signs such as "Blind Pedestrian Crossing" and "Hidden Driveway" can be posted without a permit, even as other permanent signs require one. Elsewhere, historic site markers—for example, "George Washington Slept Here"—are also exempt from general regulations. And similarly, the federal Highway Beautification Act limits signs along interstate highways unless, for instance, they direct travelers to "scenic and historical attractions" or advertise free coffee.

Given the Court's analysis, many sign ordinances of that kind are now in jeopardy. * * * The consequence—unless courts water down strict scrutiny to something unrecognizable—is that our communities will find themselves in an unenviable bind: They will have to either repeal the exemptions that allow for helpful signs on streets and sidewalks, or else lift their sign restrictions altogether and resign themselves to the resulting clutter.

Although the majority insists that applying strict scrutiny to all such ordinances is "essential" to protecting First Amendment freedoms, I find it challenging to understand why that is so. * * *

* * * Subject-matter regulation, in other words, may have the intent or effect of favoring some ideas over others. When that is realistically possible—when the restriction "raises the specter that the Government may effectively drive certain ideas or viewpoints from the marketplace"—we insist that the law pass the most demanding constitutional test

But when that is not realistically possible, we may do well to relax our guard so that "entirely reasonable" laws imperiled by strict scrutiny can survive. * * * To do its intended work, of course, the category of content-based regulation triggering strict scrutiny must sweep more broadly than the actual harm; that category exists to create a buffer zone guaranteeing that the government cannot favor or disfavor certain viewpoints. But that buffer zone need not extend forever. We can administer our content-regulation doctrine with a dose of common sense, so as to leave standing laws that in no way implicate its intended function. * * *

NOTES ON REED

1. *Defining Content Neutrality.* The majority defines content neutrality very narrowly. To be content neutral, a law must neither (a) draw any distinctions based on communicative content, nor (b) have a purpose related to communicative content. Any other regulation of private speech is subject to strict scrutiny. Absent a compelling interest, if the state allows any category of messages, it must allow all categories of messages equally, even if there seems to be a commonsense justification for treating some messages (such as address signs) differently.

2. *Why Not Allow Commonsense Distinctions?* Consider a law that allows owners to illuminate their house numbers but not other kinds of signs. Why should that be subject to strict scrutiny? Is the reason that there might be some discriminatory intent behind theses seemingly innocuous distinctions that would be difficult to establish more directly? (Perhaps the city wanted to prevent illumination of some other particular kind of sign in drawing this distinction?) Or is the reason that cities are likely to want to allow addresses to be illuminated and that an anti-discrimination rule will then provide an opportunity for other signs to be illuminated, increasing the possibilities for communication? (Notice that these reasons are quite different: one is an effort to prevent hidden harms while the other one is an effort to open up broader channels of communication.) Or is the reason that there is something intrinsically unjust about distinctions based on communicative message, no matter how trivial they may seem? Or, finally, do we not trust judges to decide when a particular type of content distinction poses no threat to public discourse?

SECTION 2. REGULATION OF POLITICAL EXPRESSION

C. CAMPAIGN EXPENDITURES

Page 777. Insert before Section 3:

McCutcheon v. Federal Election Commission, ___ U.S. ___, 134 S.Ct. 1434 (2013). *Buckley* upheld a limit on the total contributions that an individual can make to federal candidates during an election cycle, as well the limits on contributions to individual candidates. In *McCutcheon*, the Court struck down the aggregate limit. Chief Justice Roberts' plurality opinion (joined by Scalia, Kennedy and Alito) focused on whether the aggregate limit was necessary to prevent quid pro quo corruption, which it considered the only valid purpose for campaign regulation. The plurality concluded that the risk of quid pro quo corruption was adequately addressed by the limit on contributions to each individual candidate. Because of anti-circumvention regulations adopted since *Buckley* was decided, the plurality dismissed the government's argument that the aggregate limit was necessary to prevent schemes evading the individual candidate limit. Justice Thomas concurred in the judgment, arguing that

Buckley should be overruled outright. In dissent, Justice Breyer (joined by Justices Ginsburg, Sotomayor, and Kagan), argued as in *Citizens United* that corruption included broader forms of influence peddling than simple bribery, and that the aggregate limit was in fact required to prevent circumvention of the individual limits. Breyer also chided the majority for deciding factual issues about the potential for circumvention without any evidentiary hearing in the lower court, while Roberts responded that the parties had not pressed for a remand on this basis.

The following case was a departure from the strong trend of invalidating campaign finance regulations under the Roberts Court.

WILLIAMS-YULEE V. FLORIDA BAR
___ U.S. ___, 135 S.Ct. 1656 (2015)

CHIEF JUSTICE ROBERTS delivered the opinion of the Court, except as to Part II.

Our Founders vested authority to appoint federal judges in the President, with the advice and consent of the Senate, and entrusted those judges to hold their offices during good behavior. The Constitution permits States to make a different choice, and most of them have done so. In 39 States, voters elect trial or appellate judges at the polls. In an effort to preserve public confidence in the integrity of their judiciaries, many of those States prohibit judges and judicial candidates from personally soliciting funds for their campaigns. We must decide whether the First Amendment permits such restrictions on speech.

We hold that it does. Judges are not politicians, even when they come to the bench by way of the ballot. And a State's decision to elect its judiciary does not compel it to treat judicial candidates like campaigners for political office. A State may assure its people that judges will apply the law without fear or favor—and without having personally asked anyone for money. We affirm the judgment of the Florida Supreme Court.

[Part I provides background on judicial elections in Florida, including a corruption scandal. Williams-Yulee decided to run for a seat on the county court and then sent out a fundraising letter. She lost the primary and then was subject to an ethics proceeding by the Florida Bar for violating Canon 7C(1), which prohibits direct requests for campaign contributions by candidates for judicial office. Part II of the opinion, which was joined by only three Justices, reaffirmed that restrictions on the speech of judicial candidates are subject to strict scrutiny. Justice Breyer and Ginsburg argued for allowing greater latitude to states for regulation in the context of judicial elections. The following portions of the opinion were joined by five Justices, however.]

The Florida Bar faces a demanding task in defending Canon 7C(1) against Yulee's First Amendment challenge. We have emphasized that "it is the rare case" in which a State demonstrates that a speech restriction is narrowly tailored to serve a compelling interest. Here, Canon 7C(1) advances the State's compelling interest in preserving public confidence in the integrity of the judiciary, and it does so through means narrowly tailored to avoid unnecessarily abridging speech. This is therefore one of the rare cases in which a speech restriction withstands strict scrutiny.

The Florida Supreme Court adopted Canon 7C(1) to promote the State's interests in "protecting the integrity of the judiciary" and "maintaining the public's confidence in an impartial judiciary." The way the Canon advances those interests is intuitive: Judges, charged with exercising strict neutrality and independence, cannot supplicate campaign donors without diminishing public confidence in judicial integrity. This principle dates back at least eight centuries to Magna Carta, which proclaimed, "To no one will we sell, to no one will we refuse or delay, right or justice." The same concept underlies the common law judicial oath, which binds a judge to "do right to all manner of people . . . without fear or favour, affection or ill-will," and the oath that each of us took to "administer justice without respect to persons, and do equal right to the poor and to the rich." Simply put, Florida and most other States have concluded that the public may lack confidence in a judge's ability to administer justice without fear or favor if he comes to office by asking for favors.

The interest served by Canon 7C(1) has firm support in our precedents. We have recognized the "vital state interest" in safeguarding "public confidence in the fairness and integrity of the nation's elected judges." * * *

The parties devote considerable attention to our cases analyzing campaign finance restrictions in political elections. But a State's interest in preserving public confidence in the integrity of its judiciary extends beyond its interest in preventing the appearance of corruption in legislative and executive elections. As we explained in *White,* States may regulate judicial elections differently than they regulate political elections, because the role of judges differs from the role of politicians. Politicians are expected to be appropriately responsive to the preferences of their supporters. Indeed, such "responsiveness is key to the very concept of self-governance through elected officials." The same is not true of judges. In deciding cases, a judge is not to follow the preferences of his supporters, or provide any special consideration to his campaign donors. A judge instead must "observe the utmost fairness," striving to be "perfectly and completely independent, with nothing to influence or controul him but God and his conscience." * * *

The vast majority of elected judges in States that allow personal solicitation serve with fairness and honor. But "[e]ven if judges were able to refrain from favoring donors, the mere possibility that judges' decisions may be motivated by the desire to repay campaign contributions is likely to undermine the public's confidence in the judiciary." In the eyes of the public, a judge's personal solicitation could result (even unknowingly) in "a possible temptation . . . which might lead him not to hold the balance nice, clear and true." That risk is especially pronounced because most donors are lawyers and litigants who may appear before the judge they are supporting.

The concept of public confidence in judicial integrity does not easily reduce to precise definition, nor does it lend itself to proof by documentary record. But no one denies that it is genuine and compelling. In short, it is the regrettable but unavoidable appearance that judges who personally ask for money may diminish their integrity that prompted the Supreme Court of Florida and most other States to sever the direct link between judicial candidates and campaign contributors. As the Supreme Court of Oregon explained, "the spectacle of lawyers or potential litigants directly handing over money to judicial candidates should be avoided if the public is to have faith in the impartiality of its judiciary." * * *

Yulee acknowledges the State's compelling interest in judicial integrity. She argues, however, that the Canon's failure to restrict other speech equally damaging to judicial integrity and its appearance undercuts the Bar's position. In particular, she notes that Canon 7C(1) allows a judge's campaign committee to solicit money, which arguably reduces public confidence in the integrity of the judiciary just as much as a judge's personal solicitation. Yulee also points out that Florida permits judicial candidates to write thank you notes to campaign donors, which ensures that candidates know who contributes and who does not. [The Court did not find that these aspects of the law were fatal flaws, because the state had focused on the category of judicial speech posing the greatest appearance of impropriety.]

* * * Yulee argues that the Canon cannot constitutionally be applied to her chosen form of solicitation: a letter posted online and distributed via mass mailing. No one, she contends, will lose confidence in the integrity of the judiciary based on personal solicitation to such a broad audience.

This argument misperceives the breadth of the compelling interest that underlies Canon 7C(1). Florida has reasonably determined that personal appeals for money by a judicial candidate inherently create an appearance of impropriety that may cause the public to lose confidence in the integrity of the judiciary. That interest may be implicated to varying degrees in particular contexts, but the interest remains whenever the public perceives the judge personally asking for money.

Moreover, the lines Yulee asks us to draw are unworkable. Even under her theory of the case, a mass mailing would create an appearance of impropriety if addressed to a list of all lawyers and litigants with pending cases. So would a speech soliciting contributions from the 100 most frequently appearing attorneys in the jurisdiction. Yulee says she might accept a ban on one-to-one solicitation, but is the public impression really any different if a judicial candidate tries to buttonhole not one prospective donor but two at a time? Ten? Yulee also agrees that in person solicitation creates a problem. But would the public's concern recede if the request for money came in a phone call or a text message?

We decline to wade into this swamp. The First Amendment requires that Canon 7C(1) be narrowly tailored, not that it be "perfectly tailored."

JUSTICE SCALIA, joined by JUSTICE THOMAS, dissenting.

Because Canon 7C(1) restricts fully protected speech on the basis of content, it presumptively violates the First Amendment. We may uphold it only if the State meets its burden of showing that the Canon survives strict scrutiny—that is to say, only if it shows that the Canon is narrowly tailored to serve a compelling interest. I do not for a moment question the Court's conclusion that States have different compelling interests when regulating judicial elections than when regulating political ones. Unlike a legislator, a judge must be impartial—without bias for or against any party or attorney who comes before him. I accept for the sake of argument that States have a compelling interest in ensuring that its judges are *seen* to be impartial. I will likewise assume that a judicial candidate's request to a litigant or attorney presents a danger of coercion that a political candidate's request to a constituent does not. But Canon 7C(1) does not narrowly target concerns about impartiality or its appearance; it applies even when the person asked for a financial contribution has no chance of ever appearing in the candidate's court. And Florida does not invoke concerns about coercion, presumably because the Canon bans solicitations regardless of whether their object is a lawyer, litigant, or other person vulnerable to judicial pressure. So Canon 7C(1) fails exacting scrutiny and infringes the First Amendment. This case should have been just that straightforward. * * *

This Court has not been shy to enforce the First Amendment in recent Terms—even in cases that do not involve election speech. It has accorded robust protection to depictions of animal torture, sale of violent video games to children, and lies about having won military medals. Who would have thought that the same Court would today exert such heroic efforts to save so plain an abridgement of the freedom of speech? It is no great mystery what is going on here. The judges of this Court, like the judges of the Supreme Court of Florida who promulgated Canon 7C(1), evidently consider the preservation of public respect for the courts a policy objective of the highest order. So it is—but so too are preventing animal torture, protecting the innocence of children, and honoring valiant soldiers. The Court did not relax the Constitution's guarantee of freedom of speech when legislatures pursued those goals; it should not relax the guarantee when the Supreme Court of Florida pursues this one. The First Amendment is not abridged for the benefit of the Brotherhood of the Robe.

JUSTICE KENNEDY, dissenting.

The dissenting opinion by Justice Scalia gives a full and complete explanation of the reasons why the Court's opinion contradicts settled First Amendment principles. This separate dissent is written to underscore the irony in the Court's having concluded that the very First Amendment protections judges must enforce should be lessened when a judicial candidate's own speech is at issue. It is written to underscore, too, the irony in the Court's having weakened the rigors of the First Amendment in a case concerning elections, a paradigmatic forum for speech and a process intended to protect freedom in so many other manifestations.

First Amendment protections are both personal and structural. Free speech begins with the right of each person to think and then to express his or her own ideas. Protecting this personal sphere of intellect and conscience, in turn, creates structural safeguards for many of the processes that define a free society. The individual speech here is political speech. The process is a fair election. These realms ought to be the last place, not the first, for the * * *

With all due respect for the Court, it seems fair and necessary to say its decision rests on two premises, neither one correct. One premise is that in certain elections—here an election to choose the best qualified judge—the public lacks the necessary judgment to make an informed choice. Instead, the State must protect voters by altering the usual dynamics of free speech. The other premise is that since judges should be accorded special respect and dignity, their election can be subject to certain content-based rules that would be unacceptable in other elections. In my respectful view neither premise can justify the speech restriction at issue here. Although States have a compelling interest in seeking to ensure the appearance and the reality of an impartial judiciary, it does not follow that the State may alter basic First Amendment principles in pursuing that goal.

While any number of troubling consequences will follow from the Court's ruling, a simple example can suffice to illustrate the dead weight its decision now ties to public debate. Assume a judge retires, and two honest lawyers, Doe and Roe, seek the vacant position. Doe is a respected, prominent lawyer who has been active in the community and is well known to business and civic leaders. Roe, a lawyer of extraordinary ability and high ethical standards, keeps a low profile. As soon as Doe announces his or her candidacy, a campaign committee organizes of its own accord and begins raising funds. But few know or hear about Roe's potential candidacy, and no one with resources or connections is available to assist in raising the funds necessary for even a modest plan to speak to the electorate. Today the Court says the State can censor Roe's speech, imposing a gag on his or her request for funds, no matter how close Roe is to the potential benefactor or donor. The result is that Roe's personal freedom, the right of speech, is cut off by the State.

The First Amendment consequences of the Court's ruling do not end with its denial of the individual's right to speak. For the very purpose of the candidate's fundraising was to facilitate a larger speech process: an election campaign. By cutting off one candidate's personal freedom to speak, the broader campaign debate that might have followed—a debate that might have been informed by new ideas and insights from both candidates—now is silenced.

JUSTICE ALITO, dissenting.

I largely agree with what I view as the essential elements of the dissents filed by Justices Scalia and Kennedy. The Florida rule before us regulates speech that is part of the process of selecting those who wield the power of the State. Such speech lies at the heart of the protection provided by the First Amendment. The Florida rule regulates that speech based on content and must therefore satisfy strict scrutiny. This means that it must be narrowly tailored to further a compelling state interest. Florida has a compelling interest in making sure that its courts decide cases impartially and in accordance with the law and that its citizens have no good reason to lack confidence that its courts are performing their proper role. But the Florida rule is not narrowly tailored to serve that interest.

Indeed, this rule is about as narrowly tailored as a burlap bag. It applies to all solicitations made in the name of a candidate for judicial office—including, as was the case here, a mass mailing. It even applies to an ad in a newspaper. It applies to requests for contributions in any amount, and it applies even if the person solicited is not a lawyer, has never had any interest at stake in any case in the court in question, and has no prospect of ever having any interest at stake in any litigation in that court. If this rule can be characterized as narrowly tailored, then narrow tailoring has no meaning, and strict scrutiny, which is essential to the protection of free speech, is seriously impaired.

When petitioner sent out a form letter requesting campaign contributions, she was well within her First Amendment rights. The Florida Supreme Court violated the Constitution when it imposed a financial penalty and stained her record with a finding that she had engaged in unethical conduct. I would reverse the judgment of the Florida Supreme Court.

NOTES ON WILLIAMS-YULEE *AND* JUDICIAL ELECTIONS

1.   *Narrow Tailoring.* The dissent seems right that the majority does not seem to be demanding as much precision in the fit between ends and means as in some other cases of strict scrutiny. On the other hand, once avoiding the appearance of partiality is accepted as a compelling state interest, is it possible to draw rules as precise as those that the dissenters demand?

2.   *The Paradox of Judicial Elections.* Due process requires impartial decision-makers. Judicial elections inevitably create some risk that judicial decisions will be warped by the desire to appeal to potential supporters, whether newspapers or others. If judicial candidates are dependent on campaign contributions, it is hard to see how they can be completely impartial in considering the interests of major contributors, whether they receive the contributions personally or not. As an extreme case, consider the *Caperton* case [Casebook p. 722], where the majority ruled that this appearance of special influence was grave enough to violate due process.

The dissenters seem sanguine about the possibility that judges might become as responsive to contributors as other office-holders. To the extent that the governmental interest is public confidence in the institutions of government, isn't the dissent right that this interest is neither more nor less important as applied to judges as to others? On the other hand, could the majority argue that there is a special interest in giving litigants (as opposed to the general public) confidence that there cases are being decided impartially?

SECTION 4. SPEECH WITH A GOVERNMENT NEXUS

A. PUBLIC FORUM DOCTRINE

Page 807. Insert after *Hill*:

MCCULLEN V. COAKLEY
___ U.S. ___, 134 S.Ct. 2518 (2014)

CHIEF JUSTICE ROBERTS delivered the opinion of the Court.

A Massachusetts statute makes it a crime to knowingly stand on a "public way or sidewalk" within 35 feet of an entrance or driveway to any place, other than a hospital, where abortions are performed. Petitioners are individuals who approach and talk to women outside such facilities, attempting to dissuade them from having abortions. The statute prevents petitioners from doing so near the facilities' entrances. The question presented is whether the statute violates the First Amendment. * * *

The Act exempts four classes of individuals: (1) "persons entering or leaving such facility"; (2) "employees or agents of such facility acting within the scope of their employment"; (3) "law enforcement, ambulance, firefighting, construction, utilities, public works and other municipal agents acting within the scope of their employment"; and (4) "persons using the public sidewalk or street right-of-way adjacent to such facility solely for the purpose of reaching a destination other than such facility." The legislature also retained the separate provision from the 2000 version that proscribes the knowing obstruction of access to a facility. * * *

Petitioners at all three clinics claim that the buffer zones have considerably hampered their counseling efforts. Although they have managed to conduct some counseling and to distribute some literature outside the buffer zones—particularly at the Boston clinic—they say they have had many fewer conversations and distributed many fewer leaflets since the zones went into effect.

The second statutory exemption allows clinic employees and agents acting within the scope of their employment to enter the buffer zones. Relying on this exemption, the Boston clinic uses "escorts" to greet women as they approach the clinic, accompanying them through the zones to the clinic entrance. Petitioners claim that the escorts sometimes thwart petitioners' attempts to communicate with patients by blocking petitioners from handing literature to patients, telling patients not to "pay any attention" or "listen to" petitioners, and disparaging petitioners as "crazy." * * *

By its very terms, the Massachusetts Act regulates access to "public way[s]" and "sidewalk[s]." Such areas occupy a "special position in terms of First Amendment protection" because of their historic role as sites for discussion and debate. It is no accident that public streets and sidewalks have developed as venues for the exchange of ideas. Even today, they remain one of the few places where a speaker can be confident that he is not simply preaching to the choir. With respect to other means of communication, an individual confronted with an uncomfortable message can always turn the page, change the channel, or leave the Web site. Not so on public streets and sidewalks. There, a listener often encounters speech he might otherwise tune out. In light of the First Amendment's purpose "to preserve an uninhibited marketplace of ideas in which truth will ultimately prevail," this aspect of traditional public fora is a virtue, not a vice.

In short, traditional public fora are areas that have historically been open to the public for speech activities. Thus, even though the Act says nothing about speech on its face, there is no doubt—and respondents do not dispute—that it restricts access to traditional public fora and is therefore subject to First Amendment scrutiny. See Brief for Respondents 26 (although "[b]y its terms, the Act regulates only conduct," it "incidentally regulates the place and time of protected speech"). * * *

Petitioners contend that the Act is not content neutral for two independent reasons: First, they argue that it discriminates against abortion-related speech because it establishes buffer zones only at clinics that perform abortions. Second, petitioners contend that the Act, by exempting clinic employees and agents, favors one viewpoint about abortion over the other. If either of these arguments is correct, then the Act must satisfy strict scrutiny—that is, it must be the least restrictive means of achieving a compelling state interest. Respondents do not argue that the Act can survive this exacting standard. * * *

The Act applies only at a "reproductive health care facility," defined as "a place, other than within or upon the grounds of a hospital, where abortions are offered or performed." Given this definition, petitioners argue, "virtually all speech affected by the Act is speech concerning abortion," thus rendering the Act content based.

We disagree. To begin, the Act does not draw content-based distinctions on its face. The Act would be content based if it required "enforcement authorities" to "examine the content of the message that is conveyed to determine whether" a violation has occurred. But it does not. Whether petitioners violate the Act "depends" not "on what they say," but simply on where they say it. Indeed, petitioners can violate the Act merely by standing in a buffer zone, without displaying a sign or uttering a word.

It is true, of course, that by limiting the buffer zones to abortion clinics, the Act has the "inevitable effect" of restricting abortion-related speech more than speech on other subjects. But a facially neutral law does not become content based simply because it may disproportionately affect speech on certain topics. On the contrary, "[a] regulation that serves purposes unrelated to the content of expression is deemed neutral, even if it has an incidental effect on some speakers or messages but not others." The question in such a case is whether the law is " 'justified without reference to the content of the regulated speech.' "

The Massachusetts Act is. Its stated purpose is to "increase forthwith public safety at reproductive health care facilities." Respondents have articulated similar purposes before this Court—namely, "public safety, patient access to healthcare, and the unobstructed use of public sidewalks and roadways." It is not the case that "[e]very objective indication shows that the provision's primary purpose is to restrict speech that opposes abortion."

We have previously deemed the foregoing concerns to be content neutral. Obstructed access and congested sidewalks are problems no matter what caused them. A group of individuals can obstruct clinic access and clog sidewalks just as much when they loiter as when they protest abortion or counsel patients.

To be clear, the Act would not be content neutral if it were concerned with undesirable effects that arise from "the direct impact of speech on its audience" or "[l]isteners' reactions to speech." If, for example, the speech outside Massachusetts abortion clinics caused offense or made listeners uncomfortable, such offense or discomfort would not give the Commonwealth a content-neutral justification to restrict the speech. All of the problems identified by the Commonwealth here, however, arise irrespective of any listener's reactions. Whether or not a single person reacts to abortion protestors' chants or petitioners' counseling, large crowds outside abortion clinics can still compromise public safety, impede access, and obstruct sidewalks.

Petitioners do not really dispute that the Commonwealth's interests in ensuring safety and preventing obstruction are, as a general matter, content neutral. But petitioners note that these interests "apply outside every building in the State that hosts any activity that might occasion protest or comment," not just abortion clinics. By choosing to pursue these interests only at abortion clinics, petitioners argue, the Massachusetts Legislature evinced a purpose to "single[ ] out for regulation speech about one particular topic: abortion."

We cannot infer such a purpose from the Act's limited scope. The broad reach of a statute can help confirm that it was not enacted to burden a narrower category of disfavored speech. At the same time, however, "States adopt laws to address the problems that confront them. The First Amendment does not require States to regulate for problems that do not exist." The Massachusetts Legislature amended the Act in 2007 in response to a problem that was, in its experience, limited to abortion clinics. There was a record of crowding, obstruction, and even violence outside such clinics. There were apparently no similar recurring problems associated with other kinds of healthcare facilities, let alone with "every building in the State that hosts any activity that might occasion protest or comment." In light of the limited nature of the problem, it was reasonable for the Massachusetts Legislature to enact a limited solution. When selecting among various options for combating a particular problem, legislatures should be encouraged to choose the one that restricts less speech, not more. * * *

Petitioners also argue that the Act is content based because it exempts four classes of individuals, one of which comprises "employees or agents of [a reproductive healthcare] facility acting within the scope of their employment." This exemption, petitioners say, favors one side in the abortion debate and thus constitutes viewpoint discrimination—an "egregious form of content discrimination." In particular, petitioners argue that the exemption allows clinic employees and agents—including the volunteers who "escort" patients arriving at the Boston clinic—to speak inside the buffer zones. [But the Court concluded that there is "nothing inherently suspect about providing some kind of exemption to allow individuals who work at the clinics to enter or remain within the buffer zones." However, "[i]t would be a very different question if it turned out that a clinic authorized escorts to speak about abortion inside the buffer zones." In that case, the statute would be invalid as applied because of viewpoint discrimination. No such showing was made.]

Even though the Act is content neutral, it still must be "narrowly tailored to serve a significant governmental interest." The tailoring requirement does not simply guard against an impermissible desire to censor. The government may attempt to suppress speech not only because it disagrees with the message being expressed, but also for mere convenience. Where certain speech is associated with particular problems, silencing the speech is sometimes the path of least resistance. But by demanding a close fit between ends and means, the tailoring requirement prevents the government from too readily "sacrific[ing] speech for efficiency."

For a content-neutral time, place, or manner regulation to be narrowly tailored, it must not "burden substantially more speech than is necessary to further the government's legitimate interests." Such a regulation, unlike a content-based restriction of speech, "need not be the least restrictive or least intrusive means of" serving the government's interests. But the government still "may not regulate expression in such a manner that a substantial portion of the burden on speech does not serve to advance its goals."

As noted, respondents claim that the Act promotes "public safety, patient access to healthcare, and the unobstructed use of public sidewalks and roadways." Petitioners do not dispute the significance of these interests. We have, moreover, previously recognized the legitimacy of the government's interests in "ensuring public safety and order, promoting the free flow of traffic on streets and sidewalks, protecting property rights, and protecting a woman's freedom to seek pregnancy-related services." The buffer zones clearly serve these interests.

At the same time, the buffer zones impose serious burdens on petitioners' speech. At each of the three Planned Parenthood clinics where petitioners attempt to counsel patients, the zones carve out a significant portion of the adjacent public sidewalks, pushing petitioners well back from the clinics' entrances and driveways. The zones thereby compromise petitioners' ability to initiate the close, personal conversations that they view as essential to "sidewalk counseling." * * *

Respondents also emphasize that the Act does not prevent petitioners from engaging in various forms of "protest"—such as chanting slogans and displaying signs—outside the buffer zones. That misses the point. Petitioners are not protestors. They seek not merely to express their opposition to abortion, but to inform women of various alternatives and to provide help in pursuing them. Petitioners believe that they can accomplish this objective only through personal, caring, consensual conversations. * * * It is thus no answer to say that petitioners can still be "seen and heard" by women within the buffer zones. If all that the women can see and hear are vociferous opponents of abortion, then the buffer zones have effectively stifled petitioners' message. * * *

The buffer zones burden substantially more speech than necessary to achieve the Commonwealth's asserted interests. At the outset, we note that the Act is truly exceptional: Respondents and their *amici* identify no other State with a law that creates fixed buffer zones around abortion clinics. That of course does not mean that the law is invalid. It does, however, raise concern that the Commonwealth has too readily forgone options that could serve its interests just as well, without substantially burdening the kind of speech in which petitioners wish to engage.

That is the case here. The Commonwealth's interests include ensuring public safety outside abortion clinics, preventing harassment and intimidation of patients and clinic staff, and combating deliberate obstruction of clinic entrances. The Act itself contains a separate provision, subsection (e)—unchallenged by petitioners—that prohibits much of this conduct. That provision subjects to criminal punishment "[a]ny person who knowingly obstructs, detains, hinders, impedes or blocks another person's entry to or exit from a reproductive health care facility." If Massachusetts determines that broader prohibitions along the same lines are necessary, it could enact legislation similar to the federal Freedom of Access to Clinic Entrances Act of 1994 (FACE Act), 18 U.S.C. § 248(a)(1), which subjects to both criminal and civil penalties anyone who "by force or threat of force or by physical obstruction, intentionally injures, intimidates or interferes with or attempts to injure, intimidate or interfere with any person because that person is or has been, or in order to intimidate such person or any other person or any class of persons from, obtaining or providing reproductive health services." Some dozen other States have done so. If the Commonwealth is particularly concerned about harassment, it could also consider an ordinance such as the one adopted in New York City that not only prohibits obstructing access to a clinic, but also makes it a crime "to follow and harass another person within 15 feet of the premises of a reproductive health care facility." * * *

In addition, subsection (e) of the Act, the FACE Act, and the New York City anti-harassment ordinance are all enforceable not only through criminal prosecutions but also through public and private civil actions for injunctions and other equitable relief. We have previously noted the First Amendment virtues of targeted injunctions as alternatives to broad, prophylactic measures. Such an injunction "regulates the activities, and perhaps the speech, of a group," but only "because of the group's past *actions* in the context of a specific dispute between real parties." Moreover, given the equitable nature of injunctive relief, courts can tailor a remedy to ensure that it restricts no more speech than necessary. In short, injunctive relief focuses on the precise individuals and the precise conduct causing a particular problem. The Act, by contrast, categorically excludes non-exempt individuals from the buffer zones, unnecessarily sweeping in innocent individuals and their speech. * * *

The point is not that Massachusetts must enact all or even any of the proposed measures discussed above. The point is instead that the Commonwealth has available to it a variety of approaches that appear capable of serving its interests, without excluding individuals from areas historically open for speech and debate.

JUSTICE SCALIA, with whom JUSTICE KENNEDY and JUSTICE THOMAS join, concurring in the judgment.

The majority points only to the statute's stated purpose of increasing " 'public safety' " at abortion clinics, and to the additional aims articulated by respondents before this Court—namely, protecting " 'patient access to healthcare . . . and the unobstructed use of public sidewalks and roadways.' " Really? Does a statute become "justified without reference to the content of the regulated speech" simply because the statute itself and those defending it in court *say* that it is? Every objective indication shows that the provision's primary purpose is to restrict speech that opposes abortion. [Justice Scalia stressed that the law covered all abortion clinics in the state, although only the Boston clinic had faced serious problems in maintaining order and access. He argued that this undermined the credibility of the state's claimed interest.]

Is there any serious doubt that *abortion-clinic employees or agents* "acting within the scope of their employment" near clinic entrances may— indeed, often will—speak in favor of abortion ("You are doing the right thing")? Or speak in opposition to the message of abortion opponents— saying, for example, that "this is a safe facility" to rebut the statement that it is not? The Court's contrary assumption is simply incredible. And the majority makes no attempt to establish the further necessary proposition that abortion-clinic employees and agents do not engage in nonspeech activities directed to the suppression of antiabortion speech by hampering the efforts of counselors to speak to prospective clients. Are we to believe that a clinic employee sent out to "escort" prospective clients into the building would not seek to prevent a counselor like Eleanor McCullen from communicating with them? He could pull a woman away from an approaching counselor, cover her ears, or make loud noises to drown out the counselor's pleas. * * *

There is not a shadow of a doubt that the assigned or foreseeable conduct of a clinic employee or agent can include both speaking in favor of abortion rights and countering the speech of people like petitioners. * * *

In sum, the Act should be reviewed under the strict-scrutiny standard applicable to content-based legislation. That standard requires that a regulation represent "the least restrictive means" of furthering "a compelling Government interest." Respondents do not even attempt to argue that subsection (b) survives this test. "Suffice it to say that if protecting people from unwelcome communications"—the actual purpose of the provision—"is a compelling state interest, the First Amendment is a dead letter."

Having determined that the Act is content based and does not withstand strict scrutiny, I need not pursue the inquiry [into whether the statute is narrowly tailored.] I suppose I *could* do so, * * * and if I did, I suspect I would agree with the majority that the legislation is not narrowly tailored to advance the interests asserted by respondents. But I prefer not to take part in the assembling of an apparent but specious unanimity. I leave both the plainly unnecessary and erroneous half and the arguably correct half of the Court's analysis to the majority.

[JUSTICE ALITO concurred in the judgment on the ground that the exemption for clinic employees constituted viewpoint discrimination, but agreed with the majority that in any event the statute was not narrowly tailored.]

NOTES ON MCCULLEN

1. *Realism and Judicial Review.* Whose version of the statute's purpose and effect seems most plausible—the majority's or Justice Scalia's? Note that neither side offers direct evidence about the intentions of the legislatures. Both purport to infer purpose from the face of the statute and the context, but with an important difference: the majority takes the statute as it is written, while Justice Scalia is willing to make inferences about the political dynamics. Which approach is preferable?

2. *Harassment or Outreach?* A traditional argument for protecting speech involves the ability to speakers to reach willing listeners without government interference. But the Court valorizes public forums for the ability of speakers to reach listeners who would prefer to be left alone. Should there be a constitutional right to avoid unwanted communications?

3. *Sauce for the Goose Versus Sauce for the Gander?* There is a large buffer zone excluding from the Supreme Court's grounds, including the plaza in front of the building, the following activities: "demonstrations, picketing, speechmaking, marching, holding vigils or religious services and all other like forms of conduct that involve the communication or expression of views or grievances, engaged in by one or more persons, the conduct of which is reasonably likely to draw a crowd of onlookers." Is this buffer zone constitutional?

Page 811. Insert the following before Section B:

Note that a public forum is an actual or metaphorical space that the government provides for the use of private speakers. This must be distinguished from speech by the government itself. In many cases, the nature of government speech is obvious. But as the following case shows, it can sometimes be difficult to determine whether the government is offering its own message or providing space for the messages of others.

WALKER V. TEXAS DIVISION, SONS OF CONFEDERATE VETERANS
___ U.S. ___, 135 S.Ct. 2239 (2015)

JUSTICE BREYER delivered the opinion of the Court. Texas offers automobile owners a choice between ordinary and specialty license plates. Those who want the State to issue a particular specialty plate may propose a plate design, comprising a slogan, a graphic, or (most commonly) both. If the Texas Department of Motor Vehicles Board approves the design, the State will make it available for display on vehicles registered in Texas.

In this case, the Texas Division of the Sons of Confederate Veterans proposed a specialty license plate design featuring a Confederate battle flag. The Board rejected the proposal. We must decide whether that rejection violated the Constitution's free speech guarantees. We conclude that it did not. * * *

When government speaks, it is not barred by the Free Speech Clause from determining the content of what it says. *Pleasant Grove City v. Summum,* 555 U.S. 460, 467–468, 129 S.Ct. 1125, 172 L.Ed.2d 853 (2009). That freedom in part reflects the fact that it is the democratic electoral process that first and foremost provides a check on government speech.

In our view, specialty license plates issued pursuant to Texas's statutory scheme convey government speech. Our reasoning rests primarily on our analysis in *Summum,* a recent case that presented a similar problem. We conclude here, as we did there, that our precedents regarding government speech (and not our precedents regarding forums for private speech) provide the appropriate framework through which to approach the case.

In *Summum,* we considered a religious organization's request to erect in a 2.5-acre city park a monument setting forth the organization's religious tenets. In the park were 15 other permanent displays. At least 11 of these—including a wishing well, a September 11 monument, a historic granary, the city's first fire station, and a Ten Commandments monument—had been donated to the city by private entities. The religious organization argued that the Free Speech Clause required the city to display the organization's proposed monument because, by accepting a broad range of permanent exhibitions at the park, the city had created a forum for private speech in the form of monuments.

This Court rejected the organization's argument. We held that the city had not "provid[ed] a forum for private speech" with respect to monuments. Rather, the city, even when "accepting a privately donated monument and placing it on city property," had "engage[d] in expressive conduct." The speech at issue, this Court decided, was "best viewed as a form of government speech" and "therefore [was] not subject to scrutiny under the Free Speech Clause." * * *

Our analysis in *Summum* leads us to the conclusion that here, too, government speech is at issue. First, the history of license plates shows that, insofar as license plates have conveyed more than state names and vehicle identification numbers, they long have communicated messages from the States. In 1917, Arizona became the first State to display a graphic on its plates. The State presented a depiction of the head of a Hereford steer. In the years since, New Hampshire plates have featured the profile of the "Old Man of the Mountain," Massachusetts plates have included a representation of the Commonwealth's famous codfish, and Wyoming plates have displayed a rider atop a bucking bronco.

In 1928, Idaho became the first State to include a slogan on its plates. The 1928 Idaho plate proclaimed "Idaho Potatoes" and featured an illustration of a brown potato, onto which the license plate number was superimposed in green. *Id.*, at 61. The brown potato did not catch on, but slogans on license plates did. Over the years, state plates have included the phrases "North to the Future" (Alaska), "Keep Florida Green" (Florida), "Hoosier Hospitality" (Indiana), "The Iodine Products State" (South Carolina), "Green Mountains" (Vermont), and "America's Dairyland" (Wisconsin). States have used license plate slogans to urge action, to promote tourism, and to tout local industries. * * *

Second, Texas license plate designs "are often closely identified in the public mind with the [State]." Each Texas license plate is a government article serving the governmental purposes of vehicle registration and identification. The governmental nature of the plates is clear from their faces: The State places the name "TEXAS" in large letters at the top of every plate. Moreover, the State requires Texas vehicle owners to display license plates, and every Texas license plate is issued by the State. Texas also owns the designs on its license plates, including the designs that Texas adopts on the basis of proposals made by private individuals and organizations. Texas dictates the manner in which drivers may dispose of unused plates.

* * *

Indeed, a person who displays a message on a Texas license plate likely intends to convey to the public that the State has endorsed that message. If not, the individual could simply display the message in question in larger letters on a bumper sticker right next to the plate. But the individual prefers a license plate design to the purely private speech expressed through bumper stickers. That may well be because Texas's license plate designs convey government agreement with the message displayed.

Third, Texas maintains direct control over the messages conveyed on its specialty plates. Texas law provides that the State "has sole control over the design, typeface, color, and alphanumeric pattern for all license plates." The Board must approve every specialty plate design proposal before the design can appear on a Texas plate. And the Board and its predecessor have actively exercised this authority. Texas asserts, and SCV concedes, that the State has rejected at least a dozen proposed designs. * * *

SCV believes that Texas's specialty license plate designs are not government speech, at least with respect to the designs (comprising slogans and graphics) that were initially proposed by private parties. According to SCV, the State does not engage in expressive activity through such slogans and graphics, but rather provides a forum for private speech by making license plates available to display the private parties' designs. We cannot agree.

We have previously used what we have called "forum analysis" to evaluate government restrictions on purely private speech that occurs on government property. But forum analysis is misplaced here. Because the State is speaking on its own behalf, the First Amendment strictures that attend the various types of government-established forums do not apply. * * *

The fact that private parties take part in the design and propagation of a message does not extinguish the governmental nature of the message or transform the government's role into that of a mere forum-provider. In *Summum,* private entities "financed and donated monuments that the government accept[ed] and display[ed] to the public." Here, similarly, private parties propose designs that Texas may accept and display on its license plates. In this case, as in *Summum,* the "government entity may exercise [its] freedom to express its views" even "when it receives assistance from private sources for the purpose of delivering a government-controlled message." And in this case, as in *Summum,* forum analysis is inapposite. * * *

Our determination that Texas's specialty license plate designs are government speech does not mean that the designs do not also implicate the free speech rights of private persons. We have acknowledged that drivers who display a State's selected license plate designs convey the messages communicated through those designs. And we have recognized that the First Amendment stringently limits a State's authority to compel a private party to express a view with which the private party disagrees. But here, compelled private speech is not at issue. And just as Texas cannot require SCV to convey "the State's ideological message," SCV cannot force Texas to include a Confederate battle flag on its specialty license plates.

JUSTICE ALITO, joined by **CHIEF JUSTICE ROBERTS, JUSTICE SCALIA,** and **JUSTICE KENNEDY,** dissenting.

Here is a test. Suppose you sat by the side of a Texas highway and studied the license plates on the vehicles passing by. You would see, in addition to the standard Texas plates, an impressive array of specialty plates. (There are now more than 350 varieties.) You would likely observe plates that honor numerous colleges and universities. You might see plates bearing the name of a high school, a fraternity or sorority, the Masons, the Knights of Columbus, the Daughters of the American Revolution, a realty company, a favorite soft drink, a favorite burger restaurant, and a favorite NASCAR driver.

As you sat there watching these plates speed by, would you really think that the sentiments reflected in these specialty plates are the views of the State of Texas and not those of the owners of the cars? If a car with a plate that says "Rather Be Golfing" passed by at 8:30 am on a Monday morning, would you think: "This is the official policy of the State—better to golf than to work?" * * * And when a car zipped by with a plate that reads "NASCAR—24 Jeff Gordon," would you think that Gordon (born in

California, raised in Indiana, resides in North Carolina) is the official favorite of the State government?

This capacious understanding of government speech takes a large and painful bite out of the First Amendment. Specialty plates may seem innocuous. They make motorists happy, and they put money in a State's coffers. But the precedent this case sets is dangerous. While all license plates unquestionably contain *some* government speech (*e.g.,* the name of the State and the numbers and/or letters identifying the vehicle), the State of Texas has converted the remaining space on its specialty plates into little mobile billboards on which motorists can display their own messages. And what Texas did here was to reject one of the messages that members of a private group wanted to post on some of these little billboards because the State thought that many of its citizens would find the message offensive. That is blatant viewpoint discrimination. * * *

I begin with history. As we said in *Summum,* governments have used monuments since time immemorial to express important government messages, and there is no history of governments giving equal space to those wishing to express dissenting views, and members of the public understand this.

The history of messages on license plates is quite different. After the beginning of motor vehicle registration in 1917, more than 70 years passed before the proliferation of specialty plates in Texas. It was not until the 1990's that motorists were allowed to choose from among 10 messages, such as "Read to Succeed" and "Keep Texas Beautiful."

Up to this point, the words on the Texas plates can be considered government speech. The messages were created by the State, and they plausibly promoted state programs. But when, at some point within the last 20 years or so, the State began to allow private entities to secure plates conveying their own messages, Texas crossed the line.

The contrast between the history of public monuments, which have been used to convey government messages for centuries, and the Texas license plate program could not be starker. * * *

What Texas has done by selling space on its license plates is to create what we have called a limited public forum. It has allowed state property (*i.e.,* motor vehicle license plates) to be used by private speakers according to rules that the State prescribes. Under the First Amendment, however, those rules cannot discriminate on the basis of viewpoint. But that is exactly what Texas did here. The Board rejected Texas SCV's design, "specifically the confederate flag portion of the design, because public comments have shown that many members of the general public find the design offensive, and because such comments are reasonable." These statements indisputably demonstrate that the Board denied Texas SCV's design because of its viewpoint.

NOTES ON WALKER AND GOVERNMENT SPEECH

1. *Category Confusion?* It seems unlikely that Texas could ban bumper stickers portraying the Confederate flag. It seems equally clear that Texas is not compelled to use the flag as an insignia on state vehicles. Thus, the question is whether the license plate is more like a bumper sticker or a state insignia. That question divides the Court 5–4. One might wonder, however, whether this categorizing effort is really the best way to decide whether rejection of the CVS license plate design is consistent with First Amendment values. The structure of current doctrine, however, seems to make it difficult for the Court to approach cases in such functional terms.

2. *Some Historical Context.* The Court's decision was released on June 18, 2015. The night before, a white man entered a Bible study session at a black church in Charleston, South Carolina. He opened fire, and killed eighteen people, killing nine of them. Richard Fuasset, John Eligon, Jason Horowitz and Frances Roblesa, *Hectic Day at Charleston Church, and Then a Hellish Visitor*, N.Y. Times (June 30, 2015). The killer's White Supremacist background sparked a debate about racism, and about the Confederate flag in particular. Within five days, the state had decided to take down the Confederate flag that had flown outside South Carolina's capitol for decades. Michael Barbaro and Jonathan Martin, *5 Days That Left a Confederate Flag Wavering, and Likely to Fall*, N.Y. Times (June 28, 2015). All of those events took place too late to have impacted the Court's decision, but they may help place it in historic context. Note that Justice Thomas was the fifth vote in the case; his understanding of the meaning of the Confederate flag may well have been shaped by his experience of growing up as an African-American in the South.

3. *The First Amendment and the Commercial State.* It appears that the state's purpose is neither to provide a communication for private parties nor to convey its own messages, but simply to make money. This blurring of the line between governance and private enterprise presents challenges for traditional constitutional analysis. In that sense, the license plates might be analogized to the T-shirts that might be on sale in a gift shop in a public building. A private shop owner would certainly be selective in its choices of T-shirts, based on factors such as how popular the images on a shirt would be with buyers, whether controversial shirts would fit the store's image, etc. Would a state-owned gift shop be entitled to make similar choices? How would the *Walker* majority and dissent analyze the problem?

B. GOVERNMENT-SUPPORTED SPEECH

Page 812. Insert at the end of the Note on Public Employee Speech:

A related issue relating to employee speech is whether public employees can be required to pay union dues. In *Abood v. Detroit Bd. of Education*, 431 U.S. 209 (1977), the Court upheld state laws that require nonmember employees to pay an "agency fee" for the union's collective bargaining services, since they benefit from the collective bargaining agreement. In *Harris v. Quinn*, 134 S.Ct. 2618 (2014), the Court said that given what it considered the shaky foundation of *Abood*, it would not extend the *Abood* holding to quasi-public workers such as home care workers paid by Medicaid but chosen by the patient. The dissenters defended *Abood* and argued for its extension.

The continued vitality of *Abood* is unclear after *Harris*, and some public employee unions are concerned that their own viability could be threatened if *Abood* were to be overruled. Note, however, that even if *Abood* was overruled, the state could avoid any First Amendment problem by agreeing to pay a service fee for all workers directly to the union, so that the union's fee for its members would include only non-bargaining expenses. Assuming this approach was allowed by state law, it would raise no First Amendment problem since the money would no longer be part of the non-member's salary. Because government funds not linked to any individual worker would be used, workers could not complain about compelled speech even though economically the outcome is indistinguishable from an agency fee.

Pages 816–819. Replace *Velasquez* and the Notes after the opinion with the following:

AGENCY FOR INTERNATIONAL DEVELOPMENT V. ALLIANCE FOR OPEN SOCIETY INT'L, INC.
___ U.S. ___, 133 S.Ct. 2321 (2013)

CHIEF JUSTICE ROBERTS delivered the opinion of the Court.

The United States Leadership Against HIV/AIDS, Tuberculosis, and Malaria Act of 2003 (Leadership Act), 22 U.S.C. § 7601 et seq., outlined a comprehensive strategy to combat the spread of HIV/AIDS around the world. As part of that strategy, Congress authorized the appropriation of billions of dollars to fund efforts by nongovernmental organizations to assist in the fight. The Act imposes two related conditions on that funding: First, no funds made available by the Act "may be used to promote or advocate the legalization or practice of prostitution or sex trafficking." § 7631(e). And second, no funds may be used by an organization "that does not have a policy explicitly opposing prostitution and sex trafficking." § 7631(f). This case concerns the second of these conditions, referred to as the Policy Requirement. The question is whether that funding condition violates a recipient's First Amendment rights. * * *

Respondents are a group of domestic organizations engaged in combating HIV/AIDS overseas. In addition to substantial private funding, they receive billions annually in financial assistance from the United States, including under the Leadership Act. Their work includes programs aimed at limiting injection drug use in Uzbekistan, Tajikistan, and Kyrgyzstan, preventing mother-to-child HIV transmission in Kenya, and promoting safer sex practices in India. Respondents fear that adopting a policy explicitly opposing prostitution may alienate certain host governments, and may diminish the effectiveness of some of their programs by making it more difficult to work with prostitutes in the fight against HIV/AIDS. They are also concerned that the Policy Requirement may require them to censor their privately funded discussions in publications, at conferences, and in other forums about how best to prevent the spread of HIV/AIDS among prostitutes. * * *

The Policy Requirement mandates that recipients of Leadership Act funds explicitly agree with the Government's policy to oppose prostitution and sex trafficking. It is, however, a basic First Amendment principle that "freedom of speech prohibits the government from telling people what they must say." *Rumsfeld v. Forum for Academic and Institutional Rights, Inc.*, 547 U.S. 47 (2006) (citing *West Virginia Bd. of Ed. v. Barnette*, 319 U.S. 624 (1943), and *Wooley v. Maynard*, 430 U.S. 705 (1977)). "At the heart of the First Amendment lies the principle that each person should decide for himself or herself the ideas and beliefs deserving of expression, consideration, and adherence." *Turner Broadcasting System, Inc. v. FCC*, 512 U.S. 622 (1994. Were it enacted as a direct regulation of speech, the Policy Requirement would plainly violate the First Amendment. The question is whether the Government may nonetheless impose that requirement as a condition on the receipt of federal funds. * * *

As a general matter, if a party objects to a condition on the receipt of federal funding, its recourse is to decline the funds. This remains true when the objection is that a condition may affect the recipient's exercise of its First Amendment rights. See, e.g., *United States v. American Library Assn., Inc.*, 539 U.S. 194 (2003) (plurality opinion) (rejecting a claim by public libraries that conditioning funds for Internet access on the libraries' installing filtering software violated their First Amendment rights, explaining that "[t]o the extent that libraries wish to offer unfiltered access, they are free to do so without federal assistance"); *Regan v. Taxation With Representation of Wash.*, 461 U.S. 540, 546 (1983) (dismissing "the notion that First Amendment rights are somehow not fully realized unless they are subsidized by the State" (internal quotation marks omitted)).

At the same time, however, we have held that the Government " 'may not deny a benefit to a person on a basis that infringes his constitutionally protected . . . freedom of speech even if he has no entitlement to that benefit.' " In some cases, a funding condition can result in an unconstitutional burden on First Amendment rights.

The dissent thinks that can only be true when the condition is not relevant to the objectives of the program (although it has its doubts about that), or when the condition is actually coercive, in the sense of an offer that cannot be refused. See post (opinion of SCALIA, J.). Our precedents, however, are not so limited. In the present context, the relevant distinction that has emerged from our cases is between conditions that define the limits of the government spending program—those that specify the activities Congress wants to subsidize—and conditions that seek to leverage funding to regulate speech outside the contours of the program itself. The line is hardly clear, in part because the definition of a particular program can always be manipulated to subsume the challenged condition. We have held, however, that "Congress cannot recast a condition on funding as a mere definition of its program in every case, lest the First Amendment be reduced to a simple semantic exercise." *Legal Services Corporation v. Velazquez*, 531 U.S. 533, 547 (2001).

A comparison of two cases helps illustrate the distinction: In *Regan v. Taxation With Representation of Washington*, the Court upheld a requirement that nonprofit organizations seeking tax-exempt status under 26 U.S.C. § 501(c)(3) not engage in substantial efforts to influence legislation. The tax-exempt status, we explained, "ha[d] much the same effect as a cash grant to the organization." And by limiting § 501(c)(3) status to organizations that did not attempt to influence legislation, Congress had merely "chose[n] not to subsidize lobbying." In rejecting the nonprofit's First Amendment claim, the Court highlighted * * * the fact that the condition did not prohibit that organization from lobbying Congress altogether. By returning to a "dual structure" it had used in the past—separately incorporating as a § 501(c)(3) organization and § 501(c)(4) organization—the nonprofit could continue to claim § 501(c)(3) status for its nonlobbying activities, while attempting to influence legislation in its § 501(c)(4) capacity with separate funds. Ibid. Maintaining such a structure, the Court noted, was not "unduly burdensome." The condition thus did not deny the organization a government benefit "on account of its intention to lobby."

In *FCC v. League of Women Voters of California*, by contrast, the Court struck down a condition on federal financial assistance to noncommercial broadcast television and radio stations that prohibited all editorializing, including with private funds. Even a station receiving only one percent of its overall budget from the Federal Government, the Court explained, was "barred absolutely from all editorializing." Unlike the situation in *Regan*, the law provided no way for a station to limit its use of federal funds to non-editorializing activities, while using private funds "to make known its views on matters of public importance." The prohibition thus went beyond ensuring that federal funds not be used to subsidize "public broadcasting station editorials," and instead leveraged the federal funding to regulate the stations' speech outside the scope of the program.

Our decision in *Rust v. Sullivan* elaborated on the approach reflected in *Regan* and *League of Women Voters*. In *Rust*, we considered Title X of the Public Health Service Act, a Spending Clause program that issued grants to nonprofit health-care organizations "to assist in the establishment and operation of voluntary family planning projects [to] offer a broad range of acceptable and effective family planning methods and services." The organizations received funds from a variety of sources other than the Federal Government for a variety of purposes. The Act, however, prohibited the Title X federal funds from being "used in programs where abortion is a method of family planning." Ibid. (internal quotation marks omitted). To enforce this provision, HHS regulations barred Title X projects from advocating abortion as a method of family planning, and required grantees to ensure that their Title X projects were " 'physically and financially separate' " from their other projects that engaged in the prohibited activities—group of Title X funding recipients brought suit, claiming the regulations imposed an unconstitutional condition on their First Amendment rights. We rejected their claim.

We explained that Congress can, without offending the Constitution, selectively fund certain programs to address an issue of public concern, without funding alternative ways of addressing the same problem. In Title X, Congress had defined the federal program to encourage only particular family planning methods. The challenged regulations were simply "designed to ensure that the limits of the federal program are observed," and "that public funds [are] spent for the purposes for which they were authorized."

In making this determination, the Court stressed that "Title X expressly distinguishes between a Title X grantee and a Title X project." The regulations governed only the scope of the grantee's Title X projects, leaving it "unfettered in its other activities." I "The Title X grantee can continue to . . . engage in abortion advocacy; it simply is required to conduct those activities through programs that are separate and independent from the project that receives Title X funds." Because the regulations did not "prohibit[ ] the recipient from engaging in the protected conduct outside the scope of the federally funded program," they did not run afoul of the First Amendment.

As noted, the distinction drawn in these cases—between conditions that define the federal program and those that reach outside it—is not always self-evident. As Justice Cardozo put it in a related context, "Definition more precise must abide the wisdom of the future." *Steward Machine Co. v. Davis*, 301 U.S. 548, 591 (1937). Here, however, we are confident that the Policy Requirement falls on the unconstitutional side of the line.

To begin, it is important to recall that the Leadership Act has two conditions relevant here. The first—unchallenged in this litigation—prohibits Leadership Act funds from being used "to promote or advocate the legalization or practice of prostitution or sex trafficking." 22 U.S.C.

§ 7631(e). The Government concedes that § 7631(e) by itself ensures that federal funds will not be used for the prohibited purposes

The Policy Requirement therefore must be doing something more— and it is. The dissent views the Requirement as simply a selection criterion by which the Government identifies organizations "who believe in its ideas to carry them to fruition." As an initial matter, whatever purpose the Policy Requirement serves in selecting funding recipients, its effects go beyond selection. The Policy Requirement is an ongoing condition on recipients' speech and activities, a ground for terminating a grant after selection is complete. In any event, as the Government acknowledges, it is not simply seeking organizations that oppose prostitution. Rather, it explains, "Congress has expressed its purpose 'to eradicate' prostitution and sex trafficking, 22 U.S.C. § 7601(23), and it wants recipients to adopt a similar stance." This case is not about the Government's ability to enlist the assistance of those with whom it already agrees. It is about compelling a grant recipient to adopt a particular belief as a condition of funding.

By demanding that funding recipients adopt—as their own—the Government's view on an issue of public concern, the condition by its very nature affects "protected conduct outside the scope of the federally funded program." A recipient cannot avow the belief dictated by the Policy Requirement when spending Leadership Act funds, and then turn around and assert a contrary belief, or claim neutrality, when participating in activities on its own time and dime. By requiring recipients to profess a specific belief, the Policy Requirement goes beyond defining the limits of the federally funded program to defining the recipient.

The Government contends that the affiliate guidelines, established while this litigation was pending, save the program. Under those guidelines, funding recipients are permitted to work with affiliated organizations that do not abide by the condition, as long as the recipients retain "objective integrity and independence" from the unfettered affiliates. The Government suggests the guidelines alleviate any unconstitutional burden on the respondents' First Amendment rights by allowing them to either: (1) accept Leadership Act funding and comply with Policy Requirement, but establish affiliates to communicate contrary views on prostitution; or (2) decline funding themselves (thus remaining free to express their own views or remain neutral), while creating affiliates whose sole purpose is to receive and administer Leadership Act funds, thereby "cabin[ing] the effects" of the Policy Requirement within the scope of the federal program.

Neither approach is sufficient. When we have noted the importance of affiliates in this context, it has been because they allow an organization bound by a funding condition to exercise its First Amendment rights outside the scope of the federal program. Affiliates cannot serve that purpose when the condition is that a funding recipient espouse a specific belief as its own. If the affiliate is distinct from the recipient, the arrangement does not afford a means for the recipient to express its beliefs. If the affiliate is more clearly identified with the recipient, the recipient can express those beliefs only at the price of evident hypocrisy. The guidelines themselves make that clear.

The Government suggests that the Policy Requirement is necessary because, without it, the grant of federal funds could free a recipient's private funds "to be used to promote prostitution or sex trafficking." That argument assumes that federal funding will simply supplant private funding, rather than pay for new programs or expand existing ones. The Government offers no support for that assumption as a general matter, or any reason to believe it is true here. And if the Government's argument were correct, *League of Women Voters* would have come out differently, and much of the reasoning of *Regan* and *Rust* would have been beside the point. * * *

Pressing its argument further, the Government contends that "if organizations awarded federal funds to implement Leadership Act programs could at the same time promote or affirmatively condone prostitution or sex trafficking, whether using public or private funds, it would undermine the government's program and confuse its message opposing prostitution and sex trafficking." But the Policy Requirement goes beyond preventing recipients from using private funds in a way that would undermine the federal program. It requires them to pledge allegiance to the Government's policy of eradicating prostitution. As to that, we cannot improve upon what Justice Jackson wrote for the Court 70 years ago: "If there is any fixed star in our constitutional constellation, it is that no official, high or petty, can prescribe what shall be orthodox in politics, nationalism, religion, or other matters of opinion or force citizens to confess by word or act their faith therein."

The Policy Requirement compels as a condition of federal funding the affirmation of a belief that by its nature cannot be confined within the scope of the Government program. In so doing, it violates the First Amendment and cannot be sustained.

KAGAN, J., took no part in the consideration or decision of this case.

JUSTICE SCALIA, with whom JUSTICE THOMAS joins dissenting.

The Leadership Act provides that "any group or organization that does not have a policy explicitly opposing prostitution and sex trafficking" may not receive funds appropriated under the Act. 22 U.S.C. § 7631(f). This Policy Requirement is nothing more than a means of selecting suitable agents to implement the Government's chosen strategy to eradicate HIV/AIDS. That is perfectly permissible under the Constitution.

The First Amendment does not mandate a viewpoint-neutral government. Government must choose between rival ideas and adopt some as its own: competition over cartels, solar energy over coal, weapon development over disarmament, and so forth. Moreover, the government may enlist the assistance of those who believe in its ideas to carry them to fruition; and it need not enlist for that purpose those who oppose or do not support the ideas. That seems to me a matter of the most common common sense. For example: One of the purposes of America's foreign-aid programs is the fostering of good will towards this country. If the organization Hamas—reputed to have an efficient system for delivering welfare—were excluded from a program for the distribution of U.S. food assistance, no one could reasonably object. And that would remain true if Hamas were an organization of United States citizens entitled to the protection of the Constitution. So long as the unfunded organization remains free to engage in its activities (including anti-American propaganda) "without federal assistance," refusing to make use of its assistance for an enterprise to which it is opposed does not abridge its speech. And the same is true when the rejected organization is not affirmatively opposed to, but merely unsupportive of, the object of the federal program, which appears to be the case here. (Respondents do not promote prostitution, but neither do they wish to oppose it.) A federal program to encourage healthy eating habits need not be administered by the American Gourmet Society, which has nothing against healthy food but does not insist upon it.

The argument is that this commonsense principle will enable the government to discriminate against, and injure, points of view to which it is opposed. * * * The constitutional prohibition at issue here is not a prohibition against discriminating against or injuring opposing points of view, but the First Amendment's prohibition against the coercing of speech. I am frankly dubious that a condition for eligibility to participate in a minor federal program such as this one runs afoul of that prohibition even when the condition is irrelevant to the goals of the program. Not every disadvantage is a coercion.

But that is not the issue before us here. Here the views that the Government demands an applicant forswear—or that the Government insists an applicant favor—are relevant to the program in question. The program is valid only if the Government is entitled to disfavor the opposing view (here, advocacy of or toleration of prostitution). And if the program can disfavor it, so can the selection of those who are to administer the program. There is no risk that this principle will enable the Government to discriminate arbitrarily against positions it disfavors. It would not, for example, permit the Government to exclude from bidding on defense contracts anyone who refuses to abjure prostitution. But here a central part of the Government's HIV/AIDS strategy is the suppression of prostitution, by which HIV is transmitted. It is entirely reasonable to admit to participation in the program only those who believe in that goal. * * *

Of course the most obvious manner in which the admission to a program of an ideological opponent can frustrate the purpose of the program is by freeing up the opponent's funds for use in its ideological opposition. To use the Hamas example again: Subsidizing that organization's provision of social services enables the money that it would otherwise use for that purpose to be used, instead, for anti-American propaganda. Perhaps that problem does not exist in this case since the respondents do not affirmatively promote prostitution. But the Court's analysis categorically rejects that justification for ideological requirements in all cases, demanding "record indica[tion]" that "federal funding will simply supplant private funding, rather than pay for new programs." Ante, at 14. This seems to me quite naive. Money is fungible. The economic reality is that when NGOs can conduct their AIDS work on the Government's dime, they can expend greater resources on policies that undercut the Leadership Act. The Government need not establish by record evidence that this will happen. To make it a valid consideration in determining participation in federal programs, it suffices that this is a real and obvious risk. * * *

The Court's opinion contains stirring quotations * * *. They serve only to distract attention from the elephant in the room: that the Government is not forcing anyone to say anything. What Congress has done here—requiring an ideological commitment relevant to the Government task at hand—is approved by the Constitution itself. Americans need not support the Constitution; they may be Communists or anarchists. But "[t]he Senators and Representatives . . . , and the Members of the several State Legislatures, and all executive and judicial Officers, both of the United States and of the several States, shall be bound by Oath or Affirmation, to support [the] Constitution." U.S. Const., Art. VI, cl. 3. The Framers saw the wisdom of imposing affirmative ideological commitments prerequisite to assisting in the government's work. And so should we.

NOTES

1.   *A Unified Test.* In *AID*, the Court finally seems to have settled on a First Amendment test for funding conditions relating to speech. The downside is that, as Chief Justice Roberts concedes, applying the test may not always be difficult. We've already seen a similar problem before, where we saw that subject matter limits in defining a limited public forum are fine, but subject matter carve-outs from the forum are not. Yet, the distinction between the two situations can be elusive. But at least the Court has now provided a framework in which to conduct the argument.

2.   *Should Coercion Be the Test?* Justice Scalia argues that, at least when the condition is relevant to the goal of a government program, the text should

be coercion. But he does not explain why as a general matter coercion should be the test for funding conditions. After all, the word "coercion" does not appear in the First Amendment. Instead, it forbids abridging the freedom of speech. Is it implausible to say that a person's freedom of speech has been "abridged" if they are required express a view or refrain from expressing a view in order to participate in a government program?

3.   *The Oath of Office as an Analogy.* How good an analogy is the oath of office? Employees have a duty of loyalty toward their employers, and this is especially true for the employers' officers and directors. But this isn't true of independent contractors. Also, doesn't the new regulation allowing the use of affiliates underlie this argument? After all, this mechanism is designed to allow grants to go to recipients who actually do not share the government's purpose but are willing to go through a charade to meet the law's requirements. So the regulation seems ill-suited to test for genuine enthusiasm about the abortion funding restriction.

SECTION 7. THE RELIGION CLAUSES

A. FREE EXERCISE

Page 849. Insert after the Notes on *Hosanna-Tabor*:

Recall that in the aftermath of *Smith*, Congress passed the Religious Freedom Restoration Act, which the Court then declared unconstitutional as applied to the states. RFRA does, however, remain in effect with regard to the federal government. In Burwell v. Hobby Lobby Stores, ___ U.S. ___, 134 S.Ct. 2751 (2014), a five-Justice majority held that RFRA immunized a closely held corporation from being required to provide contraception coverage to female employees. The majority concluded that RFRA protected the religious scruples of the owners, who sincerely objected to providing insurance for actions by employees that violated their religious views. The majority found that the government had a less restrictive alternative: extending to for-profit corporations an optional mechanism already provided to non-profit religious organizations. Justice Kennedy concurred to emphasize the narrowness of the decision in applying only to contraception (indeed, on the facts, only to forms of contraception that operate after intercourse has already occurred). He also stressed the existence of the off-the-rack accommodation already devised by the government. The four dissenters expressed concern that the Court had opened the door for corporations to object to coverage for a wide range of medical procedures and to claim religious exemptions from anti-discrimination and other laws. They also suggested that publicly held corporations might well try to take advantage of the ruling.

Burwell makes it clear that, as a practical matter, *Smith* has no significance as applied to the federal government, given the existence of RCRA. State governments, however, retain more discretion regarding religious exemptions.

B. THE ESTABLISHMENT CLAUSE

2. Government Endorsement of Religion

Page 866. Insert at end of Note 3:

The Court has continued to find line drawing difficult in considering arguable governmental endorsements of religion. In Town of Greece, N.Y. v. Galloway, ___ U.S. ___, 134 S.Ct. 1811 (2014), the town board began public meetings with prayers by local ministers, some of which were sectarian. Given the long tradition of legislative prayers, the plurality opinion (by Justice Kennedy) did not find problematic the city's failure to broaden the roster of invitees to include more non-Christians or by the sectarian nature of the prayers. Concurring, Justice Scalia and Thomas found that the prayers were not comparable to coercive state establishments of the Founding era, even assuming that the Establishment Clause was incorporated into the Fourteenth Amendment. The dissenting Justices pointed out that citizens were required to attend board meetings on occasion in order to obtain zoning variances or other actions, and that non-Christians in the audience would undoubtedly perceive a message of exclusion from the succession of Christian ministers.

CHAPTER 7

FEDERALISM: CONGRESSIONAL POWER AND STATE AUTHORITY

■ ■ ■

SECTION 3. CONGRESSIONAL AUTHORITY TO PROMOTE CIVIL RIGHTS

C. CONGRESSIONAL POWER TO RESPOND TO DISCRIMINATION AGAINST WOMEN AND TO PROTECT FUNDAMENTAL RIGHTS

Page 1015. Insert the following Case and Notes at the end of Section 3, right after Problem 7–6:

SHELBY COUNTY, ALABAMA V. HOLDER
570 U.S. ___, 133 S.Ct. 2612 (2013)

CHIEF JUSTICE ROBERTS delivered the opinion of the Court.

[As illustrated in the *Katzenbach* Cases and *City of Rome* in the Casebook (pp. 952–66), § 5 of the Voting Rights Act of 1965 imposed preclearance requirements on jurisdictions defined in § 4(b) as those states or political subdivisions that on November 1, 1964 maintained a test or device that limited voting *and* had voting levels lower than 50% of the eligible voters in the 1964 election. Congress reauthorized the Act with minimal changes to the § 4(b) coverage formula in 1970 and 1975 (notably, to include language barriers to the definition of tests or devices limiting voting opportunities, which added Texas, Arizona, and Alaska to the roster of covered jurisdictions), and with no changes to the formula in 1982, and 2006. In 2006, Congress significantly expanded the § 5 preclearance restrictions. Shelby County fell under the coverage formula of § 4(b) but objected to preclearance on the ground that this portion of the Voting Rights Act was unconstitutional.]

Nearly 50 years later, [the § 5 preclearance requirements for covered jurisdictions] are still in effect; indeed, they have been made more stringent, and are now scheduled to last until 2031. There is no denying, however, that the conditions that originally justified these measures no longer characterize voting in the covered jurisdictions. By 2009, "the racial gap in voter registration and turnout [was] lower in the States originally covered by § 5 than it [was] nationwide." *Northwest Austin Municipal Util. Dist. No. One* v. *Holder*, 557 U.S. 193, 203–204 (2009) (Casebook, p. 1014).[1] Since that time, Census Bureau data indicate that African-American voter turnout has come to exceed white voter turnout in five of the six States originally covered by § 5,with a gap in the sixth State of less than one half of one percent. See Dept. of Commerce, Census Bureau, Reported Voting and Registration, by Sex, Race and Hispanic Origin, for States (Nov. 2012) (Table 4b). * * *

[II.] In *Northwest Austin*, we stated that "the Act imposes current burdens and must be justified by current needs." And we concluded that "a departure from the fundamental principle of equal sovereignty requires a showing that a statute's disparate geographic coverage is sufficiently related to the problem that it targets." *Ibid.* These basic principles guide our review of the question before us. [The Chief Justice set forth the well-established federalist structure of government and the substantial "autonomy" the states have in structuring their electoral processes, especially in state elections.]

Not only do States retain sovereignty under the Constitution, there is also a "fundamental principle of *equal* sovereignty" among the States. *Northwest Austin* (emphasis added). Over a hundred years ago, this Court explained that our Nation "was and is a union of States, equal in power, dignity and authority." *Coyle* v. *Smith*, 221 U.S. 559, 567 (1911). Indeed, "the constitutional equality of the States is essential to the harmonious operation of the scheme upon which the Republic was organized." *Id.,* at 580. *Coyle* concerned the admission of new States, and *Katzenbach* rejected the notion that the principle operated as a *bar* on differential treatment outside that context. At the same time, as we made clear in *Northwest Austin*, the fundamental principle of equal sovereignty remains highly pertinent in assessing subsequent disparate treatment of States.

The Voting Rights Act sharply departs from these basic principles. It suspends "*all* changes to state election law—however innocuous—until they have been precleared by federal authorities in Washington, D.C." States must beseech the Federal Government for permission to implement laws that they would otherwise have the right to enact and execute on their own, subject of course to any injunction in a § 2 action. The Attorney General has 60 days to object to a preclearance request, longer if he requests more information. See 28 CFR §§ 51.9, 51.37. If a State seeks preclearance from a three judge court, the process can take years.

---

[1]   [Eds.] In *Northwest Austin*, the Court faced a "serious" constitutional challenge to §§ 4–5 but declined to address it, because there was a statutory ground for giving relief to a local government objecting to preclearance. To avoid the serious constitutional problems with §§ 4(b) and 5, the Court interpreted the "bailout" provision in § 4(a) broadly. Shelby County did not seek bailout under § 4(a), and so its challenge did not offer the Court a statutory solution.

And despite the tradition of equal sovereignty, the Act applies to only nine States (and several additional counties). While one State waits months or years and expends funds to implement a validly enacted law, its neighbor can typically put the same law into effect immediately, through the normal legislative process. [Invoking these background principles, the Chief Justice explained that *Katzenbach*'s willingness to uphold the extraordinary requirements in §§ 4–5 was premised upon their temporary remedial features.]

Nearly 50 years later, things have changed dramatically. Shelby County contends that the preclearance requirement, even without regard to its disparate coverage, is now unconstitutional. Its arguments have a good deal of force. In the covered jurisdictions, "[v]oter turnout and registration rates now approach parity. Blatantly discriminatory evasions of federal decrees are rare. And minority candidates hold office at unprecedented levels." *Northwest Austin.* The tests and devices that blocked access to the ballot have been forbidden nationwide for over 40 years. See § 6, 84 Stat. 315; § 102, 89 Stat. 400. [The Chief Justice summed up the progress by reference to data on voting turn-out, by race, that was compiled by the House and Senate Judiciary Committees for the 2006 reauthorization:]

	1965			2004		
	White	Black	Gap	White	Black	Gap
Alabama	69.2	19.3	49.9	73.8	72.9	0.9
Georgia	62.[6]	27.4	35.2	63.5	64.2	-0.7
Louisiana	80.5	31.6	48.9	75.1	71.1	4.0
Mississippi	69.9	6.7	63.2	72.3	76.1	-3.8
South Carolina	75.7	37.3	38.4	74.4	71.1	3.3
Virginia	61.1	38.3	22.8	68.2	57.4	10.8

See S. Rep. No. 109–295, p. 11 (2006); H. R. Rep. No. 109–478, at 12.

[In light of these data, the Chief Justice found Congress's reauthorization of the Voting Rights Act, with no change in the coverage formula, in 1982 and 2006 astonishing. In Part III of his opinion, the Chief Justice explained that applying the old 1965 formula to impose preclearance obligations on states, like Alabama, that had not used voting tests since 1965 and that now had virtually complete parity in racial voting levels over several election cycles, was constitutionally unsustainable. The Fifteenth Amendment was intended to ensure voting rights now and in the future, not to punish jurisdictions for past discriminations.]

[The government argued that Congress compiled an extensive record of continuing evasions by the covered jurisdictions.] The court below and the parties have debated what that record shows * * *. Regardless of how to look at the record, however, no one can fairly say that it shows anything approaching the "pervasive," "flagrant," "widespread," and "rampant" discrimination that faced Congress in 1965, and that clearly distinguished the covered jurisdictions from the rest of the Nation at that time. *Katzenbach*; *Northwest Austin.*

But a more fundamental problem remains: Congress did not use the record it compiled to shape a coverage formula grounded in current conditions. It instead reenacted a formula based on 40-year-old facts having no logical relation to the present day. The dissent relies on "second generation barriers," which are not impediments to the casting of ballots, but rather electoral arrangements that affect the weight of minority votes. That does not cure the problem. Viewing the preclearance requirements as targeting such efforts simply highlights the irrationality of continued reliance on the § 4 coverage formula, which is based on voting tests and access to the ballot, not vote dilution. We cannot pretend that we are reviewing an updated statute, or try our hand at updating the statute ourselves, based on the new record compiled by Congress. Contrary to the dissent's contention, we are not ignoring the record; we are simply recognizing that it played no role in shaping the statutory formula before us today. * * *

[THE CHIEF JUSTICE concluded with an invitation to Congress to reconsider the coverage formula and enact one that remedies current rather than historical impediments to exercise of the franchise by racial minorities.]

[JUSTICE THOMAS wrote a concurring opinion agreeing with the Chief Justice that the coverage formula in § 4 goes beyond Congress's Fifteenth Amendment authority, but also arguing that the preclearance requirements of § 5 are unconstitutional as well. The "extraordinary" burdens imposed by § 5 would be unconstitutional even if § 4 could be more narrowly tailored, Justice Thomas concluded.]

JUSTICE GINSBURG, with whom JUSTICE BREYER, JUSTICE SOTOMAYOR, and JUSTICE KAGAN join, dissenting.

In the Court's view, the very success of § 5 of the Voting Rights Act demands its dormancy. Congress was of another mind. Recognizing that large progress has been made, Congress determined, based on a voluminous record, that the scourge of discrimination was not yet extirpated. The question this case presents is who decides whether, as currently operative, § 5 remains justifiable, this Court, or a Congress charged with the obligation to enforce the post-Civil War Amendments "by appropriate legislation." [XV Am., § 2.] With overwhelming support in both Houses, Congress concluded that, for two prime reasons, § 5 should continue in force, unabated. First, continuance would facilitate completion of the impressive gains thus far made; and second, continuance would guard against backsliding. Those assessments were well within Congress' province to make and should elicit this Court's unstinting approbation. * * *

After considering the full legislative record, Congress made the following findings: The VRA has directly caused significant progress in eliminating first-generation barriers to ballot access, leading to a marked increase in minority voter registration and turnout and the number of minority elected officials. 2006 Reauthorization § 2(b)(1). But despite this progress, "second generation barriers constructed to prevent minority voters from fully participating in the electoral process" continued to exist, as well as racially polarized voting in the covered jurisdictions, which increased the political vulnerability of racial and language minorities in those jurisdictions. §§ 2(b)(2)–(3). Extensive "[e]vidence of continued discrimination," Congress concluded, "clearly show[ed] the continued need for Federal oversight" in covered jurisdictions. §§ 2(b)(4)–(5). The overall record demonstrated to the federal lawmakers that, "without the continuation of the Voting Rights Act of 1965 protections, racial and language minority citizens will be deprived of the opportunity to exercise their right to vote, or will have their votes diluted, undermining the significant gains made by minorities in the last 40 years." § 2(b)(9).

Based on these findings, Congress reauthorized preclearance for another 25 years, while also undertaking to reconsider the extension after 15 years to ensure that the provision was still necessary and effective. [These findings, supported by exhaustive legislative hearings and factual materials assembled for Congress, are entitled to the Court's deference, argued Justice Ginsburg. This is particularly true where Congress is implementing the Fifteenth Amendment, whose text borrows the expansive language of § 2. Cf. *McCulloch* (an example of liberal construction for Congress's discretion in implementing core constitutional grants of authority).]

I begin with the evidence on which Congress based its decision to continue the preclearance remedy. The surest way to evaluate whether that remedy remains in order is to see if preclearance is still effectively preventing discriminatory changes to voting laws. See *City of Rome* (identifying "information on the number and types of submissions made by covered jurisdictions and the number and nature of objections interposed by the Attorney General" as a primary basis for upholding the 1975 reauthorization). On that score, the record before Congress was huge. In fact, Congress found there were *more* DOJ objections between 1982 and 2004 (626) than there were between 1965 and the 1982 reauthorization (490). 1 Voting Rights Act: Evidence of Continued Need, Hearing before the Subcommittee on the Constitution of the House Committee on the Judiciary, 109th Cong., 2d Sess., p. 172 (2006) (hereinafter Evidence of Continued Need).

All told, between 1982 and 2006, DOJ objections blocked over 700 voting changes based on a determination that the changes were discriminatory. H.R. Rep. No. 109–478, at 21. Congress found that the majority of DOJ objections included findings of discriminatory intent, and that the changes blocked by preclearance were "calculated decisions to keep minority voters from fully participating in the political process." H.R. Rep. 109–478, at 21. On top of that, over the same time period the DOJ and private plaintiffs succeeded in more than 100 actions to enforce the § 5 preclearance requirements. 1 Evidence of Continued Need 186, 250.

In addition to blocking proposed changes through preclearing, DOJ may request more information from a jurisdiction proposing a change. In turn, the jurisdiction may modify or withdraw the proposed change. The number of such modifications or withdrawals provides an indication of how many discriminatory proposals are deterred without need for formal objection. Congress received evidence that more than 800 proposed changes were altered or withdrawn since the last reauthorization in 1982. H.R. Rep. No. 109–478, at 40–41. Congress also received empirical studies finding that DOJ's requests for more information had a significant effect on the degree to which covered jurisdictions "compl[ied] with their obligatio[n]" to protect minority voting rights. 2 Evidence of Continued Need 2555. * * *

The number of discriminatory changes blocked or deterred by the preclearance requirement suggests that the state of voting rights in the covered jurisdictions would have been significantly different absent this remedy. Surveying the type of changes stopped by the preclearance procedure conveys a sense of the extent to which § 5 continues to protect minority voting rights. Set out below are characteristic examples of changes blocked in the years leading up to the 2006 reauthorization:

- In 1995, Mississippi sought to reenact a dual voter registration system, "which was initially enacted in 1892 to disenfranchise Black voters," and for that reason, was struck down by a federal court in 1987. H.R. Rep. No. 109–478, at 39. * * *

- In 2006, this Court found that Texas' attempt to redraw a congressional district to reduce the strength of Latino voters bore "the mark of intentional discrimination that could give rise to an equal protection violation," and ordered the district redrawn in compliance with the VRA. *League of United Latin American Citizens* v. *Perry*, 548 U.S. 399, 440 (2006). In response, Texas sought to undermine this Court's order by curtailing early voting in the district, but was blocked by an action to enforce the § 5 preclearance requirement. See Order in *League of United Latin American Citizens* v. *Texas*, No. 06–cv–1046 (WD Tex.), Doc. 8.

- In 2003, after African-Americans won a majority of the seats on the school board for the first time in history, Charleston County, South Carolina, proposed an at-large voting mechanism for the board. The proposal, made without consulting any of the African-American members of the school board, was found to be an " 'exact replica' " of an earlier voting scheme that, a federal court had determined, violated the VRA. 811 F. Supp. 2d 424, 483 (DDC 2011). See also S. Rep. No. 109–295, at 309. DOJ invoked § 5 to block the proposal. * * *

[These examples, and others invoked by Justice Ginsburg, were only the "tip of the iceberg," as Congress received and credited ample evidence that covered jurisdictions evaded the VRA through subtle as well as blatant measures. Justice Ginsburg then considered evidence that § 4(b)'s coverage formula still addressed current and not just historical needs for remedy.]

There is no question, moreover, that the covered jurisdictions have a unique history of problems with racial discrimination in voting. Consideration of this long history, still in living memory, was altogether appropriate. The Court criticizes Congress for failing to recognize that "history did not end in 1965." But the Court ignores that "what's past is prologue." W. Shakespeare, The Tempest, act 2, sc. 1. And "[t]hose who cannot remember the past are condemned to repeat it." 1 G. Santayana, The Life of Reason 284 (1905). Congress was especially mindful of the need to reinforce the gains already made and to prevent backsliding. 2006 Reauthorization § 2(b)(9).

Of particular importance, even after 40 years and thousands of discriminatory changes blocked by preclearance, conditions in the covered jurisdictions demonstrated that the formula was still justified by "current needs." *Northwest Austin*. Congress learned of these conditions through a report, known as the Katz study, that looked at § 2 suits between 1982 and 2004. To Examine the Impact and Effectiveness of the Voting Rights Act: Hearing before the Subcommittee on the Constitution of the House Committee on the Judiciary, 109th Cong., 1st Sess., pp. 964–1124 (2005) (hereinafter Impact and Effectiveness). Because the private right of action authorized by § 2 of the VRA applies nationwide, a comparison of § 2 lawsuits in covered and noncovered jurisdictions provides an appropriate yardstick for measuring differences between covered and noncovered jurisdictions. If differences in the risk of voting discrimination between covered and noncovered jurisdictions had disappeared, one would expect that the rate of successful § 2 lawsuits would be roughly the same in both areas. The study's findings, however, indicated that racial discrimination in voting remains "concentrated in the jurisdictions singled out for preclearance." *Northwest Austin*.

Although covered jurisdictions account for less than 25 percent of the country's population, the Katz study revealed that they accounted for 56 percent of successful § 2 litigation since 1982. Impact and Effectiveness 974. Controlling for population, there were nearly *four* times as many successful § 2 cases in covered jurisdictions as there were in noncovered jurisdictions. The Katz study further found that § 2 lawsuits are more likely to succeed when they are filed in covered jurisdictions than in noncovered jurisdictions. Impact and Effectiveness 974. From these findings—ignored by the Court—Congress reasonably concluded that the coverage formula continues to identify the jurisdictions of greatest concern.

[Justice Ginsburg also invoked evidence before Congress that voting in the covered jurisdictions was more racially polarized than elsewhere in the country. H.R. Rep. No. 109–478, at 34–35. And she observed that the § 4 coverage regime was far from static, contrary to the Court's suggestions. Section 4(a), expanded in 1982, allows jurisdictions to bail out of § 4(b)'s coverage if they can demonstrate a history of voting regularity. Indeed, more than 200 jurisdictions have bailed out of the VRA since the 1982 Reauthorization.

[Justice Ginsburg took the Court to task for its treatment of the Court's own precedents for analyzing constitutional issues. Shelby County's challenge was a facial one: under the Court's precedents, such a challenge can succeed *only* if the challenger can show there is "no set of circumstances" to which the statute can constitutionally be applied. *United States* v. *Salerno*, 481 U.S. 739, 745 (1987). Why did the Court not engage the *Salerno* analysis? Apparently because Alabama is the classic case where the "old" formula applies in full force.]

Although circumstances in Alabama have changed, serious concerns remain. Between 1982 and 2005, Alabama had one of the highest rates of successful § 2 suits, second only to its VRA-covered neighbor Mississippi. In other words, even while subject to the restraining effect of § 5, Alabama was found to have "deni[ed] or abridge[d]" voting rights "on account of race or color" more frequently than nearly all other States in the Union. * * * Alabama's sorry history of § 2 violations alone provides sufficient justification for Congress' determination in 2006 that the State should remain subject to § 5's preclearance requirement.

A few examples suffice to demonstrate that, at least in Alabama, the "current burdens" imposed by § 5's preclearance requirement are "justified by current needs." *Northwest Austin.* In the interim between the VRA's 1982 and 2006 reauthorizations, this Court twice confronted purposeful racial discrimination in Alabama. In *Pleasant Grove* v. *United States*, 479 U.S. 462 (1987), the Court held that Pleasant Grove—a city in Jefferson County, Shelby County's neighbor—engaged in purposeful discrimination by annexing all-white areas while rejecting the annexation request of an adjacent black neighborhood. The city had "shown unambiguous opposition to racial integration, both before and after the passage of the federal civil rights laws," and its strategic annexations appeared to be an attempt "to provide for the growth of a monolithic white voting block" for "the impermissible purpose of minimizing future black voting strength." [Justice Ginsburg cited a second Supreme Court case and other court cases where Alabama was successfully charged with blatant violations of the Fifteenth Amendment and the VRA.]

A recent FBI investigation provides a further window into the persistence of racial discrimination in state politics. See *United States* v. *McGregor*, 824 F. Supp. 2d 1339, 1344–1348 (MD Ala. 2011). Recording devices worn by state legislators cooperating with the FBI's investigation captured conversations between members of the state legislature and their political allies. The recorded conversations are shocking. Members of the state Senate derisively refer to African-Americans as "Aborigines" and talk openly of their aim to quash a particular gambling-related referendum because the referendum, if placed on the ballot, might increase African-American voter turnout. *Id.*, at 1345–1346 (internal quotation marks omitted). See also *id.*, at 1345 (legislators and their allies expressed concern that if the referendum were placed on the ballot, " '[e]very black, every illiterate' would be 'bused [to the polls] on HUD financed buses' "). These conversations occurred not in the 1870's, or even in the 1960's, they took place in 2010. * * *

The sad irony of today's decision lies in its utter failure to grasp why the VRA has proven effective. The Court appears to believe that the VRA's success in eliminating the specific devices extant in 1965 means that preclearance is no longer needed. With that belief, and the argument derived from it, history repeats itself. The same assumption—that the problem could be solved when particular methods of voting discrimination are identified and eliminated—was indulged and proved wrong repeatedly prior to the VRA's enactment. Unlike prior statutes, which singled out particular tests or devices, the VRA is grounded in Congress' recognition of the "variety and persistence" of measures designed to impair minority voting rights. *Katzenbach*. In truth, the evolution of voting discrimination into more subtle second-generation barriers is powerful evidence that a remedy as effective as preclearance remains vital to protect minority voting rights and prevent backsliding. * * *

NOTES ON SHELBY COUNTY

1. *The Doctrinal Debate.* Does the Chief Justice have satisfactory answers to the doctrinal issues raised by Justice Ginsburg's dissenting opinion? To her examination of the record? The Chief Justice's primary strategy is to escape from the overwhelming congressional record of § 5 violations by Alabama and other covered jurisdictions, by leaving § 5 intact as

a formal matter, and only striking down § 4(b)'s coverage formula. Is that a successful strategy, in your view?

Consider the Court's failure to engage Justice Ginsburg's charge that the majority was violating the doctrine established by *United States* v. *Salerno*, 481 U.S. 739, 745 (1987). That is, Shelby County's challenge to the VRA was a facial challenge; under *Salerno,* the challenger was required to show that there was "no set of circumstances" to which the VRA could constitutionally be applied. This seems hard to accomplish, as Justice Ginsburg demonstrated. How should the Chief Justice have responded? Does his response hinge upon his clever choice to focus his constitutional fire on § 4(b), and not § 5?

2.   *The Equality of the States as a Strong Background Norm.* The Chief Justice's opinion in *Shelby County* is now a citation for a constitutional norm that all states must, presumptively, be treated the same. What is the source of this norm? It does not appear anywhere in the Constitution, or even in *The Federalist.* The Chief Justice cites *Coyle* v. *Smith* but immediately concedes that *Coyle* created the "equal footing doctrine," relating to the admission of new states under U.S. Const., art. IV, § 3, cl. 1; see Sonia Sotomayor de Noonen, Note, *Statehood and the Equal Footing Doctrine: The Case for Puerto Rican Seabed Rights*, 88 Yale L.J. 825 (1979) (demonstrating that the equal footing doctrine does not prevent different treatment for new states, grounded upon demonstrated need).

Justices Scalia and Thomas are strong adherents to the disciplining mechanism of "original meaning," but how can they join an opinion that relies centrally on an idea that has no textual basis in the Constitution? Moreover, they object to nontextual constitutional precepts on this ground as well: without a basis in the constitutional text, these precepts are ungrounded and prey to ad hoc judicial efforts to make up the rules as new cases arise.

How far does the Court's state equal treatment precept extend? For example, if Congress decided that all nuclear waste materials would be stored in Nevada, over the objections of its citizens, would *Shelby County* stand in the way? Would the Court require Congress to spread the waste proportionately among all 50 states? Does it make a difference in your analysis that Article I, § 9, cl. 4 of the Constitution imposes a proportionality requirement upon "direct" taxation by the federal government? Why is there need for a Direct Taxation Clause in the Constitution of 1789 if it already embodied a background norm of state equal treatment? The Sixteenth Amendment negated the Direct Taxation Clause: How does this affect the willingness of a strict textualist to create a norm of state equal treatment?

3.   *The End of the Second Reconstruction?* Note the parallel to the Court's evolving *Brown II* jurisprudence, set forth in Chapter 2, § 2C2 of the Casebook. Justices Scalia and Thomas have insisted in the *Brown II* cases that there is a laches limitation to constitutional remedies: once extraordinary remedies have been implemented for a period of time, and jurisdictions have formally acquiesced in them, courts must relinquish jurisdiction, even if (de facto) racial segregation continues. See also *Parents Involved in Community*

Schools v. Seattle School District No. 1 (Casebook, pp. 333–53), where the Court rebuked local efforts to create integrated schools through race-sensitive criteria.

In *Shelby County*, the Court majority reveals a similar impatience with longstanding remediation by Congress (rather than the Court) and terminates the process upon a finding that covered jurisdictions have formally acquiesced in the remedies. As in the school segregation cases, the liberal Justices dissent, on the ground that there is evidence of continuing exclusions based upon race. In the school context, the winding down of judicial monitoring has coincided with rising levels of segregation—precisely the phenomenon Justice Ginsburg warns will happen in the voting context.

Press accounts within days of the Court's decision announced that several southern states planned to implement new voter identification and other restrictive laws; some states will redistrict in the wake of the Court's ruling. Before *Shelby County,* all such actions would have required preclearance, and therefore a review and often negotiation process with the Department of Justice. After *Shelby County,* such laws might still be challenged under § 2, which the Court left in place but has interpreted narrowly.

Is this process a judicial renunciation of the Reconstruction Amendments? Or, less dramatically, a retreat from the deployment of significant judicial resources to solve a problem that seems intractable? Or a confession of pessimism that the federal government can assure progress in race relations through the dialectic approach pioneered in the *Brown II* cases and then expanded to focus on the Department of Justice in the VRA?

SECTION 4. BEYOND THE COMMERCE AND CIVIL RIGHTS ENFORCEMENT POWERS

C. THE TREATY POWER

Page 1031. Delete Problem 7–8 and insert the following materials at the end of Section 4:

Bond v. United States

134 S.Ct. 2077 (2014)

In 1997, the Senate ratified the Convention on the Prohibition of the Development, Production, Stockpiling, and Use of Chemical Weapons and on Their Destruction. S. Treaty Doc. No. 103–21, 1974 U. N. T. S. 317. To fulfill the United States' obligations under the Convention, Congress enacted the Chemical Weapons Convention Implementation Act of 1998. 112 Stat. 2681–856. The Act forbids any person knowingly "to develop, produce, otherwise acquire, transfer directly or indirectly, receive, stockpile, retain, own, possess, or use, or threaten to use, any chemical weapon." 18 U.S.C. § 229(a)(1). It defines "chemical weapon" in relevant part as "[a] toxic chemical and its precursors, except where intended for a purpose not prohibited under this

chapter as long as the type and quantity is consistent with such a purpose."
§ 229F(1)(A).

When Carol Anne Bond, a microbiologist, learned that her best friend was pregnant with a child whose father was her own husband, Bond spread an arsenic-based chemical on the other woman's car door, the front door of her house, and her mailbox. Bond's hope was to harass the cheating friend and make her sick, but the only injury sustained by the other woman was a slight burn on one finger. Because the chemical was "toxic," however, federal prosecutors charged Bond with two counts of violating the 1998 Implementation Act. Bond responded that Congress had no authority to adopt this statute. On appeal, the Government relied on Congress's Treaty Power, as understood in *Missouri v. Holland*. Bond urged the Court to overrule *Holland*.

Writing for the Court, **CHIEF JUSTICE ROBERTS** declined to rule on the constitutional issue, because a statutory issue resolved the case: Bond did not fall within the ambit of the statute. To be sure, she had used a chemical considered "toxic" under the Convention and as defined by the Implementation Act, but a literal application of the statute "would 'dramatically intrude[ ] upon traditional state criminal jurisdiction,' and we avoid reading statutes to have such reach in the absence of a clear indication that they do. *United States* v. *Bass*, 404 U.S. 336, 350 (1971)."

The Court held that that "it is appropriate to refer to basic principles of federalism embodied in the Constitution to resolve ambiguity in a federal statute. In this case, the ambiguity derives from the improbably broad reach of the key statutory definition given the term—'chemical weapon'—being defined; the deeply serious consequences of adopting such a boundless reading; and the lack of any apparent need to do so in light of the context from which the statute arose—a treaty about chemical warfare and terrorism. We conclude that, in this curious case, we can insist on a clear indication that Congress meant to reach purely local crimes, before interpreting the statute's expansive language in a way that intrudes on the police power of the States. See *Bass*."

Joined by Justices Thomas and Alito, **JUSTICE SCALIA** rejected the Court's interpretation of the statute, for it clearly covered Bond's vengeful activities. But Justice Scalia (joined by Justice Thomas) concurred in the Court's judgment on the ground that the Treaty Clause vests no authority in Congress to adopt statutes that do not fall within one of its enumerated powers (such as the Commerce Clause power, which had been waived as a basis for the statute in this appeal). Justices Scalia and Thomas would have overruled *Missouri v. Holland*.

Justice Scalia rejected the Government's *Holland*-based argument that the 1998 Implementation Act was "necessary and proper" to carry out Congress's and the President's exercise of the Treaty Power set forth in Article II. Under the Necessary and Proper Clause, Congress has the authority to facilitate treaty-making, such as funding presidential treaty negotiators. "But a power to help the President *make* treaties is not a power to *implement* treaties already made. See generally Rosenkranz, Executing the Treaty Power,

118 Harv. L. Rev. 1867 (2005) [Casebook, p. 1029]. Once a treaty has been made, Congress's power to do what is 'necessary and proper' to assist the making of treaties drops out of the picture. To legislate compliance with the United States' treaty obligations, Congress must rely upon its independent (though quite robust) Article I, § 8, powers."

Justice Scalia warned that strict compliance with the Constitution's structure is especially important in an era when treaties have become multilateral regulatory regimes, requiring signatories to regulate private businesses and persons as well as public activities. The constitutional limitations protecting private persons against federal governmental regulation, such as the limits enforced in *Lopez* and *Morrison*, would be easily negated under the Government's reading of *Missouri v. Holland.*

Thus, Justice Scalia worried about "the possibilities of what the Federal Government may accomplish, with the right treaty in hand, are endless and hardly farfetched. It could begin, as some scholars have suggested, with abrogation of this Court's constitutional rulings. For example, the holding that a statute prohibiting the carrying of firearms near schools went beyond Congress's enumerated powers, *Lopez*, could be reversed by negotiating a treaty with Latvia providing that neither sovereign would permit the carrying of guns near schools. Similarly, Congress could reenact the invalidated part of the Violence Against Women Act of 1994 that provided a civil remedy for victims of gender motivated violence, just so long as there were a treaty on point—and some authors think there already is, see MacKinnon, The Supreme Court, 1999 Term, Comment,114 Harv. L. Rev. 135, 167 (2000)."

In a separate concurring opinion, **JUSTICE THOMAS** (joined by Justices Scalia and Alito) argued for a narrow understanding of the Treaty Power itself. In other words, the President and the Senate have no authority to enter into a treaty that does not have a "nexus to foreign relations." Such a limitation on the Federal Government's treaty power is needed not only to preserve "the basic constitutional distinction between domestic and foreign powers, see *Curtiss-Wright Export Corp.* [Casebook, pp. 1190–91]," but also to protect the personal liberties that derive from the Constitution's diffusion of sovereign power, argued Justice Thomas. "And a treaty-based police power would pose an even greater threat when exercised through a self-executing treaty because it would circumvent the role of the House of Representatives in the legislative process."

Justice Thomas surveyed the leading pre-1789 treatises by Grotius, Pufendorf, and Vattel, as well as contemporary dictionaries and practice. When they adopted the Constitution in 1789, We the People would have understood the power to make "treaties" to have been a power to enter into agreements relating to "international intercourse" (i.e., war and peace, alliances with other countries, foreign trade) and *not* a power to regulate domestic activities. So the United States could have entered into a treaty binding signatory nations to cease using chemical weapons, but no one in 1789 would have thought a treaty could make chemistry-based harassment by private persons a crime (the Bond case).

Justice Thomas argued that this original meaning was consistent with the actual ratifying debates as well. "In essays during the ratification campaign in New York, James Madison took the view that the Treaty Power was inherently limited. The Federal Government's powers, Madison wrote, 'will be exercised principally on external objects, as war, peace, negotiation, and foreign commerce'—the traditional subjects of treaty-making. The Federalist No. 45. If the 'external' Treaty Power contained a capacious domestic regulatory authority, that would plainly conflict with Madison's firm understanding that '[t]he powers delegated by the proposed Constitution to the Federal Government, are few and defined.' *Ibid.* Madison evidently saw no conflict, however, because the Treaty Power included authority to 'regulate the intercourse with foreign nations' rather than all domestic affairs. [The Federalist] No. 42." Madison elaborated on this position during the Virginia ratifying convention, which contained the most detailed discussion of the Treaty Power.

In an extensive discussion, Justice Thomas invoked Hamilton and other Framers, as well as post-ratification practice (such as the congressional debates over the Jay Treaty in 1796) and judicial precedent. Indeed, *Missouri v. Holland* is consistent with this understanding of the Treaty Power, for the treaty in that case covered only *migratory birds,* namely, those traversing national borders.

In a separate concurring opinion, **JUSTICE ALITO** agreed with Justice Scalia that the 1998 Implementation Act reached Bond's conduct but concurred in the Court's judgment because he found the statute unconstitutional. He did not have to reach the issue of overruling *Missouri v. Holland,* because he (like Justice Thomas) viewed the Treaty Power as limited to matters of "international intercourse."

Query: Unlike the commentators discussed in Casebook, pp. 1028–31, Justice Alito would narrow Congress's authority without overruling *Missouri v. Holland.* How about that as a constitutional strategy? Does Justice Thomas's original meaning case for such a position strike you as persuasive? Does Justice Thomas's precept for treaty invalidity represent an easily justiciable standard?

For example, can the United States enter into a treaty prohibiting torture by government officials? How is that a regulation of "international intercourse"? If an anti-torture treaty falls outside the Treaty Power, then hundreds of treaties are invalid: To what extent does the nation's practice in the last century augur against such a ruling? If an anti-torture treaty falls within the Treaty Power, then why shouldn't a treaty aimed at violence against women?

United States v. Windsor

133 S.Ct. 2675 (2013)

Edith Windsor was legally married to her life partner, Thea Spyer, at the time her partner died. Nonetheless, pursuant to § 3 of the Defense of Marriage Act, Windsor did not have the benefit of the spousal exclusion for federal estate tax purposes and had to pay $363,000 in estate taxes that a different-sex married couple would have owed. Windsor challenged DOMA § 3 as an unconstitutional discrimination against her. The Supreme Court sustained Windsor's challenge, and we excerpt the Court's debate in Chapters 4 (the equal protection issue) and 9 (the constitutional standing issues) of this Supplement.

In Part III of his opinion for the Court, **JUSTICE KENNEDY** prefaced his discussion of the merits of the challenge to DOMA with a discussion of federalism. "By history and tradition the definition and regulation of marriage, as will be discussed in more detail, has been treated as being within the authority and realm of the separate States. Yet it is further established that Congress, in enacting discrete statutes, can make determinations that bear on marital rights and privileges."

Thus, Congress has not always felt confined to "marriages" as defined by state law. "In addressing the interaction of state domestic relations and federal immigration law Congress determined that marriages 'entered into for the purpose of procuring an alien's admission [to the United States] as an immigrant' will not qualify the noncitizen for that status, even if the noncitizen's marriage is valid and proper for state-law purposes. 8 U.S.C. § 1186a(b)(1). And in establishing income-based criteria for Social Security benefits, Congress decided that although state law would determine in general who qualifies as an applicant's spouse, common-law marriages also should be recognized, regardless of any particular State's view on these relationships. 42 U.S.C. § 1382c(d)(2)."

Justice Kennedy observed, however, that "DOMA has a far greater reach; for it enacts a directive applicable to over 1,000 federal statutes and the whole realm of federal regulations. And its operation is directed to a class of persons that the laws of New York, and of 11 other States, have sought to protect." This is significant, because "regulation of domestic relations" is "an area that has long been regarded as a virtually exclusive province of the States." *Sosna* v. *Iowa*, 419 U.S. 393, 404 (1976).

"The recognition of civil marriages is central to state domestic relations law applicable to its residents and citizens. See *Williams* v. *North Carolina*, 317 U.S. 287, 298 (1942) ('Each state as a sovereign has a rightful and legitimate concern in the marital status of persons domiciled within its borders'). The definition of marriage is the foundation of the State's broader authority to regulate the subject of domestic relations with respect to the '[p]rotection of offspring, property interests, and the enforcement of marital responsibilities.' *Ibid.* '[T]he states, at the time of the adoption of the

Constitution, possessed full power over the subject of marriage and divorce . . . [and] the Constitution delegated no authority to the Government of the United States on the subject of marriage and divorce.' *Haddock* v. *Haddock*, 201 U.S. 562, 575 (1906)."

For this reason, the large majority of federal statutes defer to state policy decisions with respect to domestic relations. E.g., *De Sylva* v. *Ballentine*, 351 U.S. 570 (1956) (Copyright Act). See also See *Ankenbrandt* v. *Richards*, 504 U.S. 689, 703 (1992) (federal courts generally abstain from adjudicating issues of marital or parental status or rights). From the very beginning of the Nation, "the common understanding was that the domestic relations of husband and wife and parent and child were matters reserved to the States." *Ohio ex rel. Popovici* v. *Agler*, 280 U.S. 379, 383–384 (1930)." Accordingly, each state has constructed the eligibility and rules for marriage in distinctive ways.

"Against this background DOMA rejects the long established precept that the incidents, benefits, and obligations of marriage are uniform for all married couples within each State, though they may vary, subject to constitutional guarantees, from one State to the next. Despite these considerations, it is unnecessary to decide whether this federal intrusion on state power is a violation of the Constitution because it disrupts the federal balance. The State's power in defining the marital relation is of central relevance in this case quite apart from principles of federalism. Here the State's decision to give this class of persons the right to marry conferred upon them a dignity and status of immense import. When the State used its historic and essential authority to define the marital relation in this way, its role and its power in making the decision enhanced the recognition, dignity, and protection of the class in their own community. DOMA, because of its reach and extent, departs from this history and tradition of reliance on state law to define marriage.

"[D]iscriminations of an unusual character especially suggest careful consideration to determine whether they are obnoxious to the constitutional provision." *Romer* v. *Evans*, 517 U.S. 620, 633 (1996) (quoting *Louisville Gas & Elec. Co.* v. *Coleman*, 277 U.S. 32, 37–38 (1928)). * * *

"The States' interest in defining and regulating the marital relation, subject to constitutional guarantees, stems from the understanding that marriage is more than a routine classification for purposes of certain statutory benefits. * * * By its recognition of the validity of same-sex marriages performed in other jurisdictions and then by authorizing same-sex unions and same-sex marriages, New York sought to give further protection and dignity to that bond. For same-sex couples who wished to be married, the State acted to give their lawful conduct a lawful status. This status is a far-reaching legal acknowledgment of the intimate relationship between two people, a relationship deemed by the State worthy of dignity in the community equal with all other marriages. It reflects both the community's considered perspective on the historical roots of the institution of marriage and its evolving understanding of the meaning of equality." In Part IV of his opinion for the Court, excerpted in Chapter 4 of this Supplement, Justice Kennedy ruled that DOMA § 3 violated the equal protection guarantee of the Fifth Amendment.

Four Justices dissented from Justice Kennedy's disposition; their arguments are excerpted an analyzed in Chapters 4 and 9 of this Supplement. But each of the dissenting opinions also addressed the Court's federalism discussion. CHIEF JUSTICE ROBERTS'S dissenting opinion said this: "The Court does not have before it, and the logic of its opinion does not decide, the distinct question whether the States, in the exercise of their 'historic and essential authority to define the marital relation,' may continue to utilize the traditional definition of marriage." Indeed, the Chief Justice maintained, the constitutionality of state (rather than national) discriminations in the definition of marriage ought to find support in the Court's analysis. "Thus, while '[t]he State's power in defining the marital relation is of central relevance' to the majority's decision to strike down DOMA here, that power will come into play on the other side of the board in future cases about the constitutionality of state marriage definitions. So too will the concerns for state diversity and sovereignty that weigh against DOMA's constitutionality in this case." Similar sentiments were expressed in the dissenting opinion of JUSTICE ALITO, joined by Justice Thomas.

In his dissenting opinion, JUSTICE SCALIA (also joined by Justice Thomas), opined that the Court's federalism discussion had no logical relevance to its constitutional holding. So why did the Court devote almost seven pages of its opinion to federalism? "My guess is that the majority, while reluctant to suggest that defining the meaning of 'marriage' in federal statutes is unsupported by any of the Federal Government's enumerated powers, nonetheless needs some rhetorical basis to support its pretense that today's prohibition of laws excluding same-sex marriage is confined to the Federal Government (leaving the second, state-law shoe to be dropped later, maybe next Term). But I am only guessing."

NOTES ON THE DOMA CASE AND FEDERALISM

1. *What Role Does the Federalism Discussion Play in the Court's Disposition in* Windsor? It appears that no Justice believed that DOMA § 3 was beyond the authority of Congress to legislate. If DOMA § 3 had defined marriage in federal statutes and regulations, across the board, as always *including* same-sex couples, would that inclusion have been unconstitutional, or constitutionally problematic in any way? At oral argument, the Solicitor General readily conceded that this would have been perfectly constitutional.

So what role, precisely, does the federalism discussion play in the Court's disposition? Put together Part III of *Windsor,* excerpted here, and Part IV, excerpted in Chapter 4 of this Supplement. Does the federalism discussion set up the equal protection discussion in any way? Consider *Village of Arlington Heights v. Metropolitan Housing Development Corp.*, 429 U.S. 252 (1977) (excerpted in Casebook, pp. 238–40), where the Court articulated a variety of considerations that might be the basis for a finding of "discriminatory intent" under *Washington v. Davis*.

2. *Federalism Values and the Next Round of Equal Protection Challenges to State Marriage Exclusions.* Is Justice Kennedy's federalism analysis relevant to federal challenges to mini-DOMAs, namely, state exclusions of same-sex couples from their marriage laws (most mini-DOMAs are encoded in state constitutions)? Ought this analysis render federal courts more reluctant to strike down mini-DOMAs? The Court expresses no opinion on this matter, but the Chief Justice and Justices Thomas and Alito argue that federal courts ought to attend to the federalism reasoning, and give states a wider berth to exclude lesbian and gay couples from marriage than the Court gives the federal government.

Evaluate this last point in light of the constitutional values served by federalism (Casebook, pp. 897–900):

(1) **Liberty.** Does the "double security" promised by the Framers for people's "liberty" find protection in state regulatory authority to define civil marriage restrictively? Whose "liberty" matters: the liberty of lesbian and gay couples to enter civil marriage, or the liberty of parents and churches that do not want state validation of such relationships? If both, how does the liberty value of federalism cut in this debate?

(2) **Republicanism.** Not only are more citizens politically engaged at the state and local level, but the marriage equality issue has engaged the voters directly and deeply in most states, through ballot initiatives and referenda. California's Proposition 8 is an example. In 2012, marriage equality prevailed in all four states with ballot initiatives or referenda. DOMA resolved the marriage issue in a sweeping way at the national level. The *Windsor* dissenters argued that federal courts should be more reluctant to take this issue away from the political process at the state level.

(3) **Diversity.** Perhaps most important, leaving the marriage equality debate with the states, rather than imposing a national solution, would allow a diversity of regimes that would satisfy most Americans *and* provide useful information for undecided citizens to form or reform their views. As of July 25, 2014, nineteen states (and the District of Columbia) offer marriage licenses to same-sex couples, and another three offer civil unions or another form of recognition. Most LGBT citizens live in those states—while most citizens opposed to gay marriage on religious or other grounds live in nonrecognition states. What is wrong, the Chief Justice implores, with letting the democratic process work through this issue, state by state?

Do these federalism values affect your thinking about whether the denial of marriage equality by state constitutions and laws violates the Fourteenth Amendment? As you know, the Court in *Obergefell v. Hodges* (liberally excerpted in Chapter 4 of this Supplement) struck down the remaining state exclusions of same-sex couples from their marriage laws. Was that result inevitable after *Windsor*?

3. *The Future of DOMA § 2?* Only DOMA § 3 was in question in *Windsor*. Section 2 of DOMA provides that states do not have to recognize same-sex marriages authorized by other states. As a federalism matter, this issue is governed by Article IV, § 1. The Full Faith & Credit Clause, which requires interstate recognition of public acts, records, and judgments has not been applied with coercive force to marriage licenses. Note also the Give Effect Clause, which authorizes Congress to "prescribe" the "Effect" of interstate acts, records, and judgments.

Most choice of law scholars believe that DOMA § 2 made no change in the established law: both before and after DOMA, states do not have to recognize other state marriages, as a matter of constitutional compulsion. But § 2 was part of the package supported by President Clinton and Congress to belittle gay marriage. Congress and Clinton did not reinforce state freedom not to recognize other states' marriages generally—they only went after despised gay marriages. Perhaps the normal presumption of severability might be overcome here, or § 2 might be a separate violation of the Fifth Amendment. For prescient analysis, see Andrew Koppelman, *Dumb and DOMA: Why the Defense of Marriage Act Is Unconstitutional,* 83 Iowa L. Rev. 1 (1997).

Most of the plaintiff couples in *Obergefell v. Hodges* (Chapter 4 of this Supplement) were legally married in another jurisdiction and were complaining that Ohio, Kentucky, and Tennessee refused to recognize their valid marriages. Justice Kennedy's opinion for the Court ruled that state nonrecognition of valid out-of-state same-sex marriages violated the Fourteenth Amendment for the same reasons the state exclusions were in violation. The four dissenters disagreed. Is DOMA § 2 now unconstitutional? Does the Give Effect Clause of Article IV make no difference in your analysis?

Note, further, that the Court in *Obergefell* asked for separate briefing and argument on the issue of interstate recognition. The Justices contemplated the possibility that Ohio (Jim Obergefell's state) could refuse to give Obergefell a marriage license, but could not refuse to recognize his valid marriage in Maryland. No Justice took this position in the end—but is this kind of compromise resolution not suggested by *Windsor*? Craft an argument that the Chief Justice could have made under Article IV.

SECTION 6. NATIONAL LIMITATIONS UPON STATE REGULATORY AUTHORITY

B. DORMANT COMMERCE CLAUSE DOCTRINE

1. Discrimination Commerce Clause Doctrine

Page 1121. Add the following Case right after the Note on Interstate Taxation of Interstate Commerce:

Comptroller of the Treasury of Maryland v. Wynne

135 S.Ct. 1787 (2015)

Maryland's personal income tax on state residents consists of a "state" income tax and a "county" income tax. Residents who pay income tax to another jurisdiction for income earned in that other jurisdiction are allowed a credit against the "state" tax but not the "county" tax. Nonresidents who earn income from sources within Maryland must pay the "state" income tax, and nonresidents not subject to the county tax must pay a "special nonresident tax" in lieu of the "county" tax. Brian and Karen Wynne were a Maryland married couple with income from many other jurisdictions; they challenged the state's refusal to give them credit against the county tax for similar taxes paid to other jurisdictions.

JUSTICE ALITO, writing for a narrowly divided Court, ruled that this tax scheme violated the Dormant Commerce Clause, under the *Complete Auto Transit* test, refined for tax challenges by what the Court has called the "internal consistency" test. This test, which helps courts identify tax schemes that discriminate against interstate commerce, "looks to the structure of the tax at issue to see whether its identical application by every State in the Union would place interstate commerce at a disadvantage." *Oklahoma Tax Comm'n v. Jefferson Lines, Inc.,* 514 U.S. 179, 185 (1986).

"By hypothetically assuming that every State has the same tax structure, the internal consistency test allows courts to isolate the effect of a defendant State's tax scheme. This is a virtue of the test because it allows courts to distinguish between (1) tax schemes that inherently discriminate against interstate commerce without regard to the tax policies of other States, and (2) tax schemes that create disparate incentives to engage in interstate commerce (and sometimes result in double taxation) only as a result of the interaction of two different but nondiscriminatory and internally consistent schemes. The first category of taxes is typically unconstitutional; the second is not. Tax schemes that fail the internal consistency test will fall into the first category, not the second: '[A]ny cross-border tax disadvantage that remains after application of the [test] cannot be due to tax disparities' but is instead attributable to the taxing State's discriminatory policies alone." See *J. D. Adams Mfg. Co.* v. *Storen,* 304 U.S. 307 (1938) (striking down Indiana statute taxing an in-state company's out-of-state gross receipts without providing a credit for taxes paid in other jurisdiction).

"Maryland's income tax scheme fails the internal consistency test. A simple example illustrates the point. Assume that every State imposed the following taxes, which are similar to Maryland's 'county' and 'special nonresident' taxes: (1) a 1.25% tax on income that residents earn in State, (2) a 1.25% tax on income that residents earn in other jurisdictions, and (3) a 1.25% tax on income that nonresidents earn in State. Assume further that two taxpayers, April and Bob, both live in State A, but that April earns her income in State A whereas Bob earns his income in State B. In this circumstance, Bob will pay more income tax than April solely because he earns income interstate. Specifically, April will have to pay a 1.25% tax only once, to State A. But Bob will have to pay a 1.25% tax twice: once to State A, where he resides, and once to State B, where he earns the income.

"Critically—and this dispels a central argument made by petitioner and the principal dissent—the Maryland scheme's discriminatory treatment of interstate commerce is not simply the result of its interaction with the taxing schemes of other States. Instead, the internal consistency test reveals what the undisputed economic analysis shows: Maryland's tax scheme is inherently discriminatory and operates as a tariff. This identity between Maryland's tax and a tariff is fatal because tariffs are '[t]he paradigmatic example of a law discriminating against interstate commerce.' *West Lynn* [Casebook, p. 1137]."

Justice Alito also rejected the argument, posed by the Solicitor General as well as the dissenting Justices, that constitutional scrutiny may be abated because the "discriminatory" tax fell upon state individual residents (insiders) like the Wynnes, rather than out-of-state corporations (outsiders). "The argument is that this Court need not be concerned about state laws that burden the interstate activities of individuals because those individuals can lobby and vote against legislators who support such measures. But if a State's tax unconstitutionally discriminates against interstate commerce, it is invalid regardless of whether the plaintiff is a resident voter or nonresident of the State. This Court has thus entertained and even sustained dormant Commerce Clause challenges by individual residents of the State that imposed the alleged burden on interstate commerce, *Department of Revenue of Ky. v. Davis*, 553 U.S. 328, 336 (2008) [Casebook, p. 1119]; *Granholm v. Heald*, 544 U.S. 460, 469 (2005) [Casebook, p. 1133], and we have also sustained such a challenge to a tax whose burden was borne by in-state consumers, *Bacchus Imports, Ltd. v. Dias*, 468 U.S. 263, 272 (1984)."

JUSTICE SCALIA (joined by Justice Thomas) dissented, on the ground that the "negative Commerce Clause" is a "judicial fraud." It is not grounded in the text or original meaning of the Constitution, and judges should not expand the Dormant Commerce Clause case law any further. Also dissenting, **JUSTICE THOMAS** (joined by Justice Scalia) found the negative understanding of the Commerce Clause inconsistent with the Constitution's regulation of state taxation through the Import Export Clause.

JUSTICE GINSBURG (joined by Justices Scalia and Kagan) dissented from the majority's application of the Court's Dormant Commerce Clause precedents. "Today's decision veers from a principle of interstate and international taxation repeatedly acknowledged by this Court: A nation or State 'may tax *all* the income of its residents, even income earned outside the taxing jurisdiction.' *Oklahoma Tax Comm'n* v. *Chickasaw Nation*, 515 U.S. 450, 462–463 (1995). In accord with this principle, the Court has regularly rejected claims that taxes on a resident's out-of-state income violate the Due Process Clause for lack of a sufficient 'connection' to the taxing State. *Quill Corp.* v. *North Dakota*, 504 U.S. 298, 306 (1992). But under dormant Commerce Clause jurisprudence, the Court decides, a State is not really empowered to tax resident's income from whatever source derived. In taxing personal income, the Court holds, source-based authority, *i.e.,* authority to tax commerce conducted within a State's territory, boxes in the taxing authority of a taxpayer's domicile.

"As I see it, nothing in the Constitution or in prior decisions of this Court dictates that one of two States, the domiciliary State or the source State, must recede simply because both have lawful tax regimes reaching the same income. True, Maryland elected to deny a credit for income taxes paid to other States in computing a resident's county tax liability. It is equally true, however, that the other States that taxed the Wynnes' income elected not to offer them a credit for their Maryland county income taxes. In this situation, the Constitution does not prefer one lawful basis for state taxation of a person's income over the other. Nor does it require one State, in this case Maryland, to limit its residence-based taxation, should the State also choose to exercise, to the full extent, its source-based authority. States often offer their residents credits for income taxes paid to other States, as Maryland does for state income tax purposes. States do so, however, as a matter of tax 'policy,' not because the Constitution compels that course."

As a general matter, "States have long favored their residents over nonresidents in the provision of local services. See *Reeves, Inc.* v. *Stake*, 447 U.S. 429, 442 (1980) (such favoritism does not violate the Commerce Clause). Excluding nonresidents from these services, this Court has observed, is rational for it is residents 'who fund the state treasury and whom the State was created to serve.' A taxpayer's home State, then, can hardly be faulted for making support of local government activities an obligation of every resident, regardless of any obligations residents may have to *other* States. Residents, moreover, possess political means, not shared by outsiders, to ensure that the power to tax their income is not abused. 'It is not,' this Court has observed, 'a purpose of the Commerce Clause to protect state residents from their own state taxes.' *Goldberg* v. *Sweet*, 488 U.S. 252, 266 (1989). The reason is evident. Residents are 'insider[s] who presumably [are] able to complain about and change the tax through the [State's] political process.' *Ibid.* Nonresidents, by contrast, are not similarly positioned to 'effec[t] legislative change.' *Ibid.* As Chief Justice Marshall, developer of the Court's Commerce Clause jurisprudence, reasoned: 'In imposing a tax the legislature acts upon its constituents. This is in general a sufficient security against erroneous and oppressive taxation.' *McCulloch* v. *Maryland*. The 'people of a State' can thus 'res[t] confidently on the interest of the legislator, and on the influence of the constituents over their representative, to guard them against . . . abuse" of the "right of taxing themselves and their property.' "

Additionally, Justice Ginsburg pointed to the longstanding state adherence to the rule invalidated in this case, namely, granting tax credits to residents who pay taxes elsewhere. "As Justice Holmes stated over a century ago, in regard to a 'mode of taxation . . . of long standing, . . . the fact that the system has been in force for a very long time is of itself a strong reason . . . for leaving any improvement that may be desired to the legislature.' *Paddell* v. *City of New York*, 211 U.S. 446, 448 (1908). Only recently, this Court followed that sound advice in resisting a dormant Commerce Clause challenge to a taxing practice with a pedigree as enduring as the practice in this case. See *Department of Revenue of Ky.* v. *Davis*, 553 U.S. 328, 356–357 (2008) [Casebook, p. 1119]. Surely that advice merits application here, where the challenged tax draws support from both historical practice and numerous decisions of this Court.

"The majority rejects Justice Holmes' counsel, observing that most States, over time, have chosen not to exercise plenary authority to tax residents' worldwide income. The Court, however, learns the wrong lesson from the 'independent *policy* decision[s]' States have made. This history demonstrates not that States 'doub[t]' their 'constitutiona[l]' authority to tax residents' income, wherever earned, as the majority speculates, but that the very political processes the Court disregards as 'fanciful' have in fact worked to produce policies the Court ranks as responsible—all the more reason to resist this Court's heavy-handed supervision."

Queries: What distinguishes *Wynne* from *United Haulers* [Casebook, p. 1116]. Justice Alito, a vigorous enforcer of the Dormant Commerce Clause precedents, wrote for the Court in *Wynne* but dissented in *United Haulers* and in *Davis* [Casebook, p. 1119]. Why would the Chief Justice, for example, vote differently in *Wynne* and *United Haulers*?   Justice Ginsburg's dissenting opinion makes out a good case for the proposition (strongly echoed by Justice Scalia's dissent) that the Court's Dormant Commerce Clause jurisprudence has "jumped the shark" and has ventured into aggressive judicial management of state tax policy.

C.   SHOULD THE DORMANT COMMERCE CLAUSE BE LAID TO REST? ALTERNATE LIMITATIONS ON THE STATES

Page 1141. Add the following paragraphs right before the heading for The Import-Export Clause:

Justices Thomas and Scalia continued their attack on the "negative Commerce Clause" in *Comptroller of the Treasury of Maryland v. Wynne*,

135 S.Ct. 1787 (2015), the interstate taxation case excerpted earlier in this chapter of the Supplement. In separate dissenting opinions (each joined by the other), Thomas and Scalia maintained that the Court's jurisprudence is inconsistent with the original meaning of the Constitution. As they had argued previously, the Commerce Clause contains no "negative" language vetoing state regulation, and other provisions of the Constitution do regulate discriminatory state economic regulations and taxation.

In *Wynne,* these Justices made out a more detailed case for the further proposition that in the founding era many states had taxes and regulations that did discriminate against interstate commercial activities and investments. Not only did the ratification debates say nothing about these laws, but they persevered after the Constitution of 1789 went into effect. For decades, no one suggested that such laws violated the Constitution. It was not until 1873 that the Supreme Court ruled that some laws of this nature did violate the Constitution.

In his dissenting opinion, Justice Thomas said that he would not vote to invalidate a law for violating the Court's made-up "negative" Commerce Clause. In his dissenting opinion, Justice Scalia labeled the "negative" Commerce Clause a "judicial fraud," yet conceded that, for reasons of *stare decisis*, he would agree to invalidation of a state law openly discriminating against interstate commerce *or* falling within the four corners of one of the Court's Dormant Commerce Clause precedents. As pointed out in the Casebook, p. 1121, there are zealous enforcers of the Dormant Commerce Clause on the Court, namely, Justices Alito and Kennedy. And there are zealous opponents, namely, Justices Scalia and Thomas. Among the middle group on the Court, however, it appears that Justices Ginsburg and Kagan may be reluctant enforcers at best.

Note that Justice Alito's opinion for the Court abandoned one justification for the Dormant Commerce Clause, namely, the process (representation-reinforcement) argument that the doctrine protects "outsiders" against predation by rent-seeking state "insiders." The Court emphasized two other justifications for the doctrine—namely, *stare decisis* and the Constitution's anti-balkinization (anti-tariff) purpose. Does this limited defense of Dormant Commerce Clause doctrine render it more vulnerable to its critics inside and outside the Court?

Is the Dormant Commerce Clause in more danger than ever before? If you were on the Court, would you be inclined to abrogate this line of cases? Or interpret the case law conservatively? If so, are the other constitutional protections against state intrusions onto interstate commerce (the balkanization concern) sufficient protections? Consider the possibilities in the materials that follow.

CHAPTER 8

SEPARATION OF POWERS

■ ■ ■

SECTION 1. ISSUES OF EXECUTIVE AGGRANDIZEMENT (IMPERIAL PRESIDENCY)

A. THE POST-NEW DEAL FRAMEWORK

Page 1189. Insert the following Case and Notes at the end of Section 1(A), right after Problem 8–1:

UNITED STATES V. NOEL CANNING
572 U.S. ___, 134 S.Ct. 2550 (2014)

JUSTICE BREYER delivered the opinion of the Court.

Ordinarily the President must obtain "the Advice and Consent of the Senate" before appointing an "Office[r] of the United States." U.S. Const., Art. II, § 2, cl. 2. But the Recess Appointments Clause creates an exception. It gives the President alone the power "to fill up all Vacancies that may happen during the Recess of the Senate, by granting Commissions which shall expire at the End of their next Session." Art. II, § 2, cl. 3. We here consider three questions about the application of this Clause.

The first concerns the scope of the words "recess of the Senate." Does that phrase refer only to an inter-session recess (*i.e.,* a break between formal sessions of Congress), or does it also include an intra-session recess, such as a summer recess in the midst of a session? We conclude that the Clause applies to both kinds of recess.

The second question concerns the scope of the words "vacancies that may happen." Does that phrase refer only to vacancies that first come into existence during a recess, or does it also include vacancies that arise prior to a recess but continue to exist during the recess? We conclude that the Clause applies to both kinds of vacancy.

The third question concerns calculation of the length of a "recess." The President made the appointments here at issue on January 4, 2012. At that time the Senate was in recess pursuant to a December 17, 2011, resolution providing for a series of brief recesses punctuated by "*pro forma* session[s]," with "no business . . . transacted," every Tuesday and Friday through January 20, 2012. S. J., 112th Cong., 1st Sess., 923 (2011) (hereinafter 2011

119

S. J.). In calculating the length of a recess are we to ignore the *pro forma* sessions, thereby treating the series of brief recesses as a single, month-long recess? We conclude that we cannot ignore these *pro forma* sessions.

Our answer to the third question means that, when the appointments before us took place, the Senate was in the midst of a 3-day recess. Three days is too short a time to bring a recess within the scope of the Clause. Thus we conclude that the President lacked the power to make the recess appointments here at issue.

[II] Before turning to the specific questions presented, we shall mention two background considerations that we find relevant to all three. First, *the Recess Appointments Clause sets forth a subsidiary, not a primary, method for appointing officers of the United States.* The immediately preceding Clause—Article II, Section 2, Clause 2—provides the primary method of appointment. It says that the President "shall nominate, *and by and with the Advice and Consent of the Senate*, shall appoint Ambassadors, other public Ministers and Consuls, Judges of the supreme Court, and all other Officers of the United States" (emphasis added).

The Federalist Papers make clear that the Founders intended this method of appointment, requiring Senate approval, to be the norm (at least for principal officers). Alexander Hamilton wrote that the Constitution vests the power of *nomination* in the President alone because "one man of discernment is better fitted to analise and estimate the peculiar qualities adapted to particular offices, than a body of men of equal, or perhaps even of superior discernment." The Federalist No. 76, p. 510 (J. Cooke ed. 1961).

At the same time, the need to secure Senate approval provides "an excellent check upon a spirit of favoritism in the President, and would tend greatly to preventing the appointment of unfit characters from State prejudice, from family connection, from personal attachment, or from a view to popularity." *Id.,* at 513.

Thus the Recess Appointments Clause reflects the tension between, on the one hand, the President's continuous need for "the assistance of subordinates," *Myers* v. *United States*, 272 U.S. 52, 117 (1926), and, on the other, the Senate's practice, particularly during the Republic's early years, of meeting for a single brief session each year, see Art. I, § 4, cl. 2; Amdt. 20, § 2 (requiring the Senate to "assemble" only "once in every year"). We seek to interpret the Clause as granting the President the power to make appointments during a recess but not offering the President the authority routinely to avoid the need for Senate confirmation.

Second, *in interpreting the Clause, we put significant weight upon historical practice.* For one thing, the interpretive questions before us concern the allocation of power between two elected branches of Government. Long ago Chief Justice Marshall wrote that "a doubtful question, one on which human reason may pause, and the human judgment be suspended, in the decision of which the great principles of liberty are not concerned, but the respective powers of those who are equally the representatives of the people, are to be adjusted; if not put at rest by the practice of the government, ought to receive a considerable impression from that practice." *McCulloch* v. *Maryland*, 4 Wheat. 316, 401 (1819).

And we later confirmed that "[l]ong settled and established practice is a consideration of great weight in a proper interpretation of constitutional provisions" regulating the relationship between Congress and the President. *The Pocket Veto Case*, 279 U.S. 655, 689 (1929); see also *id.,* at 690 ("[A] practice of at least twenty years duration 'on the part of the executive department, acquiesced in by the legislative department, . . . is entitled to great regard in determining the true construction of a constitutional provision the phraseology of which is in any respect of doubtful meaning'" (quoting *State* v. *South Norwalk*, 77 Conn. 257, 264, 58 A. 759, 761 (1904))). * * *

There is a great deal of history to consider here. Presidents have made recess appointments since the beginning of the Republic. Their frequency suggests that the Senate and President have recognized that recess appointments can be both necessary and appropriate in certain circumstances. We have not previously interpreted the Clause, and, when doing so for the first time in more than 200 years, we must hesitate to upset the compromises and working arrangements that the elected branches of Government themselves have reached.

[III] The first question concerns the scope of the phrase *"the recess* of the Senate." Art. II, § 2, cl. 3 (emphasis added). The Constitution provides for congressional elections every two years. And the 2-year life of each elected Congress typically consists of two formal 1-year sessions, each separated from the next by an "inter-session recess." The Senate or the House of Representatives announces an inter-session recess by approving a resolution stating that it will "adjourn *sine die," i.e.,* without specifying a date to return (in which case Congress will reconvene when the next formal session is scheduled to begin). The Senate and the House also take breaks in the midst of a session.

The Senate or the House announces any such "intra-session recess" by adopting a resolution stating that it will "adjourn" to a fixed date, a few days or weeks or even months later. All agree that the phrase "the recess of the Senate" covers inter-session recesses. The question is whether it includes intra-session recesses as well. In our view, the phrase "the recess" includes an intra-session recess of substantial length. Its words taken literally can refer to both types of recess. Founding-era dictionaries define the word "recess," much as we do today, simply as "a period of cessation from usual work." 13 The Oxford English Dictionary 322–323 (2d ed. 1989) (hereinafter OED) (citing 18th-and 19th-century sources for that definition of "recess"). The Founders themselves used the word to refer to intra-session, as well as to intersession, breaks. See, *e.g.,* 3 Records of the Federal Convention of 1787, p. 76 (M. Farrand rev. 1966) (hereinafter Farrand) (letter from George Washington to John Jay using "the recess" to refer to an intra-session break of the Constitutional Convention).

We recognize that the word "the" in "*the* recess" might suggest that the phrase refers to the single break separating formal sessions of Congress. * * * But the word can also refer "to a term used generically or universally." 17 OED 879. The Constitution, for example, directs the Senate to choose a President *pro tempore* "in *the* Absence of the Vice-President." Art. I, § 3, cl. 5 (emphasis added). And the Federalist Papers refer to the chief magistrate of an ancient Achaean league who "administered the government in *the* recess of the Senate." The Federalist No. 18, at 113 (J. Madison) (emphasis added). Reading "the" generically in this way, there is no linguistic problem applying the Clause's phrase to both kinds of recess. And, in fact, the phrase "the recess" was used to refer to intra-session recesses at the time of the founding. See, *e.g.,* 3 Farrand 76 (letter from Washington to Jay); New Jersey Legislative-Council Journal, 5th Sess., 1st Sitting 70, 2d Sitting 9 (1781) (twice referring to a 4-month, intra-session break as "the Recess").

The constitutional text is thus ambiguous. And we believe the Clause's purpose demands the broader interpretation. The Clause gives the President authority to make appointments during "the recess of the Senate" so that the President can ensure the continued functioning of the Federal Government when the Senate is away. The Senate is equally away during both an inter-session and an intra-session recess, and its capacity to participate in the appointments process has nothing to do with the words it uses to signal its departure.

History also offers strong support for the broad interpretation. We concede that pre-Civil War history is not helpful. But it shows only that Congress generally took long breaks between sessions, while taking no significant intra-session breaks at all (five times it took a break of a week or so at Christmas). * * * In 1867 and 1868, Congress for the first time took substantial, nonholiday intra-session breaks, and President Andrew Johnson made dozens of recess appointments. The Federal Court of Claims upheld one of those specific appointments, writing "[w]e have *no doubt* that a vacancy occurring while the Senate was thus temporarily adjourned" during the "first session of the Fortieth Congress" was "legally filled by appointment of the President alone." *Gould* v. *United States*, 19 Ct. Cl. 593, 595–596 (1884) (emphasis added). Attorney General Evarts also issued three opinions concerning the constitutionality of President Johnson's appointments, and it apparently did not occur to him that the distinction between intra-session and inter-session recesses was significant. See 12 Op. Atty. Gen. 449 (1868); 12 Op. Atty. Gen. 455 (1868); 12 Op. Atty. Gen. 469 (1868). Similarly, though the 40th Congress impeached President Johnson on charges relating to his appointment power, he was not accused of violating the Constitution by making intra-session recess appointments. Hartnett, Recess Appointments of Article III Judges: Three Constitutional Questions, 26 Cardozo L. Rev. 377, 409 (2005).

In all, between the founding and the Great Depression, Congress took substantial intra-session breaks (other than holiday breaks) in four years: 1867, 1868, 1921, and 1929. And in each of those years the President made intra-session recess appointments. [Justice Breyer included an Appendix to his opinion for the Court, with documentation of recess appointments.]

Since 1929, and particularly since the end of World War II, Congress has shortened its inter-session breaks as it has taken longer and more frequent intra-session breaks; Presidents have correspondingly made more intra-session recess appointments. Indeed, if we include military appointments, Presidents have made thousands of intra-session recess appointments. President Franklin Roosevelt, for example, commissioned Dwight Eisenhower as a permanent Major General during an intra-session recess; President Truman made Dean Acheson Under Secretary of State; and President George H. W. Bush reappointed Alan Greenspan as Chairman of the Federal Reserve Board.

Not surprisingly, the publicly available opinions of Presidential legal advisers that we have found are nearly unanimous in determining that the Clause authorizes these appointments. In 1921, for example, Attorney General Daugherty advised President Harding that he could make intra-session recess appointments. He reasoned:

"If the President's power of appointment is to be defeated because the Senate takes an adjournment to a specified date, the painful and inevitable result will be measurably to prevent the exercise of governmental functions. I can not bring myself to believe that the framers of the Constitution ever intended such a catastrophe to happen." 33 Op. Atty. Gen. 20, 23.

We have found memoranda offering similar advice to President Eisenhower and to every President from Carter to the present. * * *

Similarly, in 1940 the Senate helped to enact a law regulating the payment of recess appointees, and the Comptroller General of the United States has interpreted that law functionally. An earlier 1863 statute had denied pay to individuals appointed to fill up vacancies first arising prior to the beginning of a recess. The Senate Judiciary Committee then believed that those vacancies fell outside the scope of the Clause. In 1940, however, the Senate amended the law to permit many of those recess appointees to be paid. Act of July 11, 1940, 54 Stat. 751. Interpreting the amendments in

1948, the Comptroller General—who, unlike the Attorney General, is an "officer of the Legislative Branch," *Bowsher*—wrote:

> "I think it is clear that [the Pay Act amendments'] primary purpose was to relieve 'recess appointees' of the burden of serving without compensation during periods when the Senate is not actually sitting and is not available to give its advice and consent in respect to the appointment, irrespective of whether the recess of the Senate is attributable to a final adjournment *sine die* or to an adjournment to a specified date." 28 Comp. Gen. 30, 37.

[Justice Breyer concluded that historical practice supported presidential appointments during intra-session recesses but further ruled that the President could not act when the Senate is in recess for fewer than 3 days, as the Constitution (Article I, § 5, cl. 4) bars the Senate from adjourning for more than 3 days without the consent of the House. Additionally, the Court ruled,] in light of historical practice, that a recess of more than 3 days but less than 10 days is presumptively too short to fall within the Clause. We add the word "presumptively" to leave open the possibility that some very unusual circumstance—a national catastrophe, for instance, that renders the Senate unavailable but calls for an urgent response—could demand the exercise of the recess-appointment power during a shorter break.

[IV] [The second issue was whether the "Vacancies that may *happen*" must be vacancies that arise during the recess, and not vacancies that persist during the recess. Justice Breyer favored the latter, broader interpretation.] We believe that the Clause's language, read literally, permits, though it does not naturally favor, our broader interpretation. We concede that the most natural meaning of "happens" as applied to a "vacancy" (at least to a modern ear) is that the vacancy "happens" when it initially occurs. But that is not the only possible way to use the word.

Thomas Jefferson wrote that the Clause is "certainly susceptible of [two] constructions." Letter to Wilson Cary Nicholas (Jan. 26, 1802), in 36 Papers of Thomas Jefferson 433 (B. Oberg ed., 2009). It "may mean 'vacancies that may happen to be' or 'may happen to fall' " during a recess. *Ibid.* Jefferson used the phrase in the first sense when he wrote to a job seeker that a particular position was unavailable, but that he (Jefferson) was "happy that *another vacancy happens* wherein I can . . . avail the public of your integrity & talents," for "the office of Treasurer of the US. *is vacant* by the resignation of Mr. Meredith." Letter to Thomas Tudor Tucker (Oct. 31, 1801), in 35 *id.*, at 530 (B. Oberg ed. 2008) (emphasis added).

Similarly, when Attorney General William Wirt advised President Monroe to follow the broader interpretation, he wrote that the "expression seems not perfectly clear. It may mean 'happen to take place:' that is, '*to originate*,' " or it "may mean, also, without violence to the sense, 'happen to exist.' " 1 Op. Atty. Gen. 631, 631–632 (1823). The broader interpretation, he added, is "most accordant with" the Constitution's "reason and spirit." *Id.,* at 632. * * *

The Clause's purpose strongly supports the broader interpretation. That purpose is to permit the President to obtain the assistance of subordinate officers when the Senate, due to its recess, cannot confirm them. Attorney General Wirt clearly described how the narrower interpretation would undermine this purpose:

> "Put the case of a vacancy occurring in an office, held in a distant part of the country, on the last day of the Senate's session. Before the vacancy is made known to the President, the Senate rises. The office may be an important one; the vacancy may paralyze a whole line of action in some essential branch of our internal police; the public interests may imperiously demand that it shall be immediately filled. But the vacancy happened to occur during the session of the Senate; and if the President's power is to be limited to such vacancies only as happen to occur during the recess of the Senate, the vacancy in the case put must continue, however ruinous the consequences may be to the public." 1 Op. Atty. Gen., at 632.

[What does history have to teach us? Justice Breyer found little relevant practice from the Washington, Adams, and Jefferson Administrations.] But the evidence suggests that James Madison—as familiar as anyone with the workings of the Constitutional Convention— appointed Theodore Gaillard to replace a district judge who had left office before a recess began. It also appears that in 1815 Madison signed a bill that created two new offices prior to a recess which he then filled later during the recess. See Act of Mar. 3, ch. 95, 3 Stat. 235; S. J. 13th Cong., 3d Sess., 689–690 (1815); 3 S. Exec. J. 19 (1828) (for Monday, Jan. 8, 1816). He also made recess appointments to "territorial" United States attorney and marshal positions, both of which had been created when the Senate was in session more than two years before. Act of Feb. 27, 1813, ch. 35, 2 Stat. 806; 3 S. Exec. J. 19.

[Upon the advice of Attorney General Wirt, the Monroe Administration followed the same understanding, as did every other Attorney General to opine on this issue.] Indeed, as early as 1862, Attorney General Bates advised President Lincoln that his power to fill pre-recess vacancies was "settled . . . as far . . . as a constitutional question can be settled," 10 Op. Atty. Gen., at 356, and a century later Acting Attorney General Walsh gave President Eisenhower the same advice "without any doubt," 41 Op. Atty. Gen., at 466. * * *

* * * No one disputes that every President since James Buchanan has made recess appointments to preexisting vacancies. * * *

[Did the Senate object? Not early on.] Then in 1863 the Senate Judiciary Committee disagreed with the broad interpretation. It issued a report concluding that a vacancy "must have its inceptive point after one session has closed and before another session has begun." S. Rep. No. 80, 37th Cong., 3d Sess., p. 3. And the Senate then passed the Pay Act, which provided that "no money shall be paid . . . as a salary, to any person appointed during the recess of the Senate, to fill a vacancy . . . which . . . existed while the Senate was in session." Act of Feb. 9, 1863, § 2, 12 Stat. 646. [Justice Breyer minimized the extent to which the 1863 Pay Act was a constitutional pushback from the Senate.]

In any event, the Senate subsequently abandoned its hostility. In the debate preceding the 1905 Senate Report regarding President Roosevelt's "constructive" recess appointments, Senator Tillman—who chaired the Committee that authored the 1905 Report—brought up the 1863 Report, and another Senator responded: "Whatever that report may have said in 1863, I do not think that has been the view the Senate has taken" of the issue. 38 Cong. Rec. 1606 (1904). Senator Tillman then agreed that "the Senate has acquiesced" in the President's "power to fill" pre-recess vacancies. *Ibid.* And Senator Tillman's 1905 Report described the Clause's purpose in terms closely echoing Attorney General Wirt. 1905 Senate Report, at 2 ("Its sole purpose was to render it *certain* that at all times there should be, whether the Senate was in session or not, an officer for every office" (emphasis added)).

[The President continued to make recess appointments for vacancies that arose before the recesses.] Then in 1940 Congress amended the Pay Act to authorize salary payments (with some exceptions) where (1) the "vacancy arose within thirty days prior to the termination of the session," (2) "at the termination of the session" a nomination was "pending," or (3) a nominee was "rejected by the Senate within thirty days prior to the termination of the session." Act of July 11, 54 Stat. 751 (codified, as amended, at 5 U.S.C. § 5503). All three circumstances concern a vacancy that did not initially occur during a recess but happened to exist during that recess. By paying salaries to this kind of recess appointee, the 1940 Senate (and later Senates) in effect supported the President's interpretation of the Clause.

[V] The third question concerns the calculation of the length of the Senate's "recess." On December 17, 2011, the Senate by unanimous consent adopted a resolution to convene "*pro forma* session[s]" only, with "no business . . . transacted," on every Tuesday and Friday from December 20, 2011, through January 20, 2012. At the end of each *pro forma* session, the Senate would "adjourn until" the following *pro forma* session. *Ibid.* During that period, the Senate convened and adjourned as agreed. It held *pro forma* sessions on December 20, 23, 27, and 30, and on January 3, 6, 10, 13, 17, and 20; and at the end of each *pro forma* session, it adjourned until the time and date of the next. The President made the recess appointments before us on January 4, 2012, in between the January 3 and the January 6 *pro forma* sessions. We must determine the significance of these sessions— that is, whether, for purposes of the Clause, we should treat them as periods when the Senate was in session or as periods when it was in recess. If the former, the period between January 3 and January 6 was a 3-day recess, which is too short to trigger the President's recess-appointment power. If the latter, however, then the 3-day period was part of a much longer recess during which the President did have the power to make recess appointments.

[The Court unanimously rejected the Solicitor General's argument that the *pro forma* sessions did not count as sessions, and hence did not break up the periods of recess.] We hold that, for purposes of the Recess Appointments Clause, the Senate is in session when it says it is, provided that, under its own rules, it retains the capacity to transact Senate business. The Senate met that standard here.

The standard we apply is consistent with the Constitution's broad delegation of authority to the Senate to determine how and when to conduct its business. The Constitution explicitly empowers the Senate to "determine the Rules of its Proceedings." Art. I, § 5, cl. 2. And we have held that "all matters of method are open to the determination" of the Senate, as long as there is "a reasonable relation between the mode or method of proceeding established by the rule and the result which is sought to be attained" and the rule does not "ignore constitutional restraints or violate fundamental rights." *United States* v. *Ballin*, 144 U.S. 1, 5 (1892).

In addition, the Constitution provides the Senate with extensive control over its schedule. There are only limited exceptions. See Amdt. 20, § 2 (Congress must meet once a year on January 3, unless it specifies another day by law); Art. II, § 3 (Senate must meet if the President calls it into special session); Art. I, § 5, cl. 4 (neither House may adjourn for more than three days without consent of the other). The Constitution thus gives the Senate wide latitude to determine whether and when to have a session, as well as how to conduct the session. This suggests that the Senate's determination about what constitutes a session should merit great respect. [Accordingly, Justice Breyer ruled that the Senate was in session during the *pro forma* sessions and, hence, that the short breaks between *pro forma* sessions could not trigger the Recess Appointments Clause.]

[VI] The Recess Appointments Clause responds to a structural difference between the Executive and Legislative Branches: The Executive Branch is perpetually in operation, while the Legislature only acts in intervals separated by recesses. The purpose of the Clause is to allow the Executive to continue operating while the Senate is unavailable. We believe that the Clause's text, standing alone, is ambiguous. It does not resolve whether the President may make appointments during intra-session recesses, or whether he may fill pre-recess vacancies. But the broader reading better serves the Clause's structural function. Moreover, that broader reading is reinforced by centuries of history, which we are hesitant to disturb. We thus hold that the Constitution empowers the President to fill any existing vacancy during any recess—intra-session or inter-session—of sufficient length.

[Joined by **CHIEF JUSTICE ROBERTS and JUSTICES THOMAS and ALITO, JUSTICE SCALIA** rejected the Court's analysis and maintained that the Recess Appointments Clause allowed presidential appointments *only* for vacancies that *arise* during *inter-session* recesses. Because these Justices agreed that the Obama appointments in this case violated the Constitution, they concurred in the Court's judgment. We discuss many of Justice Scalia's arguments in the Notes that follow.]

NOTES ON THE RECESS APPOINTMENTS CASE: THE MANY FACES OF HISTORY IN CONSTITUTIONAL INTERPRETATION

Noel Canning reflects the important role history sometimes plays in the Supreme Court's interpretation of the Constitution's structure and particular provisions.

1. *Original Meaning of Constitutional Text.* Like the Justices in the Second Amendment Cases, *Heller* (2008) and *McDonald* (2010) (Casebook, pp. 199–210), as well as the Brady Act Case, *Printz* (1997) (Casebook, pp. 1055–65), all nine Justices in the Recess Appointments Case trained their attention on the original meaning of the relevant text. The continued, even accelerating, rise of original meaning is significant. But it is not clear that methodology makes a difference. Original meaning theorists maintain that this interpretive approach is the only one that constrains result-oriented judges to rule neutrally and predictably. Is that correct?

Or does the debate among the Justices in *Noel Canning* support the critics, who say that original meaning inquiries are like looking out over the crowd and picking out your friends? For example, does Justice Breyer present a good case for the propositions that the "original meaning" of "recess" can include intra-session recesses and that a vacancy "happens" not only when it arises but also when it persists over time? Or is original meaning just window dressing?

As to the first issue, one historian has opined that "in government practice the phrase 'the Recess' *always* referred to the gap between sessions." Robert Natelson, *The Origins and Meaning of "Vacancies that May Happen During the Recess" in the Constitution's Recess Appointments Clause*, 37 Harv. J. L. & Pub. Pol'y 199, 213 (2014). Indeed, the Constitution uses the verb "adjourn" rather than "recess" to refer to the commencement of breaks *during* a formal legislative session. U.S. Const. art. I, § 5, cl. 1 and 4. In *Federalist* No. 67, Publius explained to the ratifying audience that appointments would require

Senate consent "during the *session* of the Senate" but would be made by the President alone "*in their recess*," apparently using the term as a break between sessions.

As to the second issue, even Justice Breyer conceded that the narrow reading of "happens" is the "most natural" one. Justice Scalia maintained that it is the only "plausible" one, a view he felt was confirmed by early practice. "In 1792, Attorney General Edmund Randolph, who had been a leading member of the Constitutional Convention, provided the Executive Branch's first formal interpretation of the Clause. He advised President Washington that the Constitution did not authorize a recess appointment to fill the office of Chief Coiner of the United States Mint, which had been created by Congress on April 2, 1792, during the Senate's session. Randolph wrote: '[I]s it a vacancy which has *happened* during the recess of the Senate? It is now the same and no other vacancy, than that, which existed on the 2nd. of April 1792. It commenced therefore on that day or may be said to have *happened* on that day.' Opinion on Recess Appointments (July 7, 1792), in 24 Papers of Thomas Jefferson 165–166 (J. Catanzariti ed. 1990). Randolph added that his interpretation was the most congruent with the Constitution's structure, which made the recess-appointment power "an exception to the general participation of the Senate.' *Ibid*." President Adams's Attorney General, Charles Lee, came to the same conclusion. Even Attorney General Wirt in 1823 admitted that the letter of the Constitution did not support his broad reading.

The asserted virtue of the original meaning methodology is that it yields more predictable interpretations and constrains judges better than any other method. Was the Court's interpretation of the Recess Appointments Clause (to include intra-session recesses of more than ten days, and sometimes for 3–10 days, to fill preexisting vacancies) *predictable*? Did the methodology *constrain* any Justice? It's hard to see how: the Court's four most conservative GOP-appointed Justices voted with the Republican Senators challenging the President's action and giving the pro-labor NLRB a hard time, while the Court's four liberal Democrat-appointed Justices (only one of whom served in the executive branch) voted with the Democratic Solicitor General on most issues and gave hundreds of recess appointees a break. For all the argumentation in the opinions, it is hard to imagine that original meaning explains the Court's judgment—and it is far from clear that any Justice really voted with nothing else in mind.

2. *Historical Purposes of Constitutional Text*. Another way that history figures into the Justices' debate in *Noel Canning* is figuring out the purpose of the Recess Appointments Clause. Indeed, because he finds the text ambiguous, Justice Breyer's opinion for the Court relies mainly on the historical purpose of the Clause. But is he any more persuasive on that front than in his treatment of original meaning?

Justice Breyer said the purpose of the Clause is to keep the government running efficiently when the Senate is not prepared to do business (and confirm appointees)—but his main evidence for that proposition is the Opinion of Attorney General Wirt other executive branch officers far removed from the founding era. Justice Scalia responded: "The majority disregards another self-evident purpose of the Clause: to preserve the Senate's role in the appointment process—which the founding generation regarded as a critical protection against 'despotism'—by clearly delineating the times when the President can appoint officers without the Senate's consent. Today's decision seriously undercuts *that* purpose."

Indeed, viewed structurally, the Constitution protects the liberty of citizens and corporations by making it harder for potentially tyrannical officials to act without the cooperation of officials in other branches. See *Federalist* No. 51 (Madison) (the Constitution's system of checks and balances provides a "double security" for citizens). Thus, the obvious purpose of the Appointments Clauses is to check the President's ability to make appointments without considering the views of the Senate; that purpose is liberty-protecting and democracy-enhancing, as it assures the country that persons acceptable to both the nationally elected President and the state-representing Senate will serve in high office. In this scheme of things, the Recess Appointments Clause is an *exception*, to accommodate practical problems when the Senate is unavailable to participate. Exceptions are supposed to be narrowly construed, not broadly, as Justice Breyer urged. And the Court's broad interpretation of the Recess Appointments Clause opens the way for the already imperial President to secure even more power vis-à-vis Congress.

Justice Scalia made another point about purposive interpretation: "The rise of intra-session adjournments has occurred in tandem with the development of modern forms of communication and transportation that mean the Senate 'is always available' to consider nominations, even when its Members are temporarily dispersed for an intra-session break. Tr. of Oral Arg. 21 (Ginsburg, J.). The Recess Appointments Clause therefore is, or rather, should be, an anachronism—'essentially an historic relic, something whose original purpose has disappeared.' *Id.*, at 19 (Kagan, J.). The need it was designed to fill no longer exists, and its only remaining use is the ignoble one of enabling the President to circumvent the Senate's role in the appointment process." Justice Breyer responded that Justice Scalia was trying to read the Recess Appointments Clause out of the Constitution—which is not correct: Justice Scalia was merely responding to the purpose argument with the observation that the *original* purpose is no longer so pressing and, hence, provides even less reason to read the Clause broadly.

Consider Justice Scalia's analysis in light of what has transpired in Washington, D.C. in the last several years—Congress has shut down. Due to hyperpartisan bickering between the parties and to the fractured GOP caucus in the House (which the Republicans have controlled since 2011), not only does Congress not enact substantive legislation anymore, but even routine legislative activities such as budgets, debt ceiling adjustments, and confirmations have slowed or stalled. Like the Bush-Cheney Administration, the Obama-Biden Administration has responded to an exacerbated congressional gridlock with aggressive executive action—including more recess appointments to positions that were once routine matters. Can you blame the Court majority for giving the President some slack, given his efforts to press onward with governance and given the contrast with an obstructionist and deeply unpopular Congress?

3.   *Practice as Constitutional Adverse Possession.* As in the Steel Seizure Case (Casebook, pp. 1175–88), the Justices in the Recess Appointments Case took a variety of positions regarding the relevance of executive practice when judges set the meaning of constitutional provisions. Justice Breyer posited that constitutional ambiguities may be resolved by consulting a longstanding presidential practice which Congress has not decisively resisted. Like Chief Justice Vinson in the Steel Seizure Case (Casebook, pp. 1184–85), Justice Breyer applied the practice-as-adverse-possession standard pretty liberally. Following Justice Frankfurter's formulation of the constitutional adverse possession idea (Casebook, pp. 1179–80), Justice Scalia opined that "where a governmental practice has been open, widespread, and unchallenged since the early days of the Republic, the practice should guide our interpretation of an ambiguous constitutional provision."

Even if the constitutional text were in any way ambiguous and even if the Breyer/Vinson standard were the proper one, Justice Scalia argued that the majority did not make its case. "Intra-session recess appointments were virtually unheard of for the first 130 years of the Republic, were deemed unconstitutional by the first Attorney General to address them [Attorney General Philander Knox in 1901], were not openly defended by the Executive until 1921 [Attorney General Harry Daughtery], were not made in significant numbers until after World War II, and have been repeatedly criticized as unconstitutional by Senators of both parties."

On the availability of recess appointments arising beforehand, Justice Scalia had an even stronger historical response. Few Presidents made such appointments in the first century of the republic—and when they did there was sometimes pushback. After President Lincoln appointed David Davis to the Supreme Court through a recess appointment to a preexisting vacancy, a number of Senators strenuously objected. And in 1863 Congress enacted the Pay Act, which provided that "no money shall be paid . . . out of the Treasury, as salary, to any person appointed during the recess of the Senate, to fill a vacancy . . . which . . . existed while the Senate was in session." Act of Feb. 9, 1863, § 2, 12 Stat. 646. Between 1863 and 1940, there were few recess appointments to fill preexisting vacancies.

As Justice Breyer observed, Congress amended the Pay Act in 1940. Under the current version of the Act, "[p]ayment for services may not be made from the Treasury of the United States to an individual appointed during a recess of the Senate to fill a vacancy" that "existed while the Senate was in session" *unless* either the vacancy arose, or a different individual's nomination to fill the vacancy was rejected, "within 30 days before the end of the session"; or a nomination was pending before the Senate at the end of the session, and the individual nominated was not himself a recess appointee. § 5503(a)(1)–(3).

And if the President fills a pre-recess vacancy under one of the circumstances specified in the Act, the law requires that he submit a nomination for that office to the Senate "not later than 40 days after the beginning of the next session." § 5503(b).

Since the 1940 Amendment to the Pay Act, Presidents have made several dozen recess appointments to fill preexisting vacancies. Even as amended, the Pay Act seems disapproving of the practice generally, and certainly regulates it stringently. (If the President has the constitutional authority described by the Court, isn't the Pay Act unconstitutional, because it burdens officials validly appointed by the President?) Senators, including the GOP Senators who participated in *Noel Canning,* have continued to object to the practice. Concluded Justice Scalia: "I can conceive of no sane constitutional theory under which this evidence of 'historical practice'—which is actually evidence of a long-simmering inter-branch conflict—would require us to defer to the views of the Executive Branch." Can you disagree with this assertion?

Return to first principles, and the Steel Seizure Case. Why should executive practice be relevant to the meaning of the Constitution? Understood thus, executive practice can easily bootstrap an institutionally biased viewpoint into the law of the land: Is that not disturbing—especially in light of the first-mover advantage the President already has and the imperial power the office has accumulated. The contrast between the President and the Senate is quite stark: the Presidency can mobilize quickly because one man or woman makes ultimate decisions, whereby the Senate cannot act on most matters (including adjournment!) without the cooperation of the House and is internally hamstrung by the filibuster and other vetogates that block legislative initiatives.

In light of these concerns, has the *Noel Canning* majority stacked the deck in its adverse possession analysis? If it has done so, perhaps that is defensible because the adverse possession idea is defensible. After all, property law, the home to rule-of-law values and bright line directives, originated the adverse possession idea, where it has served a useful role of protecting reliance interests and providing incentives for property owners to assert their rights. The big problem for adverse possession in constitutional law, however, is that it is usually easier for the President to assert executive authority than it is for a diffused and often disorganized Congress to assert its prerogatives. The easiest way for Congress to resist a presidential initiative is to refuse to fund it or to limit the initiative through a rider to an appropriations measure or even a framework statute such as the Pay Act.

What is the right answer to the Case of the Recess Appointments? Does John Hart Ely's representation-reinforcement theory have any insights here (Casebook, pp. 161–71)? How about Alexander Bickel's theory of the passive virtues: Is passivity virtuous in this kind of case?

B. FOREIGN RELATIONS AND WAR

Page 1216. Insert a new subsection B.4 at the end of subsection B.3:

4. Presidential Authority in Conducting Diplomacy

Zivotofsky v. Kerry

___ U.S. ___, 135 S.Ct. 2076 (2015)

Since 1948, the United States, acting through the President, has recognized the state of Israel but has taken no position on the delicate issue of which state has sovereignty over Jerusalem. Consistent with this policy, the State Department will not identify Israel as the nation of citizenship for anyone born in Jerusalem; the passport will simply say "Jerusalem." This is considered objectionable by many supporters of Israel.

In 2002, Congress passed the Foreign Relations Authorization Act, Fiscal Year 2003, 116 Stat. 1350. Section 214 of the Act is titled "United States Policy with Respect to Jerusalem as the Capital of Israel." Section 214(d) allows citizens born in Jerusalem to list their place of birth as "Israel." "For purposes of the registration of birth, certification of nationality, or issuance of a passport of a United States citizen born in the city of Jerusalem, the Secretary shall, upon the request of the citizen or the citizen's legal guardian, record the place of birth as Israel." Did this statutory override of State Department and Presidential policy violate Article II?

Writing for the Court, **JUSTICE KENNEDY** applied the Steel Seizure framework and found that the President's assertion of authority fell under Category 3—"measures incompatible with the expressed or implied will of Congress," which can only be allowed when the President's own constitutional authority disables Congress from acting. Unlike the Steel Seizure Case, where President Truman did not satisfy the stringent requirements of Category 3, the Court here upheld the President and ruled that the 2002 statute was invalid because Article II vested the President with exclusive authority to "recognize" foreign states.

The Constitution does not use the term "recognition," but Secretary Kerry relied on the Reception Clause, which directs that the President "shall receive Ambassadors and other public Ministers." Art. II, § 3. The Reception Clause received little attention at the Constitutional Convention, see Reinstein, Recognition: A Case Study on the Original Understanding of Executive Power, 45 U. Rich. L. Rev. 801, 860–862 (2011), and during the ratification debates, Alexander Hamilton claimed that the power to receive ambassadors was "more a matter of dignity than of authority," a ministerial duty largely "without consequence." The Federalist No. 69, p. 420 (C. Rossiter ed. 1961).

"At the time of the founding, however, prominent international scholars suggested that receiving an ambassador was tantamount to recognizing the sovereignty of the sending state. See E. de Vattel, The Law of Nations § 78, p.

461 (1758) (J. Chitty ed. 1853) ('[E]very state, truly possessed of sovereignty, has a right to send ambassadors' and 'to contest their right in this instance' is equivalent to 'contesting their sovereign dignity'); [other sources omitted]. It is a logical and proper inference, then, that a Clause directing the President alone to receive ambassadors would be understood to acknowledge his power to recognize other nations."

"This in fact occurred early in the Nation's history when President Washington recognized the French Revolutionary Government by receiving its ambassador. After this incident the import of the Reception Clause became clear—causing Hamilton to change his earlier view. He wrote that the Reception Clause 'includes th[e power] of judging, in the case of a revolution of government in a foreign country, whether the new rulers are competent organs of the national will, and ought to be recognised, or not.' See A. Hamilton, Pacificus No. 1, in The Letters of Pacificus and Helvidius 5, 13–14 (1845) (reprint 1976) (President 'acknowledged the republic of France, by the reception of its minister'). [S]ee also 3 J. Story, Commentaries on the Constitution of the United States § 1560, p. 416 (1833) ('If the executive receives an ambassador, or other minister, as the representative of a new nation . . . it is an acknowledgment of the sovereign authority *de facto* of such new nation, or party'). As a result, the Reception Clause provides support, although not the sole authority, for the President's power to recognize other nations."

Justice Kennedy found the foregoing inference supported by the President's other Article II powers. The President, "by and with the Advice and Consent of the Senate," is to "make Treaties, provided two thirds of the Senators present concur." Art. II, § 2, cl. 2. Also, "he shall nominate, and by and with the Advice and Consent of the Senate, shall appoint Ambassadors" as well as "other public Ministers and Consuls." *Ibid.*

"As a matter of constitutional structure, these additional powers give the President control over recognition decisions. At international law, recognition may be effected by different means, but each means is dependent upon Presidential power. In addition to receiving an ambassador, recognition may occur on 'the conclusion of a bilateral treaty,' or the 'formal initiation of diplomatic relations,' including the dispatch of an ambassador. The President has the sole power to negotiate treaties, and the Senate may not conclude or ratify a treaty without Presidential action. The President, too, nominates the Nation's ambassadors and dispatches other diplomatic agents. Congress may not send an ambassador without his involvement. Beyond that, the President himself has the power to open diplomatic channels simply by engaging in direct diplomacy with foreign heads of state and their ministers. The Constitution thus assigns the President means to effect recognition on his own initiative. Congress, by contrast, has no constitutional power that would enable it to initiate diplomatic relations with a foreign nation. Because these specific Clauses confer the recognition power on the President, the Court need not consider whether or to what extent the Vesting Clause, which provides that the 'executive Power' shall be vested in the President, provides further support for the President's action here. Art. II, § 1, cl. 1.

"The text and structure of the Constitution grant the President the power to recognize foreign nations and governments. The question then becomes whether that power is exclusive. The various ways in which the President may unilaterally effect recognition—and the lack of any similar power vested in Congress—suggest that it is. So, too, do functional considerations. Put simply, the Nation must have a single policy regarding which governments are legitimate in the eyes of the United States and which are not. Foreign countries need to know, before entering into diplomatic relations or commerce with the United States, whether their ambassadors will be received; whether their officials will be immune from suit in federal court; and whether they may initiate lawsuits here to vindicate their rights. These assurances cannot be equivocal."

Justice Kennedy also found it significant that "the President since the founding has exercised this unilateral power to recognize new states—and the Court has endorsed the practice. See *Banco Nacional de Cuba v. Sabbatino*, 376 U.S. 398, 410, 84 S.Ct. 923, 11 L.Ed.2d 804 (1964); [*United States v. Pink*, 315 U.S. 203, 229, 62 S.Ct. 552, 86 L.Ed. 796 (1942)]; *Williams v. Suffolk Ins. Co.*, 13 Pet. 415, 420, 10 L.Ed. 226 (1839). Texts and treatises on international law treat the President's word as the final word on recognition. See, *e.g.*, Restatement (Third) of Foreign Relations Law § 204, at 89 ('Under the Constitution of the United States the President has exclusive authority to recognize or not to recognize a foreign state or government'). In light of this authority all six judges who considered this case in the Court of Appeals agreed that the President holds the exclusive recognition power." Justice Kennedy found *Sabbatino* especially relevant, for the Court held that "[p]olitical recognition is exclusively a function of the Executive."

Secretary Kerry urged the Court to define the executive power broadly, namely, "exclusive authority to conduct diplomatic relations," along with "the bulk of foreign-affairs powers." Brief for Respondent 18, 16. The Court refused to go that far. "In a world that is ever more compressed and interdependent, it is essential the congressional role in foreign affairs be understood and respected. For it is Congress that makes laws, and in countless ways its laws will and should shape the Nation's course. The Executive is not free from the ordinary controls and checks of Congress merely because foreign affairs are at issue."

Finally, Justice Kennedy considered the extensive historical record to discern whether there had been congressional acquiescence in the exclusive power claimed by the President and the Secretary of State. As Judge Tatel had remarked in the proceedings below, what is most remarkable is that, since the Washington Administration, the President had openly claimed the exclusive authority to recognize foreign states (or not) and had not been met with a congressional statute to the contrary—until the 2002 law at issue in this case.

JUSTICE BREYER joined the opinion for the Court but noted his view, rejected by the Court in *Zivotofsky v. Clinton*, 132 S.Ct. 1441 (2012), that the controversy was a nonjusticiable political question. See Chapter 9 of the Casebook, as well as *Sabbatino*, where the Court ruled that the President's recognition of Cuba was not reviewable.

JUSTICE THOMAS concurred in part of the Court's judgment and rejected the Court's constitutional analysis. He argued that the Article II Vesting Clause ("executive power," without qualification) gives the President plenary authority to act in matters of foreign affairs or military deployment. Because Congress's Article I Vesting Clause only gives Congress "[a]ll legislative Powers herein granted," Congress can trump the President only where the Constitution has explicitly authorized congressional action, such as confirming ambassadors and providing funds for foreign affairs and military operations. See Saikrishna Prakash & Michael Ramsey, *The Executive Power Over Foreign Affairs*, 111 Yale L.J. 231, 298–346 (2001). Under his framework, Justice Thomas would have invalidated § 214(d) as applied to passports (fully within the "executive Power" as understood in 1789) but would have applied it to matters of naturalization, fully within Congress's enumerated powers. U.S. Const. art. I, § 8, cl. 4.

CHIEF JUSTICE ROBERTS (joined by Justice Alito) noted that this was the first time the Supreme Court has allowed the President to defy an explicit congressional statute regulating foreign affairs. The Court's holding was not properly attentive to the "caution" urged by Justice Jackson in Steel Seizure Category 3 cases.

JUSTICE SCALIA (joined by the Chief Justice and Justice Alito) also dissented. In a significant break from Justice Thomas's broad reading of the Article II Vesting Clause, Justice Scalia worked within the analytical structure of a balanced government, where both Congress and the President share foreign affairs authority.

"Congress's power to 'establish an uniform Rule of Naturalization,' Art. I, § 8, cl. 4, enables it to grant American citizenship to someone born abroad. The naturalization power also enables Congress to furnish the people it makes citizens with papers verifying their citizenship—say a consular report of birth abroad (which certifies citizenship of an American born outside the United States) or a passport (which certifies citizenship for purposes of international travel). As the Necessary and Proper Clause confirms, every congressional power 'carries with it all those incidental powers which are necessary to its complete and effectual execution.' *Cohens v. Virginia*, 6 Wheat. 264, 429, 5 L.Ed. 257 (1821). Even on a miserly understanding of Congress's incidental authority, Congress may make grants of citizenship 'effectual' by providing for the issuance of certificates authenticating them.

"One would think that if Congress may grant Zivotofsky a passport and a birth report, it may also require these papers to record his birthplace as 'Israel.' The birthplace specification promotes the document's citizenship-authenticating function by identifying the bearer, distinguishing people with similar names but different birthplaces from each other, helping authorities uncover identity fraud, and facilitating retrieval of the Government's citizenship records."

Having found that Congress possessed constitutional authority to enact § 214(d), Justice Scalia posed the question whether Article II trumps that authority. Without resolving the thorny question of whether Article II trumps Article I, Justice Scalia found no conflict between the legislative and executive powers at issue, because "§ 214(d) has nothing to do with recognition," the core executive power the majority jealously protected. "Section 214(d) does not require the Secretary to make a formal declaration about Israel's sovereignty over Jerusalem. And nobody suggests that international custom infers acceptance of sovereignty from the birthplace designation on a passport or birth report, as it does from bilateral treaties or exchanges of ambassadors. Recognition would preclude the United States (as a matter of international law) from later contesting Israeli sovereignty over Jerusalem. But making a notation in a passport or birth report does not encumber the Republic with any international obligations. It leaves the Nation free (so far as international law is concerned) to change its mind in the future. That would be true even if the statute required *all* passports to list 'Israel.' But in fact it requires only those passports to list 'Israel' for which the citizen (or his guardian) *requests* 'Israel'; all the rest, under the Secretary's policy, list 'Jerusalem.' It is utterly impossible for this deference to private requests to constitute an act that unequivocally manifests an intention to grant recognition.

"Section 214(d) performs a more prosaic function than extending recognition. Just as foreign countries care about what our Government has to say about their borders, so too American citizens often care about what our Government has to say about their identities."

What of the Court's concern that the nation speak in one voice on matters of foreign relations? Nonsense, replied Justice Scalia. There is nothing in the Constitution that says Congress and the President must operate along exactly the same assumptions about foreign relations matters. Consider the President's power "to make Treaties," Art. II, § 2, cl. 2. "There is no question that Congress may, if it wishes, pass laws that openly flout treaties made by the President. Would anyone have dreamt that the President may refuse to carry out such laws—or, to bring the point closer to home, refuse to execute federal courts' judgments under such laws—so that the Executive may 'speak with one voice' about the country's international obligations? To ask is to answer. Today's holding puts the implied power to recognize territorial claims (which the Court infers from the power to recognize states, which it infers from the responsibility to receive ambassadors) on a higher footing than the express power to make treaties."

Justice Scalia concluded: "In the end, the Court's decision does not rest on text or history or precedent. It instead comes down to 'functional considerations'—principally the Court's perception that the Nation 'must speak with one voice' about the status of Jerusalem. The vices of this mode of analysis go beyond mere lack of footing in the Constitution. Functionalism of the sort the Court practices today will *systematically* favor the unitary President over the plural Congress in disputes involving foreign affairs. It is possible that this approach will make for more effective foreign policy, perhaps as effective as that of a monarchy. It is certain that, in the long run, it will erode the structure of separated powers that the People established for the protection of their liberty."

NOTE ON THE PRESIDENT'S EXPANDING AUTHORITY IN FOREIGN AFFAIRS

As reflected in Justice Kennedy's opinion, as well as those of the dissenters, the Prakash and Ramsey Foreign Affairs Vesting Thesis (Casebook, pp. 1191–94) has little constituency among the Justices (except for Justice Thomas). But if you read the Reception Clause as broadly as Justice Kennedy does, and then afford the same broad reading to the Commander-in-Chief Clause, you have accepted a significant amount of little-restricted power to the President. Is this process of expanding presidential power inevitable, given the circumstances of the modern world? Can the Constitution accommodate it? Ought the Constitution set some limits? How can they be enforced?

Recall Edward Swaine's argument that decisive, initiative-seizing Presidents have deployed the Steel Seizure (Jackson) framework much more successfully than plodding Congress has been. Edward T. Swaine, *The Political Economy of* Youngstown, 83 S. Cal. L. Rev. 263 (2010) (Casebook, pp. 1187–88). Functionalism is the President's best friend in constitutional theory—a point that the Chief Justice and Justice Scalia join in making. But cf. *Chadha*, where the President's highly formalist point of view prevailed with the Justices, at the expense of Congress's enactment of legislative veto provisions.

Consider the cogency of Justice Scalia's critique of functionalism in light of the arguments made by the Obama Administration in the Libyan Bombing Problem. See Problem 8–2(c) (Casebook, pp. 1209–11). Does the majority opinion provide ammunition for the Obama Administration's narrowing interpretation of the War Powers Resolution? If a justiciable controversy had brought the Libyan Bombing Campaign to the Supreme Court after *Zivotofsky*, how would the Justices have ruled?

SECTION 2. ISSUES OF LEGISLATIVE OVERREACHING

A. "EXCESSIVE" CONGRESSIONAL DELEGATIONS AND THE ARTICLE I, SECTION 7 STRUCTURE FOR LAWMAKING

1. The Decline and Potential Revival of the Nondelegation Doctrine

Page 1238. Insert the following Case after *Whitman*:

Department of Transportation v. Association of American Railroads

135 S.Ct. 1225 (2015)

In 1970, Congress created the National Railroad Passenger Corporation (Amtrak). Congress has given Amtrak priority to use track systems owned by the freight railroads for passenger rail travel, at rates agreed to by the parties or, in case of a dispute, set by the Surface Transportation Board. In 2008, Congress gave Amtrak and the Federal Railroad Administration (FRA) joint authority to issue "metrics and standards" addressing the performance and scheduling of passenger railroad services, see § 207(a), 122 Stat. 4907, including Amtrak's on-time performance and train delays caused by host railroads. The Association of American Railroads (AAR) brought a lawsuit, claiming that the metrics and standards are unconstitutional because Congress allows and directs a private entity like Amtrak to exercise joint authority in their issuance. Its argument rested on the Fifth Amendment Due Process Clause and the constitutional provisions regarding separation of powers.

The Court of Appeals held that because "Amtrak is a private corporation with respect to Congress's power to delegate . . . authority," it cannot constitutionally be granted the "regulatory power prescribed in § 207." The lower court treated as controlling Congress's statutory directive that Amtrak "is not a department, agency, or instrumentality of the United States Government." 49 U.S.C. § 24301(a)(3)). The Court of Appeals also relied on Congress's pronouncement that Amtrak "shall be operated and managed as a for-profit corporation." § 24301(a)(2));

JUSTICE KENNEDY delivered the opinion for the Court, reversing the lower court's judgment and remanding the case for further proceedings on AAR's other constitutional claims. Justice Kennedy did not quarrel with the lower court's view that Article I does bar Congress from delegating lawmaking authority to a private entity, but ruled that Amtrak is, in fact, a government entity. "In addition to controlling Amtrak's stock and Board of Directors the political branches exercise substantial, statutorily mandated supervision over Amtrak's priorities and operations." Thus, Amtrak must submit annual reports to Congress, is subject to the Freedom of Information Act, and must maintain an inspector general, much like governmental agencies. Congress conducts frequent oversight hearings into Amtrak's budget, routes, and prices. "Given the combination of these unique features and its significant ties to the Government, Amtrak is not an autonomous private enterprise." Accord, *Lebron v. National Railroad Passenger Corp.*, 513 U.S. 374 (1995) (Amtrak is a governmental actor subject to the constraints of the First Amendment).

In a thoughtful concurring opinion, JUSTICE ALITO worried that Amtrak's status as a governmental entity did not solve all the separation of powers concerns with the statute. He had a specific list of constitutional problems to be addressed on remand.

First, once Amtrak is considered a government actor, Amtrak's officials are "officers of the United States" who must take an oath or affirmation to support the Constitution and must receive a commission. Art. VI, cl. 3; Art. II, § 3, cl. 6. But the United States conceded that Amtrak's officers do not take such an oath, nor do they enjoy such a commission. So is Amtrak unconstitutionally constituted? How can that be fixed?

Second, the statute provides that disputes between Amtrak and the FRA are to be resolved by an "arbitrator." Because that provision contemplated a legal change in status and might be promulgated by a private person (a private arbitrator), it would seem to be unconstitutional under the private nondelegation doctrine. The United States sought a narrowing interpretation, to read "arbitrator" to mean a government arbitrator, but Justice Alito doubted that this was a meaning that those words could bear. Should the arbitral process be ruled unconstitutional—or should the lower court adopt a narrowing construction?

Third, the statute's provision that Amtrak's President is appointed by Amtrak's Board of Directors would seem to violate the Appointments Clause, as well as the Article II Vesting Clause, according to Justice Alito. The United States claimed that the President is an "inferior officer," a proposition Justice Alito found dubious. But even if the Amtrak President were an "inferior officer," would a majority of the Amtrak Board be a group of officials authorized by the Appointments Clause to make such an appointment? In short, by saving the statute from the immediate nondelegation challenge, the Court may have dug a bigger constitutional hole for Amtrak.

JUSTICE THOMAS concurred in the judgment only. "We have come to a strange place in our separation-of powers jurisprudence. Confronted with a statute that authorizes a putatively private market participant to work hand-in-hand with an executive agency to craft rules that have the force and effect of law, our primary question—indeed, the primary question the parties ask us to answer—is whether that market participant is subject to an adequate measure of control by the Federal Government. We never even glance at the Constitution to see what it says about how this authority must be exercised and by whom."

Justice Thomas took sharp aim at the nondelegation doctrine as it has been applied by the Court, starting with *J. W. Hampton, Jr., & Co.* v. *United States*, 276 U.S. 394 (1928), which articulated the rule that Congress can delegate lawmaking authority to a government agency so long as the statute lays out an "intelligible principle" for the agency to apply. "Although the Court may never have intended the boundless standard the 'intelligible principle' test has become, it is evident that it does not adequately reinforce the Constitution's allocation of legislative power. I would return to the original understanding of the federal legislative power and require that the Federal Government create generally applicable rules of private conduct only through the constitutionally prescribed legislative process.

"We should return to the original meaning of the Constitution: The Government may create generally applicable rules of private conduct only through the proper exercise of legislative power. I accept that this would inhibit the Government from acting with the speed and efficiency Congress has sometimes found desirable. In anticipating that result and accepting it, I am in good company. John Locke, for example, acknowledged that a legislative body 'is usually too numerous, and so too slow for the dispatch requisite to execution.' Locke, [*Second Treatise of Civil Government*] § 160. But he saw that as a benefit for legislation, for he believed that the creation of rules of private conduct should be an irregular and infrequent occurrence. See *id.*, § 143. The Framers, it appears, were inclined to agree. As Alexander Hamilton explained in another context, 'It may perhaps be said that the power of preventing bad laws includes that of preventing good ones. . . . But this objection will have little weight with those who can properly estimate the mischiefs of that inconstancy and mutability in the laws, which form the greatest blemish in the character and genius of our governments.' The *Federalist* No. 73. I am comfortable joining his conclusion that '[t]he injury which may possibly be done by defeating a few good laws will be amply compensated by the advantage of preventing a number of bad ones.' "

No other Justice joined this concurring opinion, which makes a good case that the original meaning of the Constitution's separation of powers has long ago been breached. *Query*: But is the breach so longstanding, brigaded with public reliance, that it is too late to start enforcing the original meaning? Is there some middle ground?

CHAPTER 9

LIMITS ON THE JUDICIAL POWER

▪ ▪ ▪

SECTION 2. "CASES" OR "CONTROVERSIES"

Page 1425. Insert before Section 3:

CLAPPER V. AMNESTY INTERNATIONAL
__ U.S. __, 133 S.Ct. 1138 (2013)

JUSTICE ALITO delivered the opinion of the Court.

Section 702 of the Foreign Intelligence Surveillance Act of 1978, 50 U.S.C. § 1881a, allows the Attorney General and the Director of National Intelligence to acquire foreign intelligence information by jointly authorizing the surveillance of individuals who are not "United States persons" and are reasonably believed to be located outside the United States. Before doing so, the Attorney General and the Director of National Intelligence normally must obtain the Foreign Intelligence Surveillance Court's approval. Respondents are United States persons whose work, they allege, requires them to engage in sensitive international communications with individuals who they believe are likely targets of surveillance under § 1881a. Respondents seek a declaration that § 1881a is unconstitutional, as well as an injunction against § 1881a-authorized surveillance. The question before us is whether respondents have Article III standing to seek this prospective relief.

Respondents assert that they can establish injury in fact because there is an objectively reasonable likelihood that their communications will be acquired under § 1881a at some point in the future. But respondents' theory of future injury is too speculative to satisfy the well-established requirement that threatened injury must be "certainly impending." And even if respondents could demonstrate that the threatened injury is certainly impending, they still would not be able to establish that this injury is fairly traceable to § 1881a. As an alternative argument, respondents contend that they are suffering present injury because the risk of § 1881a-authorized surveillance already has forced them to take costly and burdensome measures to protect the confidentiality of their international communications. But respondents cannot manufacture standing by choosing to make expenditures based on hypothetical future harm that is not certainly impending. We therefore hold that respondents lack Article III standing. * * *

In 1978, after years of debate, Congress enacted the Foreign Intelligence Surveillance Act (FISA) to authorize and regulate certain governmental electronic surveillance of communications for foreign intelligence purposes.

In constructing such a framework for foreign intelligence surveillance, Congress created two specialized courts. In FISA, Congress authorized judges of the Foreign Intelligence Surveillance Court (FISC) to approve electronic surveillance for foreign intelligence purposes if there is probable cause to believe that "the target of the electronic surveillance is a foreign power or an agent of a foreign power," and that each of the specific "facilities or places at which the electronic surveillance is directed is being used, or is about to be used, by a foreign power or an agent of a foreign power." Additionally, Congress vested the Foreign Intelligence Surveillance Court of Review with jurisdiction to review any denials by the FISC of applications for electronic surveillance. * * *

When Congress enacted the FISA Amendments Act of 2008 (FISA Amendments Act), it left much of FISA intact, but it "established a new and independent source of intelligence collection authority, beyond that granted in traditional FISA." As relevant here, § 702 of FISA, which was enacted as part of the FISA Amendments Act, supplements pre-existing FISA authority by creating a new framework under which the Government may seek the FISC's authorization of certain foreign intelligence surveillance targeting the communications of non-U.S. persons located abroad. Unlike traditional FISA surveillance, § 1881a does not require the Government to demonstrate probable cause that the target of the electronic surveillance is a foreign power or agent of a foreign power. And, unlike traditional FISA, § 1881a does not require the Government to specify the nature and location of each of the particular facilities or places at which the electronic surveillance will occur. * * *

The Foreign Intelligence Surveillance Court's role includes determining whether the Government's certification contains the required elements. Additionally, the Court assesses whether the targeting procedures are "reasonably designed" (1) to "ensure that an acquisition . . . is limited to targeting persons reasonably believed to be located outside the United States" and (2) to "prevent the intentional acquisition of any communication as to which the sender and all intended recipients are known . . . to be located in the United States." The Court analyzes whether the minimization procedures "meet the definition of minimization procedures under section 1801(h) . . . , as appropriate." The Court also assesses whether the targeting and minimization procedures are consistent with the statute and the Fourth Amendment.

Respondents are attorneys and human rights, labor, legal, and media organizations whose work allegedly requires them to engage in sensitive and sometimes privileged telephone and e-mail communications with colleagues, clients, sources, and other individuals located abroad. Respondents believe that some of the people with whom they exchange foreign intelligence information are likely targets of surveillance under § 1881a. Specifically, respondents claim that they communicate by telephone and e-mail with people the Government "believes or believed to be associated with terrorist organizations," "people located in geographic areas that are a special focus" of the Government's counterterrorism or diplomatic efforts, and activists who oppose governments that are supported by the United States Government.

Respondents claim that § 1881a compromises their ability to locate witnesses, cultivate sources, obtain information, and communicate confidential information to their clients. Respondents also assert that they "have ceased engaging" in certain telephone and e-mail conversations. According to respondents, the threat of surveillance will compel them to travel abroad in order to have in-person conversations. In addition, respondents declare that they have undertaken "costly and burdensome measures" to protect the confidentiality of sensitive communications. * * *

The law of Article III standing, which is built on separation-of-powers principles, serves to prevent the judicial process from being used to usurp the powers of the political branches. In keeping with the purpose of this doctrine, "[o]ur standing inquiry has been especially rigorous when reaching the merits of the dispute would force us to decide whether an action taken by one of the other two branches of the Federal Government was unconstitutional "Relaxation of standing requirements is directly related to the expansion of judicial power," and we have often found a lack of standing in cases in which the Judiciary has been requested to review actions of the political branches in the fields of intelligence gathering and foreign affairs.

To establish Article III standing, an injury must be "concrete, particularized, and actual or imminent; fairly traceable to the challenged action; and redressable by a favorable ruling." "Although imminence is concededly a somewhat elastic concept, it cannot be stretched beyond its purpose, which is to ensure that the alleged injury is not too speculative for Article III purposes—that the injury is certainly impending." Thus, we have repeatedly reiterated that "threatened injury must be certainly impending to constitute injury in fact," and that "[a]llegations of possible future injury" are not sufficient.

Respondents assert that they can establish injury in fact that is fairly traceable to § 1881a because there is an objectively reasonable likelihood that their communications with their foreign contacts will be intercepted under § 1881a at some point in the future. This argument fails. As an initial matter, the Second Circuit's "objectively reasonable likelihood" standard is inconsistent with our requirement that "threatened injury must be certainly impending to constitute injury in fact. Furthermore, respondents' argument rests on their highly speculative fear that: (1) the Government will decide to target the communications of non-U.S. persons with whom they communicate; (2) in doing so, the Government will choose to invoke its authority under § 1881a rather than utilizing another method of surveillance; (3) the Article III judges who serve on the Foreign Intelligence Surveillance Court will conclude that the Government's proposed surveillance procedures satisfy § 1881a's many safeguards and are consistent with the Fourth Amendment; (4) the Government will succeed in intercepting the communications of respondents' contacts; and (5) respondents will be parties to the particular communications that the Government intercepts. As discussed below, respondents' theory of standing, which relies on a highly attenuated chain of possibilities, does not satisfy the requirement that threatened injury must be certainly impending. * * *

Second, even if respondents could demonstrate that the targeting of their foreign contacts is imminent, respondents can only speculate as to whether the Government will seek to use § 1881a-authorized surveillance (rather than other methods) to do so. The Government has numerous other methods of conducting surveillance, none of which is challenged here. * * *

Third, even if respondents could show that the Government will seek the Foreign Intelligence Surveillance Court's authorization to acquire the communications of respondents' foreign contacts under § 1881a, respondents can only speculate as to whether that court will authorize such surveillance. In the past, we have been reluctant to endorse standing theories that require guesswork as to how independent decisionmakers will exercise their judgment. * * *

Fourth, even if the Government were to obtain the Foreign Intelligence Surveillance Court's approval to target respondents' foreign contacts under § 1881a, it is unclear whether the Government would succeed in acquiring the communications of respondents' foreign contacts. And fifth, even if the Government were to conduct surveillance of respondents' foreign contacts, respondents can only speculate as to whether their own communications with their foreign contacts would be incidentally acquired.

Respondents' alternative argument—namely, that they can establish standing based on the measures that they have undertaken to avoid § 1881a-authorized surveillance—fares no better. Respondents assert that they are suffering ongoing injuries that are fairly traceable to § 1881a because the risk of surveillance under § 1881a requires them to take costly and burdensome measures to protect the confidentiality of their communications. Respondents claim, for instance, that the threat of surveillance sometimes compels them to avoid certain e-mail and phone conversations, to "tal[k] in generalities rather than specifics," or to travel so that they can have in-person conversations. * * *

The Second Circuit's analysis improperly allowed respondents to establish standing by asserting that they suffer present costs and burdens that are based on a fear of surveillance, so long as that fear is not "fanciful, paranoid, or otherwise unreasonable." This improperly waters down the fundamental requirements of Article III. Respondents' contention that they have standing because they incurred certain costs as a reasonable reaction to a risk of harm is unavailing—because the harm respondents seek to avoid is not certainly impending. In other words, respondents cannot manufacture standing merely by inflicting harm on themselves based on their fears of hypothetical future harm that is not certainly impending. Any ongoing injuries that respondents are suffering are not fairly traceable to § 1881a.

If the law were otherwise, an enterprising plaintiff would be able to secure a lower standard for Article III standing simply by making an expenditure based on a nonparanoid fear. As Judge Raggi accurately noted, under the Second Circuit panel's reasoning, respondents could, "for the price of a plane ticket, . . . transform their standing burden from one requiring a showing of actual or imminent . . . interception to one requiring a showing that their subjective fear of such interception is not fanciful, irrational, or clearly unreasonable." Thus, allowing respondents to bring this action based on costs they incurred in response to a speculative threat would be tantamount to accepting a repackaged version of respondents' first failed theory of standing. * * *

Respondents incorrectly maintain that "[t]he kinds of injuries incurred here—injuries incurred because of [respondents'] reasonable efforts to avoid greater injuries that are otherwise likely to flow from the conduct they challenge—are the same kinds of injuries that this Court held to support standing in cases such as" *Laidlaw* * * * As an initial matter, none of these cases holds or even suggests that plaintiffs can establish standing simply by claiming that they experienced a "chilling effect" that resulted from a governmental policy that does not regulate, constrain, or compel any action on their part. Moreover, each of these cases was very different from the present case.

In *Laidlaw*, plaintiffs' standing was based on "the proposition that a company's continuous and pervasive illegal discharges of pollutants into a river would cause nearby residents to curtail their recreational use of that waterway and would subject them to other economic and aesthetic harms." Because the unlawful discharges of pollutants were "concededly ongoing," the only issue was whether "nearby residents"—who were members of the organizational plaintiffs—acted reasonably in refraining from using the polluted area. *Laidlaw* is therefore quite unlike the present case, in which it is not "concede[d]" that respondents would be subject to unlawful surveillance but for their decision to take preventive measures. *Laidlaw* would resemble this case only if (1) it were undisputed that the Government was using § 1881a-authorized surveillance to acquire respondents' communications and (2) the sole dispute concerned the reasonableness of respondents' preventive measures.

JUSTICE BREYER, with whom **JUSTICE GINSBURG**, **JUSTICE SOTOMAYOR**, and **JUSTICE KAGAN** join, dissenting.

[U]sing the authority of § 1881a, the Government can obtain court approval for its surveillance of electronic communications between places within the United States and targets in foreign territories by showing the court (1) that "a significant purpose of the acquisition is to obtain foreign intelligence information," and (2) that it will use general targeting and privacy-intrusion minimization procedures of a kind that the court had previously approved

Several considerations, based upon the record along with commonsense inferences, convince me that there is a very high likelihood that Government, acting under the authority of § 1881a, will intercept at least some of the communications just described. First, the plaintiffs have engaged, and continue to engage, in electronic communications of a kind that the 2008 amendment, but not the prior Act, authorizes the Government to intercept. These communications include discussions with family members of those detained at Guantanamo, friends and acquaintances of those persons, and investigators, experts and others with knowledge of circumstances related to terrorist activities. These persons are foreigners located outside the United States. They are not "foreign power[s]" or "agent[s] of . . . foreign power [s]." And the plaintiffs state that they exchange with these persons "foreign intelligence information," defined to include information that "relates to" "international terrorism" and "the national defense or the security of the United States."

Second, the plaintiffs have a strong motive to engage in, and the Government has a strong motive to listen to, conversations of the kind described. A lawyer representing a client normally seeks to learn the circumstances surrounding the crime (or the civil wrong) of which the client is accused. A fair reading of the affidavit of Scott McKay, for example, taken together with elementary considerations of a lawyer's obligation to his client, indicates that McKay will engage in conversations that concern what suspected foreign terrorists, such as his client, have done; in conversations that concern his clients' families, colleagues, and contacts; in conversations that concern what those persons (or those connected to them) have said and done, at least in relation to terrorist activities; in conversations that concern the political, social, and commercial environments in which the suspected terrorists have lived and worked; and so forth. Journalists and human rights workers have strong similar motives to conduct conversations of this kind. * * *

The majority more plausibly says that the plaintiffs have failed to show that the threatened harm is "certainly impending." But, as the majority appears to concede, certainty is not, and never has been, the touchstone of standing. The future is inherently uncertain. Yet federal courts frequently entertain actions for injunctions and for declaratory relief aimed at preventing future activities that are reasonably likely or highly likely, but not absolutely certain, to take place. And that degree of certainty is all that is needed to support standing here. * * *

The majority cannot find support in cases that use the words "certainly impending" to deny standing. While I do not claim to have read every standing case, I have examined quite a few, and not yet found any such case. * * *

In sum, as the Court concedes, the word "certainly" in the phrase "certainly impending" does not refer to absolute certainty. As our case law demonstrates, what the Constitution requires is something more akin to "reasonable probability" or "high probability." The use of some such standard is all that is necessary here to ensure the actual concrete injury that the Constitution demands.

NOTES

1.   *The Plaintiffs' Dilemma.* The Court faults the plaintiffs for being unable to show that their calls have been intercepted under authority of § 1881a. But the possible existence of any surveillance of their calls, let alone the legal basis invoked by the agency in particular cases, is top secret, so there's no way the plaintiffs can offer direct evidence. Yet the Court won't let them establish their standing indirectly, so they seem to have no way of protesting what could well be a violation of their constitutional rights.

2.   *What about* Laidlaw? *Is* it fair to say that the majority distinguishes *Laidlaw* on the ground that in *Laidlaw*, there was no doubt that the defendant's conduct was taking place, and the only issue was the impact on the plaintiffs, whereas here it was unclear whether the conduct was even taking place? Doesn't that really go to the fairly traceable requirement rather than injury in fact?

3.   *What is "Imminent"?* Imminent seems to carry an implication of certainty and immediacy. Susan B. Anthony List v. Driehaus, 134 S.Ct. 2334 (2014), makes it clear that neither temporal proximity nor certainty is required in order to obtain standing. Ohio has a law prohibiting false statements in connection with elections. The lead plaintiff was accused by a candidate of making such statements, and the candidate filed a complaint with the Ohio

Elections Commission. When the candidate lost, however, the complaint was dropped. The Court nevertheless held that the plaintiff had standing to challenge the law because it said it intended to make similar statements about other candidates in the future elections, and if doing so could then face the burden of defending administrative proceedings as well as possible criminal charges. It was enough that the plaintiff established "an intention to engage in a course of conduct arguably affected with a constitutional interest, but proscribed by statute, and there exists a credible threat of prosecution thereunder."

HOLLINGSWORTH V. PERRY

___ U.S. ___, 133 S.Ct. 2652 (2013)

[An initiative measure (Proposition 8) in California limited marriage to members of the opposite sexes. After a lengthy trial, the federal district court ruled the initiative measure unconstitutional. State officials decided not to appeal. The individuals who had led the effort to place Proposition 8 on the ballot filed an appeal. The federal appellate court certified the following question to the California Supreme Court:

> "Whether under Article II, Section 8 of the California Constitution, or otherwise under California law, the official proponents of an initiative measure possess either a particularized interest in the initiative's validity or the authority to assert the State's interest in the initiative's validity, which would enable them to defend the constitutionality of the initiative upon its adoption or appeal a judgment invalidating the initiative, when the public officials charged with that duty refuse to do so."

The California Supreme Court responded that:

> "In a postelection challenge to a voter-approved initiative measure, the official proponents of the initiative are authorized under California law to appear and assert the state's interest in the initiative's validity and to appeal a judgment invalidating the measure when the public officials who ordinarily defend the measure or appeal such a judgment decline to do so."

Perry v. Brown, 52 Cal. 4th 1116, 1127, 265 P. 3d 1002, 1007 (2011). On certiorari, the Court considered whether a case or controversy continued to exist after the state officials dropped out of the case.]

CHIEF JUSTICE ROBERTS delivered the opinion of the Court.

Petitioners argue that the California Constitution and its election laws give them a " 'unique,' 'special,' and 'distinct' role in the initiative process— one 'involving both authority and responsibilities that differ from other supporters of the measure.' " True enough—but only when it comes to the process of enacting the law. Upon submitting the proposed initiative to the attorney general, petitioners became the official "proponents" of Proposition 8. As such, they were responsible for collecting the signatures required to qualify the measure for the ballot. After those signatures were collected, the proponents alone had the right to file the measure with election officials to put it on the ballot. Petitioners also possessed control over the arguments in favor of the initiative that would appear in California's ballot pamphlets.

But once Proposition 8 was approved by the voters, the measure became "a duly enacted constitutional amendment or statute." Petitioners have no role—special or otherwise—in the enforcement of Proposition 8. They therefore have no "personal stake" in defending its enforcement that is distinguishable from the general interest of every citizen of California. * * *

Without a judicially cognizable interest of their own, petitioners attempt to invoke that of someone else. They assert that even if *they* have no cognizable interest in appealing the District Court's judgment, the State of California does, and they may assert that interest on the State's behalf. * * *

Petitioners contend that this case is different, because the California Supreme Court has determined that they are "authorized under California law to appear and assert the state's interest" in the validity of Proposition 8. The court below agreed: "All a federal court need determine is that the state has suffered a harm sufficient to confer standing and that the party seeking to invoke the jurisdiction of the court is authorized by the state to represent its interest in remedying that harm." * * *

Both petitioners and respondents seek support from dicta in *Arizonans for Official English* v. *Arizona*, 520 U.S. 43. The plaintiff in *Arizonans for Official English* filed a constitutional challenge to an Arizona ballot initiative declaring English " 'the official language of the State of Arizona.' " After the District Court declared the initiative unconstitutional, Arizona's Governor announced that she would not pursue an appeal. Instead, the principal sponsor of the ballot initiative—the Arizonans for Official English Committee—sought to defend the measure in the Ninth Circuit. Analogizing the sponsors to the Arizona Legislature, the Ninth Circuit held that the Committee was "qualified to defend [the initiative] on appeal," and affirmed the District Court.

Before finding the case mooted by other events, this Court expressed "grave doubts" about the Ninth Circuit's standing analysis. We reiterated that "[s]tanding to defend on appeal in the place of an original defendant . . . demands that the litigant possess 'a direct stake in the outcome.' " We recognized that a legislator authorized by state law to represent the State's interest may satisfy standing requirements * * * , but noted that the Arizona committee and its members were "not elected representatives, and we [we}re aware of no Arizona law appointing initiative sponsors as agents of the people of Arizona to defend, in lieu of public officials, the constitutionality of initiatives made law of the State."

Petitioners argue that, by virtue of the California Supreme Court's decision, they *are* authorized to act " 'as agents of the people' of California." But that Court never described petitioners as "agents of the people," or of anyone else. * * * All that the California Supreme Court decision stands for is that, so far as California is concerned, petitioners may argue in defense of Proposition 8. This "does not mean that the proponents become de facto public officials"; the authority they enjoy is "simply the authority to participate as parties in a court action and to assert legal arguments in defense of the state's interest in the validity of the initiative measure." That interest is by definition a generalized one, and it is precisely because proponents assert such an interest that they lack standing under our precedents. * * *

More to the point, the most basic features of an agency relationship are missing here. Agency requires more than mere authorization to assert a particular interest. "An essential element of agency is the principal's right to control the agent's actions.". Yet petitioners answer to no one; they decide for themselves, with no review, what arguments to make and how to make them. Unlike California's attorney general, they are not elected at regular intervals—or elected at all. See Cal. Const., Art. V, § 11. No provision provides for their removal. As one *amicus* explains, "the proponents apparently have an unelected appointment for an unspecified period of time as defenders of the initiative, however and to whatever extent they choose to defend it."

"If the relationship between two persons is one of agency . . . , the agent owes a fiduciary obligation to the principal." 1 Restatement § 1.01, Comment *e*. But petitioners owe nothing of the sort to the people of California. Unlike California's elected officials, they have taken no oath of office. As the California Supreme Court explained, petitioners are bound simply by "the same ethical constraints that apply to all other parties in a legal proceeding." They are free to pursue a purely ideological commitment to the law's constitutionality without the need to take cognizance of resource constraints, changes in public opinion, or potential ramifications for other state priorities.

Finally, the California Supreme Court stated that "[t]he question of who should bear responsibility for any attorney fee award . . . is *entirely distinct* from the question" before it. But it is hornbook law that "a principal has a duty to indemnify the agent against expenses and other losses incurred by the agent in defending against actions brought by third parties if the agent acted with actual authority in taking the action challenged by the third party's suit." 2 Restatement § 8.14, Comment *d*. If the issue of fees is entirely distinct from the authority question, then authority cannot be based on agency. * * *

We have never before upheld the standing of a private party to defend the constitutionality of a state statute when state officials have chosen not to. We decline to do so for the first time here.

Because petitioners have not satisfied their burden to demonstrate standing to appeal the judgment of the District Court, the Ninth Circuit was without jurisdiction to consider the appeal. The judgment of the Ninth Circuit is vacated, and the case is remanded with instructions to dismiss the appeal for lack of jurisdiction.

JUSTICE KENNEDY, with whom JUSTICE THOMAS, JUSTICE ALITO, and JUSTICE SOTOMAYOR join, dissenting.

The Court's opinion is correct to state, and the Supreme Court of California was careful to acknowledge, that a proponent's standing to defend an initiative in federal court is a question of federal law. Proper resolution of the justiciability question requires, in this case, a threshold determination of state law. The state-law question is how California defines and elaborates the status and authority of an initiative's proponents who seek to intervene in court to defend the initiative after its adoption by the electorate. Those state-law issues have been addressed in a meticulous and unanimous opinion by the Supreme Court of California.

Under California law, a proponent has the authority to appear in court and assert the State's interest in defending an enacted initiative when the public officials charged with that duty refuse to do so. The State deems such an appearance essential to the integrity of its initiative process. Yet the Court today concludes that this state-defined status and this state-conferred right fall short of meeting federal requirements because the proponents cannot point to a formal delegation of authority that tracks the requirements of the Restatement of Agency. But the State Supreme Court's definition of proponents' powers is binding on this Court. And that definition is fully sufficient to establish the standing and adversity that are requisites for justiciability under Article III of the United States Constitution.

In my view Article III does not require California, when deciding who may appear in court to defend an initiative on its behalf, to comply with the Restatement of Agency or with this Court's view of how a State should make its laws or structure its government. The Court's reasoning does not take into account the fundamental principles or the practical dynamics of the initiative system in California, which uses this mechanism to control and to bypass public officials—the same officials who would not defend the initiative, an injury the Court now leaves unremedied. The Court's decision also has implications for the 26 other States that use an initiative or popular referendum system and which, like California, may choose to have initiative proponents stand in for the State when public officials decline to defend an initiative in litigation. In my submission, the Article III requirement for a justiciable case or controversy does not prevent proponents from having their day in court. * * *

The Court concludes that proponents lack sufficient ties to the state government. It notes that they "are not elected," "answer to no one," and lack " 'a fiduciary obligation' " to the State. *Ante,* at 15 (quoting 1 Restatement (Third) of Agency § 1.01, Comments *e, f* (2005)). But what the Court deems deficiencies in the proponents' connection to the State government, the State Supreme Court saw as essential qualifications to defend the initiative system. The very object of the initiative system is to establish a lawmaking process that does not depend upon state officials. In California, the popular initiative is necessary to implement "the theory that all power of government ultimately resides in the people." The right to adopt initiatives has been described by the California courts as "one of the most precious rights of [the State's] democratic process." That historic role for the initiative system "grew out of dissatisfaction with the then governing public officials and a widespread belief that the people had lost control of the political process." *Ibid.* The initiative's "primary purpose," then, "was to afford the people the ability to propose and to adopt constitutional amendments or statutory provisions that their elected public officials had refused or declined to adopt."

The California Supreme Court has determined that this purpose is undermined if the very officials the initiative process seeks to circumvent are the only parties who can defend an enacted initiative when it is challenged in a legal proceeding. Giving the Governor and attorney general this *de facto* veto will erode one of the cornerstones of the State's governmental structure. And in light of the frequency with which initiatives' opponents resort to litigation, the impact of that veto could be substantial. As a consequence, California finds it necessary to vest the responsibility and right to defend a voter-approved initiative in the initiative's proponents when the State Executive declines to do so.

Yet today the Court demands that the State follow the Restatement of Agency. There are reasons, however, why California might conclude that a conventional agency relationship is inconsistent with the history, design, and purpose of the initiative process. The State may not wish to associate itself with proponents or their views outside of the "extremely narrow and limited" context of this litigation, or to bear the cost of proponents' legal fees. The State may also wish to avoid the odd conflict of having a formal agent of the State (the initiative's proponent) arguing in favor of a law's validity while state officials (*e.g.,* the attorney general) contend in the same proceeding that it should be found invalid. * * *

Arizonans for Official English v. *Arizona*, 520 U.S. 43 (1997), is consistent with the premises of this dissent, not with the rationale of the Court's opinion. There, the Court noted its serious doubts as to the aspiring defenders' standing because there was "no Arizona law appointing initiative sponsors as agents of the people of Arizona to defend, in lieu of public officials, the constitutionality of initiatives made law of the State." The Court did use the word "agents"; but, read in context, it is evident that the Court's intention was not to demand a formal agency relationship in compliance with the Restatement. Rather, the Court used the term as shorthand for a party whom "state law authorizes" to "represent the State's interests" in court. * * *

There is much irony in the Court's approach to justiciability in this case. A prime purpose of justiciability is to ensure vigorous advocacy, yet the Court insists upon litigation conducted by state officials whose preference is to lose the case. The doctrine is meant to ensure that courts are responsible and constrained in their power, but the Court's opinion today means that a single district court can make a decision with far-reaching effects that cannot be reviewed. And rather than honor the principle that justiciability exists to allow disputes of public policy to be resolved by the political process rather than the courts, here the Court refuses to allow a State's authorized representatives to defend the outcome of a democratic election. * * *

In the end, what the Court fails to grasp or accept is the basic premise of the initiative process. And it is this. The essence of democracy is that the right to make law rests in the people and flows to the government, not the other way around. Freedom resides first in the people without need of a grant from government. The California initiative process embodies these principles and has done so for over a century. "Through the structure of its government, and the character of those who exercise government authority, a State defines itself as sovereign." *Gregory* v. *Ashcroft*, 501 U.S. 452, 460 (1991). In California and the 26 other States that permit initiatives and popular referendums, the people have exercised their own inherent sovereign right to govern themselves. The Court today frustrates that choice by nullifying, for failure to comply with the Restatement of Agency, a State Supreme Court decision holding that state law authorizes an enacted initiative's proponents to defend the law if and when the State's usual legal advocates decline to do so. The Court's opinion fails to abide by precedent and misapplies basic principles of justiciability. Those errors necessitate this respectful dissent.

UNITED STATES V. WINDSOR

___ U.S. ___, 133 S.Ct. 2675 (2013)

JUSTICE KENNEDY delivered the opinion of the Court.

Two women then resident in New York were married in a lawful ceremony in Ontario, Canada, in 2007. Edith Windsor and Thea Spyer returned to their home in New York City. When Spyer died in 2009, she left her entire estate to Windsor. Windsor sought to claim the estate tax exemption for surviving spouses. She was barred from doing so, however, by a federal law, the Defense of Marriage Act, which excludes a same-sex partner from the definition of "spouse" as that term is used in federal statutes. Windsor paid the taxes but filed suit to challenge the constitutionality of this provision. The United States District Court and the Court of Appeals ruled that this portion of the statute is unconstitutional and ordered the United States to pay Windsor a refund. [The United States took the position that DOMA was unconstitutional, but at the same time it continued to enforce the law pending judicial resolution of the issue. The Bipartisan Legal Advisory Group (BLAG) of the House of Representatives voted to intervene in the litigation to defend the constitutionality of § 3 of DOMA. The Court also appointed a law professor to act as amicus on the jurisdictional issue, since all the parties agreed the Court had jurisdiction.]

There is no dispute that when this case was in the District Court it presented a concrete disagreement between opposing parties, a dispute suitable for judicial resolution. "[A] taxpayer has standing to challenge the collection of a specific tax assessment as unconstitutional; being forced to pay such a tax causes a real and immediate economic injury to the individual taxpayer." Windsor suffered a redressable injury when she was required to pay estate taxes from which, in her view, she was exempt but for the alleged invalidity of § 3 of DOMA.

The decision of the Executive not to defend the constitutionality of § 3 in court while continuing to deny refunds and to assess deficiencies does introduce a complication. Even though the Executive's current position was announced before the District Court entered its judgment, the Government's agreement with Windsor's position would not have deprived the District Court of jurisdiction to entertain and resolve the refund suit; for her injury (failure to obtain a refund allegedly required by law) was concrete, persisting, and unredressed. The Government's position— agreeing with Windsor's legal contention but refusing to give it effect— meant that there was a justiciable controversy between the parties, despite what the claimant would find to be an inconsistency in that stance. Windsor, the Government, BLAG, and the amicus appear to agree upon that point. The disagreement is over the standing of the parties, or aspiring parties, to take an appeal in the Court of Appeals and to appear as parties in further proceedings in this Court.

The *amicus'* position is that, given the Government's concession that § 3 is unconstitutional, once the District Court ordered the refund the case should have ended; and the *amicus* argues the Court of Appeals should have dismissed the appeal. The *amicus* submits that once the President agreed with Windsor's legal position and the District Court issued its judgment, the parties were no longer adverse. From this standpoint the United States was a prevailing party below, just as Windsor was. Accordingly, the *amicus* reasons, it is inappropriate for this Court to grant certiorari and proceed to rule on the merits; for the United States seeks no redress from the judgment entered against it.

This position, however, elides the distinction between two principles: the jurisdictional requirements of Article III and the prudential limits on its exercise. The latter are "essentially matters of judicial self-governance." The Court has kept these two strands separate: "Article III standing, which enforces the Constitution's case-or-controversy requirement, see *Lujan* v. *Defenders of Wildlife,* 504 U.S. 555, 559–562 (1992); and prudential standing, which embodies 'judicially self-imposed limits on the exercise of federal jurisdiction,' *Allen* [v. *Wright,*] 468 U.S. [737,] 751 [(1984)]." *Elk Grove Unified School Dist.* v. *Newdow*, 542 U.S. 1, 11–12 (2004).

The requirements of Article III standing are familiar:

> "First, the plaintiff must have suffered an 'injury in fact'—an invasion of a legally protected interest which is (a) concrete and particularized, and (b) 'actual or imminent, not "conjectural or hypothetical." ' Second, there must be a causal connection between the injury and the conduct complained of—the injury has to be 'fairly . . . trace[able] to the challenged action of the defendant, and not . . . th[e] result [of] the independent action of some third party not before the court.' Third, it must be 'likely,' as opposed to merely 'speculative,' that the injury will be 'redressed by a favorable decision.' " *Lujan, supra,* at 560–561 (footnote and citations omitted).

Rules of prudential standing, by contrast, are more flexible "rule[s] . . . of federal appellate practice," designed to protect the courts from "decid[ing] abstract questions of wide public significance even [when] other governmental institutions may be more competent to address the questions and even though judicial intervention may be unnecessary to protect individual rights."

In this case the United States retains a stake sufficient to support Article III jurisdiction on appeal and in proceedings before this Court. The judgment in question orders the United States to pay Windsor the refund she seeks. An order directing the Treasury to pay money is "a real and immediate economic injury," indeed as real and immediate as an order directing an individual to pay a tax. That the Executive may welcome this order to pay the refund if it is accompanied by the constitutional ruling it wants does not eliminate the injury to the national Treasury if payment is made, or to the taxpayer if it is not. The judgment orders the United States to pay money that it would not disburse but for the court's order. The Government of the United States has a valid legal argument that it is injured even if the Executive disagrees with § 3 of DOMA, which results in Windsor's liability for the tax. Windsor's ongoing claim for funds that the United States refuses to pay thus establishes a controversy sufficient for Article III jurisdiction. It would be a different case if the Executive had taken the further step of paying Windsor the refund to which she was entitled under the District Court's ruling.

This Court confronted a comparable case in *INS* v. *Chadha*, 462 U.S. 919 (1983). A statute by its terms allowed one House of Congress to order the Immigration and Naturalization Service (INS) to deport the respondent Chadha. There, as here, the Executive determined that the statute was unconstitutional, and "the INS presented the Executive's views on the constitutionality of the House action to the Court of Appeals." The INS, however, continued to abide by the statute, and "the INS brief to the Court of Appeals did not alter the agency's decision to comply with the House action ordering deportation of Chadha." This Court held "that the INS was sufficiently aggrieved by the Court of Appeals decision prohibiting it from taking action it would otherwise take," regardless of whether the agency welcomed the judgment. The necessity of a "case or controversy" to satisfy Article III was defined as a requirement that the Court's " 'decision will have real meaning: if we rule for Chadha, he will not be deported; if we uphold [the statute], the INS will execute its order and deport him.' " This conclusion was not dictum. It was a necessary predicate to the Court's holding that "prior to Congress' intervention, there was adequate Art. III adverseness." The holdings of cases are instructive, and the words of *Chadha* make clear its holding that the refusal of the Executive to provide the relief sought suffices to preserve a justiciable dispute as required by Article III. In short, even where "the Government largely agree[s] with the opposing party on the merits of the controversy," there is sufficient adverseness and an "adequate basis for jurisdiction in the fact that the Government intended to enforce the challenged law against that party." * * *

While these principles suffice to show that this case presents a justiciable controversy under Article III, the prudential problems inherent in the Executive's unusual position require some further discussion. The Executive's agreement with Windsor's legal argument raises the risk that instead of a " 'real, earnest and vital controversy,' " the Court faces a "friendly, non-adversary, proceeding . . . [in which] 'a party beaten in the legislature [seeks to] transfer to the courts an inquiry as to the constitutionality of the legislative act.'" Even when Article III permits the exercise of federal jurisdiction, prudential considerations demand that the Court insist upon "that concrete adverseness which sharpens the presentation of issues upon which the court so largely depends for illumination of difficult constitutional questions." *Baker* v. *Carr*, 369 U.S. 186, 204 (1962).

There are, of course, reasons to hear a case and issue a ruling even when one party is reluctant to prevail in its position. Unlike Article III requirements—which must be satisfied by the parties before judicial consideration is appropriate—the relevant prudential factors that counsel against hearing this case are subject to "countervailing considerations [that] may outweigh the concerns underlying the usual reluctance to exert judicial power." One consideration is the extent to which adversarial presentation of the issues is assured by the participation of *amici curiae* prepared to defend with vigor the constitutionality of the legislative act. With respect to this prudential aspect of standing as well, the *Chadha* Court encountered a similar situation. It noted that "there may be prudential, as opposed to Art. III, concerns about sanctioning the adjudication of [this case] in the absence of any participant supporting the validity of [the statute]. The Court of Appeals properly dispelled any such concerns by inviting and accepting briefs from both Houses of Congress." *Chadha* was not an anomaly in this respect. The Court adopts the practice of entertaining arguments made by an *amicus* when the Solicitor General confesses error with respect to a judgment below, even if the confession is in effect an admission that an Act of Congress is unconstitutional.

In the case now before the Court the attorneys for BLAG present a substantial argument for the constitutionality of § 3 of DOMA. BLAG's sharp adversarial presentation of the issues satisfies the prudential concerns that otherwise might counsel against hearing an appeal from a decision with which the principal parties agree. Were this Court to hold that prudential rules require it to dismiss the case, and, in consequence, that the Court of Appeals erred in failing to dismiss it as well, extensive litigation would ensue. The district courts in 94 districts throughout the Nation would be without precedential guidance not only in tax refund suits but also in cases involving the whole of DOMA's sweep involving over 1,000 federal statutes and a myriad of federal regulations. * * * That numerical prediction may not be certain, but it is certain that the cost in judicial resources and expense of litigation for all persons adversely affected would be immense. True, the very extent of DOMA's mandate means that at some point a case likely would arise without the prudential concerns raised here; but the costs, uncertainties, and alleged harm and injuries likely would continue for a time measured in years before the issue is resolved. In these unusual and urgent circumstances, the very term "prudential" counsels that it is a proper exercise of the Court's responsibility to take jurisdiction. For these reasons, the prudential and Article III requirements are met here; and, as a consequence, the Court need not decide whether BLAG would have standing to challenge the District Court's ruling and its affirmance in the Court of Appeals on BLAG's own authority.

The Court's conclusion that this petition may be heard on the merits does not imply that no difficulties would ensue if this were a common practice in ordinary cases. The Executive's failure to defend the constitutionality of an Act of Congress based on a constitutional theory not yet established in judicial decisions has created a procedural dilemma. On the one hand, as noted, the Government's agreement with Windsor raises questions about the propriety of entertaining a suit in which it seeks affirmance of an order invalidating a federal law and ordering the United States to pay money. On the other hand, if the Executive's agreement with a plaintiff that a law is unconstitutional is enough to preclude judicial review, then the Supreme Court's primary role in determining the constitutionality of a law that has inflicted real injury on a plaintiff who has brought a justiciable legal claim would become only secondary to the President's. This would undermine the clear dictate of the separation-of-powers principle that "when an Act of Congress is alleged to conflict with the Constitution, '[i]t is emphatically the province and duty of the judicial department to say what the law is.' " Similarly, with respect to the legislative power, when Congress has passed a statute and a President has signed it, it poses grave challenges to the separation of powers for the Executive at a particular moment to be able to nullify Congress' enactment solely on its own initiative and without any determination from the Court.

The Court's jurisdictional holding, it must be underscored, does not mean the arguments for dismissing this dispute on prudential grounds lack substance. Yet the difficulty the Executive faces should be acknowledged. When the Executive makes a principled determination that a statute is unconstitutional, it faces a difficult choice. Still, there is no suggestion here that it is appropriate for the Executive as a matter of course to challenge statutes in the judicial forum rather than making the case to Congress for their amendment or repeal. The integrity of the political process would be at risk if difficult constitutional issues were simply referred to the Court as a routine exercise. But this case is not routine. And the capable defense of the law by BLAG ensures that these prudential issues do not cloud the merits question, which is one of immediate importance to the Federal Government and to hundreds of thousands of persons. These circumstances support the Court's decision to proceed to the merits.

JUSTICE SCALIA, with whom **JUSTICE THOMAS** joins, and with whom the **CHIEF JUSTICE** joins as to Part I [the discussion of standing excerpted below].

The Court is eager—*hungry*—to tell everyone its view of the legal question at the heart of this case. Standing in the way is an obstacle, a technicality of little interest to anyone but the people of We the People, who created it as a barrier against judges' intrusion into their lives. They gave judges, in Article III, only the "judicial Power," a power to decide not abstract questions but real, concrete "Cases" and "Controversies." Yet the plaintiff and the Government agree entirely on what should happen in this lawsuit. They agree that the court below got it right; and they agreed in the court below that the court below that one got it right as well. What, then, are we *doing* here?

The answer lies at the heart of the jurisdictional portion of today's opinion, where a single sentence lays bare the majority's vision of our role. The Court says that we have the power to decide this case because if we did not, then our "primary role in determining the constitutionality of a law" (at least one that "has inflicted real injury on a plaintiff") would "become only secondary to the President's." But wait, the reader wonders—Windsor won below, and so *cured* her injury, and the President was glad to see it. True, says the majority, but judicial review must march on regardless, lest we "undermine the clear dictate of the separation-of-powers principle that when an Act of Congress is alleged to conflict with the Constitution, it is emphatically the province and duty of the judicial department to say what the law is."

That is jaw-dropping. It is an assertion of judicial supremacy over the people's Representatives in Congress and the Executive. It envisions a Supreme Court standing (or rather enthroned) at the apex of government, empowered to decide all constitutional questions, always and everywhere "primary" in its role.

This image of the Court would have been unrecognizable to those who wrote and ratified our national charter. They knew well the dangers of "primary" power, and so created branches of government that would be "perfectly co-ordinate by the terms of their common commission," none of which branches could "pretend to an exclusive or superior right of settling the boundaries between their respective powers." [Federalist No. 49] (J. Madison). The people did this to protect themselves. They did it to guard their right to self-rule against the black-robed supremacy that today's majority finds so attractive. So it was that Madison could confidently state, with no fear of contradiction, that there was nothing of "greater intrinsic value" or "stamped with the authority of more enlightened patrons of liberty" than a government of separate and coordinate powers.

For this reason we are quite forbidden to say what the law is whenever (as today's opinion asserts) " 'an Act of Congress is alleged to conflict with the Constitution.' " We can do so only when that allegation will determine the outcome of a lawsuit, and is contradicted by the other party. The "judicial Power" is not, as the majority believes, the power " 'to say what the law is,' " giving the Supreme Court the "primary role in determining the constitutionality of laws." The majority must have in mind one of the foreign constitutions that pronounces such primacy for its constitutional court and allows that primacy to be exercised in contexts other than a lawsuit. See, *e.g.,* Basic Law for the Federal Republic of Germany, Art. 93. The judicial power as Americans have understood it (and their English ancestors before them) is the power to adjudicate, with conclusive effect, disputed government claims (civil or criminal) against private persons, and disputed claims by private persons against the government or other private persons. Sometimes (though not always) the parties before the court disagree not with regard to the facts of their case (or not *only* with regard to the facts) but with regard to the applicable law—in which event (and *only* in which event) it becomes the " 'province and duty of the judicial department to say what the law is.' "

In other words, declaring the compatibility of state or federal laws with the Constitution is not only not the "primary role" of this Court, it is not a separate, free-standing role *at all*. We perform that role incidentally—by accident, as it were—when that is necessary to resolve the dispute before us. Then, and only then, does it become " 'the province and duty of the judicial department to say what the law is.' " That is why, in 1793, we politely declined the Washington Administration's request to "say what the law is" on a particular treaty matter that was not the subject of a concrete legal controversy. And that is why, as our opinions have said, some questions of law will *never* be presented to this Court, because there will never be anyone with standing to bring a lawsuit. As Justice Brandeis put it, we cannot "pass upon the constitutionality of legislation in a friendly, non-adversary, proceeding"; absent a " 'real, earnest and vital controversy between individuals,' " we have neither any work to do nor any power to do it. Our authority begins and ends with the need to adjudge the rights of an injured party who stands before us seeking redress.

That is completely absent here. Windsor's injury was cured by the judgment in her favor. And while, in ordinary circumstances, the United States is injured by a directive to pay a tax refund, this suit is far from ordinary. Whatever injury the United States has suffered will surely not be redressed by the action that it, as a litigant, asks us to take. The final sentence of the Solicitor General's brief on the merits reads: "For the foregoing reasons, the judgment of the court of appeals *should be affirmed.*" That will not cure the Government's injury, but carve it into stone. One could spend many fruitless afternoons ransacking our library for any other petitioner's brief seeking an affirmance of the judgment against it. What the petitioner United States asks us to do in the case before us is exactly what the respondent Windsor asks us to do: not to provide relief from the judgment below but to say that that judgment was correct. And the same was true in the Court of Appeals: Neither party sought to undo the judgment for Windsor, and so that court should have dismissed the appeal (just as we should dismiss) for lack of jurisdiction. Since both parties agreed with the judgment of the District Court for the Southern District of New York, the suit should have ended there. The further proceedings have been a contrivance, having no object in mind except to elevate a District Court judgment that has no precedential effect in other courts, to one that has precedential effect throughout the Second Circuit, and then (in this Court) precedential effect throughout the United States.

We have never before agreed to speak—to "say what the law is"—where there is no controversy before us. In the more than two centuries that this Court has existed as an institution, we have never suggested that we have the power to decide a question when every party agrees with both its nominal opponent *and the court below* on that question's answer. The United States reluctantly conceded that at oral argument.

The closest we have ever come to what the Court blesses today was our opinion in *INS* v. *Chadha*, 462 U.S. 919 (1983). But in that case, two parties to the litigation disagreed with the position of the United States and with the court below: the House and Senate, which had intervened in the case. Because *Chadha* concerned the validity of a mode of congressional action— the one-house legislative veto—the House and Senate were threatened with destruction of what they claimed to be one of their institutional powers. The Executive choosing not to defend that power, we permitted the House and Senate to intervene. Nothing like that is present here.

To be sure, the Court in *Chadha* said that statutory aggrieved-party status was "not altered by the fact that the Executive may agree with the holding that the statute in question is unconstitutional." But in a footnote to that statement, the Court acknowledged Article III's separate requirement of a "justiciable case or controversy," and stated that *this* requirement was satisfied "because of the presence of the two Houses of Congress as adverse parties." Later in its opinion, the *Chadha* Court remarked that the United States' announced intention to enforce the statute also sufficed to permit judicial review, even absent congressional participation. That remark is true, as a description of the judicial review conducted in the Court of Appeals, where the Houses of Congress had not intervened. There, absent a judgment setting aside the INS order, Chadha faced deportation. This passage of our opinion seems to be addressing that initial standing in the Court of Appeals, as indicated by its quotation from the lower court's opinion. But if it was addressing standing to pursue the appeal, the remark was both the purest dictum (as congressional intervention at that point made the required adverseness "beyond doubt"), and quite incorrect. When a private party has a judicial decree safely in hand to prevent his injury, additional judicial action requires that a party injured by the decree *seek to undo it*. In *Chadha*, the intervening House and Senate fulfilled that requirement. Here no one does.

The majority's discussion of the requirements of Article III bears no resemblance to our jurisprudence. It accuses the *amicus* (appointed to argue against our jurisdiction) of "elid[ing] the distinction between . . . the jurisdictional requirements of Article III and the prudential limits on its exercise." It then proceeds to call the requirement of adverseness a "prudential" aspect of standing. *Of standing.* That is incomprehensible. A plaintiff (or appellant) can have all the standing in the world—satisfying all three standing requirements of *Lujan* that the majority so carefully quotes—and yet no Article III controversy may be before the court. Article III requires not just a plaintiff (or appellant) who has standing to complain but *an opposing party* who denies the validity of the complaint. It is not the *amicus* that has done the eliding of distinctions, but the majority, calling the quite separate Article III requirement of adverseness between the parties an element (which it then pronounces a "prudential" element) of standing. The question here is not whether, as the majority puts it, "the United States retains a stake sufficient to support Article III jurisdiction," the question is whether there is any controversy (which requires *contradiction*) between the United States and Ms. Windsor. There is not. * * *

A few words in response to the theory of jurisdiction set forth in Justice Alito's dissent: Though less far reaching in its consequences than the majority's conversion of constitutionally required adverseness into a discretionary element of standing, the theory of that dissent similarly elevates the Court to the "primary" determiner of constitutional questions involving the separation of powers, and, to boot, increases the power of the most dangerous branch: the "legislative department," which by its nature "draw[s] all power into its impetuous vortex." The Federalist, No. 48, at 309 (J. Madison). Heretofore in our national history, the President's failure to "take Care that the Laws be faithfully executed," U.S. Const., Art. II, § 3, could only be brought before a judicial tribunal by someone whose concrete interests were harmed by that alleged failure. Justice Alito would create a system in which Congress can hale the Executive before the courts not only to vindicate its own institutional powers to act, but to correct a perceived inadequacy in the execution of its laws.

JUSTICE ALITO, with whom **JUSTICE THOMAS** joins as to Parts II and III [but not as to the standing discussion excerpted below], dissenting.

The United States clearly is not a proper petitioner in this case. The United States does not ask us to overturn the judgment of the court below or to alter that judgment in any way. Quite to the contrary, the United States argues emphatically in favor of the correctness of that judgment. We have never before reviewed a decision at the sole behest of a party that took such a position, and to do so would be to render an advisory opinion, in violation of Article III's dictates. For the reasons given in Justice Scalia's dissent, I do not find the Court's arguments to the contrary to be persuasive.

Whether the Bipartisan Legal Advisory Group of the House of Representatives (BLAG) has standing to petition is a much more difficult question. It is also a significantly closer question than whether the interveners in *Hollingsworth* v. *Perry*—which the Court also decides today—have standing to appeal. It is remarkable that the Court has simultaneously decided that the United States, which "receive[d] all that [it] ha[d] sought" below, is a proper petitioner in this case but that the intervenors in *Hollingsworth*, who represent the party that lost in the lower court, are not. In my view, both the *Hollingsworth* interveners and BLAG have standing.

A party invoking the Court's authority has a sufficient stake to permit it to appeal when it has " 'suffered an injury in fact' that is caused by 'the conduct complained of' and that 'will be redressed by a favorable decision.' " In the present case, the House of Representatives, which has authorized BLAG to represent its interests in this matter, suffered just such an injury.

In *INS* v. *Chadha*, 462 U.S. 919 (1983), the Court held that the two Houses of Congress were "proper parties" to file a petition in defense of the constitutionality of the one-house veto statute, *id.*, at 930, n. 5 (internal quotation marks omitted). Accordingly, the Court granted and decided petitions by both the Senate and the House, in addition to the Executive's petition. That the two Houses had standing to petition is not surprising: The Court of Appeals' decision in *Chadha*, by holding the one-house veto to be unconstitutional, had limited Congress' power to legislate. In discussing Article III standing, the Court suggested that Congress suffered a similar injury whenever federal legislation it had passed was struck down, noting that it had "long held that Congress is the proper party to defend the validity of a statute when an agency of government, as a defendant charged with enforcing the statute, agrees with plaintiffs that the statute is inapplicable or unconstitutional."

The United States attempts to distinguish *Chadha* on the ground that it "involved an unusual statute that vested the House and the Senate themselves each with special procedural rights—namely, the right effectively to veto Executive action." But that is a distinction without a difference: just as the Court of Appeals decision that the *Chadha* Court affirmed impaired Congress' power by striking down the one-house veto, so the Second Circuit's decision here impairs Congress' legislative power by striking down an Act of Congress. The United States has not explained why the fact that the impairment at issue in *Chadha* was "special" or "procedural" has any relevance to whether Congress suffered an injury.

Indeed, because legislating is Congress' central function, any impairment of that function is a more grievous injury than the impairment of a procedural add-on. * * *

Both the United States and the Court-appointed *amicus* err in arguing that *Raines* v. *Byrd*, 521 U.S. 811 (1997), is to the contrary. In that case, the Court held that Members of Congress who had voted "nay" to the Line Item Veto Act did not have standing to challenge that statute in federal court. *Raines* is inapposite for two reasons. First, *Raines* dealt with individual Members of Congress and specifically pointed to the individual Members' lack of institutional endorsement as a sign of their standing problem: "We attach some importance to the fact that appellees have not been authorized to represent their respective Houses of Congress in this action, and indeed both Houses actively oppose their suit."

Second, the Members in *Raines*—unlike the state senators in *Coleman*—were not the pivotal figures whose votes would have caused the Act to fail absent some challenged action. Indeed, it is telling that *Raines* characterized *Coleman* as standing "for the proposition that legislators whose votes would have been sufficient to defeat (or enact) a specific legislative Act have standing to sue if that legislative action goes into effect (or does not go into effect), on the ground that their votes have been completely nullified." Here, by contrast, passage by the House was needed for DOMA to become law. * * *

I appreciate the argument that the Constitution confers on the President alone the authority to defend federal law in litigation, but in my view, as I have explained, that argument is contrary to the Court's holding in *Chadha*, and it is certainly contrary to the *Chadha* Court's endorsement of the principle that "Congress is the proper party to defend the validity of a statute" when the Executive refuses to do so on constitutional grounds. Accordingly, in the narrow category of cases in which a court strikes down an Act of Congress and the Executive declines to defend the Act, Congress both has standing to defend the undefended statute and is a proper party to do so.

NOTES

1. *Shifting Votes on Standing in* Hollingsworth *and* Windsor. The following table may help you track the different views of standing in these two cases:

Case	Justices Finding Standing	Justices Finding No Standing
Hollingsworth v. Perry	Kennedy, Thomas, Alito, Sotomayor	Roberts, Scalia, Ginsburg, Kagan, Breyer
United States v. Windsor	Kennedy, Breyer, Kagan, Ginsburg, Sotomayor, Alito (as to interveners)	Scalia, Thomas, Roberts, Alito (as to the government)

Thus, there are four groups of Justices:

1. *Finding standing in both cases*: Kennedy, Sotomayor, Alito (but only as to the interveners in *Windsor*, not the government).

2. *Finding standing in neither case*: Scalia and Roberts.

3. *Finding standing in* Windsor *but not in* Hollingsworth: Breyer, Kagan, and Ginsburg

4. *Finding standing in* Hollingsworth *but not in* Windsor: Thomas

The reasons why various Justices thought they called for different outcomes remains obscure. Yet both cases involve the continuing justiciability of a challenge to a law when the government's executive branch has failed to defend the law.

2. *Reconciling the Cases?* The main distinction between the cases seems to be that the executive branch officials representing the government wanted a judicial resolution in *Windsor* but not in *Hollingsworth*. This is reflected by the fact that the relevant officials continued to enforce the statute in the *Windsor* case but did not attempt to do so in *Hollingsworth*, and that they actually filed appeals (and a cert. petition) on behalf of the government in *Windsor* but did not file an appeal in *Hollingsworth*. Thus, in *Windsor*, the government as an entity was at least nominally before the Court and had a financial interest (since it would have to pay money if the case was affirmed). On the other hand, in *Hollingsworth*, the state was no longer a formal party, and its only continuing interest was the abstract one of having its laws upheld. Is this distinction a sufficient basis for distinguishing the cases?

An alternative but related perspective is that some of the Justices may have put the cases into two different legal frames. The California case fits into a string of cases in which legislators have tried to get standing, with the initiative proponents here having a similar position in the lawmaking process. In contrast, the DOMA case involves another recurrent situation in which the government is a party (not true in the California appeal) but chose not to defend a particular legal position. Given the different framing, it doesn't seem as much in tension with the DOMA ruling.

Or maybe the different treatment of the cases was strategic. Ginsburg, Breyer and Kagan may have felt that an incremental approach was better than deciding the constitutionality of state same-sex marriage restrictions immediately (or perhaps deciding it wrong, depending on Kennedy's view.) Perhaps Thomas wanted to reach the merits in *Hollingsworth* because the district court ruling had statewide effect, whereas in *Windsor* the district court ruling applied only to a single taxpayer.

3. *The Development of Standing.* Historically, standing law was justified on the theory that a concrete stake in the dispute was needed in order to make the case truly adversarial. By *Windsor*, however, the need for an adversarial contest has faded only into an optional element of standing, which has been recast in separation of powers terms. Consider *Windsor* in this light. Clearly the Court isn't invading the executive's powers—after all, the executive has expressly invited the Court to decide the case. But is there a risk that the executive has too much ability to recruit the Court as an ally against Congress? Yet, wasn't that line crossed in *Chadha*?

4. *An End-run Around Hollingsworth.* If the challenge to Proposition 8 had been filed in state court, the state officials would not have been able to terminate the litigation by refusing to appeal. Because the case was filed in federal court, however, the state officials gained this extra control over the litigation, to the benefit of the plaintiffs. This seems anomalous. Future initiative proponents may want to avoid this situation. Could a future initiative appoint the initiative proponents as back-up representatives of the state, who could take over the litigation if the state failed to defend or file an appeal? Would the Supreme Court defer to this appointment as being a matter of state law, or would it still view this as merely a state effort to given the initiative sponsors "a ticket to federal court"?

5. *Executive Options.* What should the executive branch do when it believes a statute is unconstitutional? Should it continue to enforce the statute, as the Obama Administration did with DOMA? Is it obligated to defend the statute in litigation? Was it appropriate for state officials to drop the case in *Hollingsworth*?

PROBLEM 9–4:
CAN CONGRESS SUE THE PRESIDENT?

The House of Representatives filed suit in late 2014 against President Obama, claiming that he unlawfully delayed implementation of part of the health care law and was also unlawfully funding part of the law in violation of the Appropriation Clause. (That clause provides: "No Money shall be drawn from the Treasury, but in Consequence of Appropriations made by Law.") Does the House have standing? In this connection, consider *Arizona State Legislature v. Arizona Independent Redistricting Comm'n*, ___ U.S. ___, 135 S.Ct. 2652 (2015), where the Court held that the state legislature had standing to challenge a popular initiative stripping it of its control over reapportionment. The legislature challenged the initiative, which transferred control over districting to an independent commission, as a violation of the Elections Clause. (That clause grants control of federal election procedures in each state to the "Legislature thereof," subject to Congressional override.) The Court rejected the constitutional claim on the merits, holding that the state initiative validly placed legislative control over redistricting in the commission. Justice Scalia argued in dissent that the legislature lacked standing. But according to the Court, the legislature did have standing because the effect of the initiative was to nullify any vote it might hold on districting, "now or in the future," depriving it of its preexisting legal powers. A footnote reserved the question of Congressional standing:

> The case before us does not touch or concern the question whether Congress has standing to bring a suit against the President. There is no federal analogue to Arizona's initiative power, and a suit between Congress and the President would raise separation-of-powers concerns absent here. The Court's standing analysis, we have noted, has been "especially rigorous when reaching the merits of the dispute would force [the Court] to decide whether an action taken by one of the other two branches of the Federal Government was unconstitutional." *Raines v. Byrd,* 521 U.S. 811, 819–820, 117 S.Ct. 2312, 138 L.Ed.2d 849 (1997).

In light of *Windsor* and *Arizona State Legislature*, should the House be granted standing against the President? Which of the House's legal claims has better prospects of surviving a standing challenge? Does the case present a political question?